How do I get a
free driving
lesson?

It's easy. Just pre-pay for 12 hours of driving tuition and we'll give you an additional hour free, plus we will discount your first 12 hours by £24*.

Best of all, we're the only national driving school exclusively using fully qualified instructors. And you'll be learning in a Ford Focus with air conditioning and power steering.

Great value. A great instructor. And a great car. You get it all .

*Terms and Conditions apply.

Just **AA**sk.

AA driving school
0800 60 70 80
www.theAA.com

Free hour when you pre-pay for 12 hours

Complete this voucher and hand it to your instructor at the start of your first lesson.

Name _____

Pupil Number (given on calling 0800 60 70 80) _____

I apply for my one hour of free driving tuition having pre-paid for 12 hours and confirm I am not an existing pupil of AA driving school.

Signed _____

For Instructor Use Only:

Instructor Name _____ Instructor Number _____

Theory CAR + HC ext.

THEORY TEST
The *OFFICIAL* Questions & Answers
AND THE
HIGHWAY CODE

AA Publishing

Produced by AA Publishing.
© Automobile Association Developments Limited 2002
Reprinted 2002
Second edition with revised questions 2003
Third edition 2004

ISBN 0 7495 4144 X

Published by AA Publishing (a trading name of Automobile Association
Developments Limited, whose registered office is Millstream,
Maidenhead Road, Windsor, SL4 5GD; registered number 1878835).
A02028

The AA's web site address is **www.theAA.com/bookshop**

The contents of this book are believed correct at the time of printing.
Nevertheless, the publishers cannot be held responsible for any errors
or omissions or for changes in the details given in this book or for the
consequences of any reliance on the information provided by the
same. This does not affect your statutory rights.

Colour separation by Keene Group, Andover
Printed in Slovenia by Mladinska Knjiga

Visit **www.thehighwaycode.gov.uk** for all the
latest information on The Highway Code

While every effort has been made to include the
widest possible range of questions available at the
time of printing, the Government may from time to
time change, add or remove questions, and the
publisher cannot be held responsible for questions
that may appear on a question paper which were
not available for inclusion in this book.

Contents

Contents PAGE

Introduction and How to use this book

Introduction

Introduction

You want to pass the driving test and take advantage of the freedom and mobility that driving a car can give you. Do the following three things and you will achieve your goal – passing the driving test.

Acquire **knowledge** of the rules through your instructor and by studying the Highway Code. A key element is to test and reinforce your knowledge.

Take the right **attitude**. Be careful, courteous and considerate to all other road users.

Learn and understand the **skills** of driving by taking lessons from a trained and fully qualified driving instructor.

We're here to help you become a careful and safe driver and we've designed this book to help you take the first steps towards achieving your goal – preparing for your **Theory Test**.

SIX ESSENTIAL STEPS TO GETTING YOUR LICENCE

1. GET YOUR PROVISIONAL LICENCE
Use form D1 from any Post Office to apply for your provisional licence. The driving licence is issued in the form of a two-part document: a photo card and paper counterpart. So that you can legally begin learning to drive, at the appropriate date, you must be in possession of the correct licence documents. Take care when completing all the forms. Many licences cannot be issued for the required date because of errors or omissions on the

application forms. You will have to provide proof of identity such as a UK passport; make sure you have all the documents needed.

2. LEARN THE HIGHWAY CODE
The Highway Code (see pages 195–290) is essential reading for all drivers not just those learning to drive. It sets out all the rules for good driving, as well as the rules for other road users such as pedestrians and motorcycle riders. When you have learned the rules you will be able to answer most of the questions in the Theory Test and be ready to start learning the driving skills you will need to pass your Practical Test.

3. APPLY FOR AND TAKE THE THEORY TEST
The driving test is in two parts, the Theory Test and the Practical Test.

Once you have a valid provisional licence you may take the Theory Test at any time, but you must pass it before you are allowed to apply for the Practical Test. However, it is important that you should not take your Theory Test too early in your course of practical lessons. This is because you need the experience of meeting real hazards while you are learning to drive, to help you pass the Hazard Perception element of the Theory Test.

You can book your Theory Test by post, by calling or online. MasterCard, Visa, Switch, Delta, Solo and Electron are accepted. Application forms are available from test centres, Approved Driving Instructors or by calling the booking number below. Forms need to be sent with a cheque, postal order or credit or debit card details. The Theory Test currently costs £18.

By Post DSA (Driving Standards Agency),
  PO Box 148, Salford, M5 3SY
By Phone 0870 010 1372
Online www.dsa.gov.uk

For more information on the Theory Test see pages 13–16.

4. START TO LEARN TO DRIVE

We recommended that you learn with an Approved Driving Instructor (ADI). Only an ADI may legally charge for providing tuition.

Choose an instructor or driving school by asking friends or relatives who they recommend. Price is important, so find out whether the school offers any discounts for blocks or courses of lessons paid in advance; if you decide to pay in advance, make sure the driving school is reputable. If lesson prices are very low, ask yourself 'why?' Check how long the lesson will last. And don't forget to ask about the car you'll be learning to drive in. Is it modern and reliable? Is it insured? Does it have dual controls?

The most efficient and cost-effective way to learn to drive is

to accept that there is no short-cut approach to learning the necessary skills. Agree with your instructor on a planned course of tuition suited to your needs, take regular lessons, and don't skip weeks and expect to pick up where you left off. Ensure the full official syllabus is covered and, as your skills develop, get as much practice as possible with a relative or friend – but make sure they are legally able to supervise your practice. They must be over 21 years of age and have held a full driving licence for at least three years.

5. APPLY FOR AND TAKE THE PRACTICAL TEST

Once you have passed the Theory Test, and with your instructor's guidance based on your progress, you can plan ahead for a suitable test date for the Practical Test.

You can book your Practical Test by calling 0870 010 1372 at any time between 8am and 6pm Monday to Friday. The tests costs £39 and you can pay using a credit or debit card. The person who books the test must be the cardholder.

Make sure you have the following details to hand when booking your Practical Test.

- Theory Test pass certificate number
- driver number shown on your licence
- driving school code number (if known)
- your preferred date
- unacceptable days or periods
- if you can accept a test at short notice
- disability or any special circumstances
- your credit/debit card details

Saturday and weekday evening tests are available at some driving test centres. The fee is higher than for a driving test during normal working hours on weekdays. Evening tests are available during the summer months only.

Telephone bookings and enquiries
0870 010 1372

Facsimile
0870 010 2372

Welsh speakers
0870 010 0372

Minicom
0870 010 7372

6. APPLY FOR YOUR FULL DRIVER'S LICENCE

To obtain a full licence you need to send your Pass Certificate, your provisional licence and a cheque for £12 to the DVLA, Swansea, within two years of passing your Practical Test.

AFTER THE PRACTICAL TEST

The Driving Standards Agency and the insurance industry recognise and seek to reward those drivers who enhance their basic skills and widen their experience by taking further training in the form of a Pass Plus scheme.

This is a six-module syllabus which covers town and rural driving, night driving, driving in adverse weather conditions, and on dual carriageways and motorways. It offers you the opportunity to gain more driving experience with the help of an instructor to hand. An increasing number of insurance companies are prepared to offer discounts to new drivers who have completed the course. There is no test to take at the end of the course.

MORE INFORMATION

For more practical information on learning to drive including the Theory Test, Hazard Perception and the Practical Test visit
www.theAA.com
and
www.dsa.gov.uk.
For information on the Pass Plus scheme visit
www.passplus.org.uk

Note: Prices are correct at the time of going to press.

How to use this book

This book is arranged in six sections.

Part 1 explains what to expect and how to prepare for the Theory Test and Hazard Perception.

Part 2 is designed to hep you understand each of the 14 topics in the Theory Test. We tell you what type of questions you can expect in each section and give lots of helpful tips.

Each topic is colour coded to its relevant section in Part 3 of this book, which contains all the Theory Test questions.

Experience has taught us that learner drivers find particular questions difficult and are often confused when they see questions which are similar. Reading through the background to each topic, before looking at the questions, will help you to avoid the pitfalls and to group questions together as you will often find several questions are asking the same thing but in a slightly different way.

Part 3 contains all the official questions for car drivers which appear in the question bank of the DSA. You could be tested on any of these questions when you take your touch-screen Theory Test.

The questions are arranged in topics, such as **Safety Margins** and **Rules of the Road**. Each theme has its own colour band to help

Talk to your driving instructor and learn about good driving practice on the road

How to use this book

you find your way around. However, as you start to work through the questions you will soon discover that similar questions on the same topic may appear in different sections. Don't be put off by this, but read each question and the choice of answers very carefully. Similar questions may be asked in a slightly different way to test your knowledge.

Most of the Theory Test questions can be answered if you learn *The Highway Code* (see below). However, you will only find the answers to some questions by talking to your driving instructor and learning about good driving practice on the road.

We've added a cross reference in blue to each question where *The Highway Code* has the answer. The cross reference is to the number of the rule you need to check, or to the annexe or section of traffic signs that will help understand the answer. You will also find lots of helpful tip boxes throughout the questions.

You'll find all the correct answers to the questions at the back of the book, that way, you can easily test yourself to see what you are getting right and what you will need to work on.

Part 4 contains the complete, official *Highway Code. The Highway Code* sets out all the rules and advice on good driving, as well as the rules for other road users such as pedestrians and motorcyclists.

It is essential reading for everybody who uses the road but particularly for learner drivers. The good news is that once you have learned the rules you will be able answer most of the questions in the Theory Test.

The rules are set out in sections, such as **Using the Road**, or **Driving in Adverse Weather Conditions**. There are also useful picture-based sections about traffic signs and road markings, and annexes at the end which give advice about topics such as **vehicle documentation** and **first aid**. At the back of this section you'll find a complete **index** to *The Highway Code*, which will help you if you want to find all the relevant rules and advice to a particular topic or word.

Part 5 is a short **glossary**, which explains some of the more difficult words and terms used in the theory questions and *The Highway Code*. It's in alphabetical order and you can use this to check if you're not sure what a **chicane** is, for example, or what **brake fade** means.

Part 6 has all the **answers** to the 893 Theory Test questions.

Part 1

The Theory Test: What to expect

The Theory Test: What to expect

You now have to pass two driving tests before you can apply for a full driving licence – the Theory Test, including Hazard Perception, and the Practical Test. The Theory Test was introduced in 1996 to check that drivers know more than just how to operate a car, and the Hazard Perception element was introduced in 2001 to test learner drivers on their hazard awareness skills.

You are strongly recommended to prepare for the Theory Test and Hazard Perception at the same time as you develop your skills behind the wheel for the Practical Test. Obviously, there are many similarities between the two tests and you need the experience of meeting real hazards in order to pass the Hazard Perception element of the Theory Test.

It is all about making you a safer driver on today's busy roads. By preparing for both tests at the same time, you will reinforce your knowledge and understanding of all aspects of driving and you will improve your chances of passing both tests first time.

WHAT TO EXPECT IN THE THEORY TEST

You will have 40 minutes to complete the questions in the test, using a touch-screen to select your answers. The test is a set of 35 questions drawn from a bank of almost a 1,000, all of which have multiple-choice answers. In order to pass the test you must answer a minimum of 30 questions correctly within the given time. The Government may change the pass mark from time to time. Your driving school or the DSA will be able to tell you if there has been a change.

The questions appear on the screen one at a time and you can return to any of the questions within the 40 minutes to re-check or alter your answers.

Preparing for the Theory Test

Read and get to know *The Highway Code*. It is included in full in this book, and many of the theory questions relate directly to it. Look at the list of topics on page 49, then read through the topic summary. Now turn to the section containing the questions. Read through the questions and tick your choice of answer(s). Now check your answer(s) against the answer section at the back of the book. If you don't understand the answer(s), look up the cross-reference(s) given in blue to *The Highway Code*. If there is no reference given and you don't understand the answer, take a note of the question and discuss it with your driving instructor.

Questions marked with an **NI** symbol are those not found in Theory Test papers in Northern Ireland.

Remember
- Don't try too many questions at once.
- Don't try to learn the answers by heart.
- The order of the questions in this book may be different from how they are arranged in the actual test – so don't try to memorise the order.

How to answer the questions

Each question has four, five or six possible answers. You must mark the boxes with the correct answer(s). Each question tells you how many answers to mark.

Study each question carefully, making sure you understand what it is asking you. Look carefully at any diagram, drawing or photograph. Before you look at the answer(s) given, decide what you think the correct answer(s) might be. You can then select the answer(s) that matches the one you had decided on. If you follow this system, you will avoid being confused by answers that appear to be similar.

WHAT TO EXPECT IN THE HAZARD PERCEPTION TEST

After a break of up to three minutes you will begin the Hazard Perception part of the test. The Hazard Perception test lasts for about 20 minutes. Before you start you will be given some instructions explaining how the test works; you'll also get a chance to practise with the computer and mouse before you start the test.

Real road scenes feature in the video clips in the Hazard Perception test

Next you will see 14 film or video clips of real street scenes with traffic such as cars, pedestrians, cyclists etc. The scenes are shot from the point of view of a driver in a car. You have to notice potential hazards that are developing on the road ahead – that is, problems that could lead to an accident. As soon as you notice a hazard developing, click the mouse. You will have plenty of time to see the hazard – but the sooner you notice it, the more marks you score.

Click the mouse when you spot potential hazards – the pedestrian crossing the side road and the cyclist approaching a parked vehicle (ringed in yellow). Click again as the hazard develops when the cyclist (ringed in red) moves out to overtake the parked vehicle

Each clip has at least one hazard in it – some clips may have more than one hazard. You have to score a minimum of 44 out of 75 to pass, but the pass mark may change so check with your instructor or the DSA before sitting your test. (Note that the computer has checks built in to show anyone trying to cheat – for example someone who keeps clicking the mouse all the time.) Be aware that, unlike the Theory Test questions, you will not have an opportunity to go back to an earlier clip and change your response, so you need to concentrate throughout the test.

Preparing for the Hazard Perception test
Who do you think have the most accidents – new or experienced drivers? New drivers have just had lessons, so they should remember how to drive safely, but in fact new drivers have the most accidents.

Learner drivers need training in how to spot hazards because they are often so busy thinking about the car's controls that they forget to watch the road and traffic – and losing concentration for even a second could prove fatal to you or another road user.

> **You have to pass both the Theory Test questions and the Hazard Perception test. At the end of the test they will tell you your scores for both parts. Even if you only failed on one part of the Theory Test, you still have to take both parts again next time.**

Proper training can help you to recognise more of the hazards that you will meet when driving and to spot those hazards earlier. So you are less likely to have an accident.

Your driving instructor has been trained to help you learn hazard perception skills and can give you plenty of practice in what to look out for when driving, how to anticipate hazards, and what action to take to deal with hazards of all kinds.

You won't be able to practise with the real video clips used in the test, of course, but training books and practice videos are available.

For more help with HAZARD PERCEPTION see pages 25–9.

Part 2

Understanding the theory behind the test

Contents

Alertness

Section 1
Alertness

The first section in the Theory Test questions is headed ALERTNESS. Alertness is a short section and is a good place to start.

- Alertness means being wide awake and concentrating on what you are doing – driving – not being distracted by mobile phones or loud music.
- Alertness means looking out for hazards.
- Alertness means noticing all road signs and road markings, and acting on the instructions and information they give.

Are you fit to drive?
'Fit' can mean:
- Did you have any alcoholic drinks before you set out?
- Are you under the influence of illegal substances (drugs)?
- Are you feeling groggy or unwell?
- Are you taking prescription medicine which could affect your ability to control the car?
- Are you too tired to drive?

It's unwise to set out on a journey if you're not well, on the basis of 'I'll see how I go – I'll probably be all right':
- your reactions are likely to be slower
- you may be unable to judge distances properly
- your actions may be less well co-ordinated than usual and it's not legal.

If you are tired open the window for a few moments to let in some fresh air. If you drive when you are too tired, you risk falling asleep

at the wheel – an all too common cause of serious accidents. Driving for long stretches on a motorway at night can be especially dangerous. If you sense that you are losing your concentration, then take a break at a motorway service station. Plan your journey ahead, giving yourself plenty of time for rest stops – at least every couple of hours.

Tackling the questions
Look at the questions in this section (pages 50–4).
You'll see that the Alertness questions are all about these:
- anticipation
- observation
- signalling
- reversing
- using your mirrors
- concentration
- getting distracted
- feeling sleepy
- using mobile phones.

DID YOU KNOW?
The main causes of distraction are:
- Loud music in the car
- Passengers (usually children)
- Events happening outside (such as accidents)
- Using a mobile phone

Now go to page 50 to test yourself on the questions about Alertness

Section 2
Attitude

The government road safety organisations believe that the ATTITUDE of learner drivers is extremely important for road safety – yours and other road users.

Attitude means
• Your frame of mind when you get in the car
• How you react when you meet hazards on the road
• How you behave towards other drivers.

Attitude is a very important part of being a good driver. Your attitude when you are driving plays a big part in ensuring your safety and that of other road users.

Do you aim to be a careful and safe driver or a fast and skilful driver? If you don't want to end up 'just another' road accident statistic then careful and safe is the way to go.

Remember
A car is not an offensive weapon, and often people don't realise what a potentially lethal machine they are in control of when they get behind the wheel. You only have to think about this to understand how important your attitude is.

You'll see that questions in this section (see pages 55–61) are concerned with encouraging you to be a careful and safe driver and cover:
• Tailgating
• Consideration for other road users, including pedestrians, buses, slow-moving vehicles and horse riders

• Driving at the right speed for the conditions
• When to flash headlights
• The right place, time and way to overtake

And remembering a few dos and don'ts will help you achieve the right attitude for driving and make passing this section of the test much easier.

Good drivers do
• Drive at the right speed and for the road and traffic conditions
• Observe speed limits
• Overtake only when it is safe to do so
• Park in correct and safe places
• Wait patiently if the driver in front is a learner or elderly or hesitant
• Look out for vulnerable road users such as cyclists, pedestrians and children
• Concentrate on their driving at all times
• Plan their journey so that they have plenty of time to get to their destination

Good drivers don't
• Allow themselves to become involved in road rage
• Break speed limits
• Drive too fast, particularly in wet, foggy or icy weather
• Accelerate or brake too harshly
• Overtake and 'cut in', forcing others to brake sharply
• Put pressure on other drivers by coming up too close behind them (this is called 'tailgating'), flashing headlights or gesturing
• Allow their attention to be distracted by passengers, mobile phones or loud music, or what is happening on the road, such as staring at an accident.

Attitude

Tailgating

Driving excessively close up behind another vehicle is known as tailgating – and it's dangerous! The car in front may stop suddenly (e.g. to avoid hitting a child or animal that has dashed out into the road); when this happens the car following runs the risk of crashing into it.

You should always leave enough space between your vehicle and the one in front, so that you can stop safely if the driver in front suddenly slows down or stops.

Rear-end shunts account for a large percentage of all accidents on the road. In these situations, the driver of the car behind is almost always judged to be the guilty party.

So tailgating can be expensive as well as dangerous.

Another time when drivers are tempted to tailgate is when attempting to pass a large slow-moving vehicle. However, keeping well back will improve your view of the road ahead, so that you're better able to judge when it's safe to overtake and the driver of the large vehicle will also be able to see you.

We get asked all the time about this

If you are being followed too closely by another driver **you** should **slow down** and increase the distance between your vehicle and the one in front. If you slow down or have to stop suddenly, the driver behind may crash into you, but you will have increased your stopping distance and will not be pushed into the vehicle in front of you.

Always remember

- Expect the unexpected, and make provision for the potential errors of other drivers – everyone makes mistakes sometimes.
- Don't create unnecessary stress for other drivers by showing your frustration in an aggressive manner.

If you are driving at the right speed for the road and weather conditions and a driver behind is trying to overtake you should pull back a bit from the vehicle in front so if the driver behind insists on overtaking, there is less risk of an accident.

Do not try to stop the car behind from overtaking. Do not move into the middle of the road or move up close to the car in front. These actions could be very dangerous.

You should not give confusing signals such as indicating left or waving the other driver on.

Now go to page 55 to test yourself on the questions about Attitude

Section 3
Safety and Your Vehicle

When you go through this section (pages 62–73) you will notice that the questions are a bit of a mixture. They cover a number of topics about SAFETY, including:

- Understanding the controls of your vehicle
- What the car's warning lights tell you
- Tyres – correct inflation, pressures and tread depths
- When to use hazard warning lights
- Passenger safety
- The environment
- Security and crime prevention

Many of the questions in this section are to do with 'legal requirements' and rules regarding parking your car and using lights. Look up all the sections in *The Highway Code* that deal with parking rules. Find out the rules for red routes, white lines and zig-zag lines as well as yellow lines.

Seat belts

If any of your passengers are young people under 14, you are responsible for making sure they are wearing seat belts. You are responsible for them by law even if you are a learner driver yourself.

Tips for this section

Know your Highway Code and you will be able to answer most of the questions in this section. In particular make sure you know the rules regarding:

- Seat belts
- Tyres
- When to use your lights, including hazard warning lights

The hazard warning system should work whether or not you have the engine switched on.

Watch out for this confusing little question

One of the most confusing questions in this section asks what kind of driving results in high fuel consumption.

The answer, of course, is **bad** driving – especially harsh braking and acceleration. This means you will use more fuel than you should and therefore cause more damage to the environment than is necessary.

BUT many people read the word 'high' as meaning 'good' – as in a level of driving skill – and so pick the wrong answer.

Don't let it be you...

Now go to page 62 to test yourself on the questions about Safety and Your Vehicle

Safety Margins

Section 4
Safety Margins

Safety margins and learner drivers
Experienced drivers are usually better than new or learner drivers at leaving good SAFETY MARGINS. Learner drivers find it harder to keep their vehicle at a safe distance from the one in front. Therefore the questions in this section (see pages 74–81) cover:
• Safe stopping distances
and
• Safe separation distances (these are the same as safety margins).

What is a safety margin?
A safety margin is the space that you need to leave between your vehicle and the one in front so that you will not crash into it if it slows downs or stops suddenly. They are also called 'separation distances' and are an important part of anticipating road and traffic hazards.

> When you are learning to drive, you can feel pressure to speed up by drivers behind you.
>
> Don't let other drivers make you cut down on your safety margins. Stay a safe distance behind the vehicle in front. Then you will have enough time to anticipate, and react to, hazards.
>
> #### The two-second rule
> In traffic that's moving at normal speed, allow at least a two-second gap between you and the vehicle in front.

Stopping distances
Many people who are taking their Theory Test often get confused about this. You will notice that some of the questions ask for your overall stopping distance and others ask for you braking distance, these are different.

Overall stopping distance or stopping distance is not the same as braking distance. Stopping distance is made up of thinking distance + braking distance.

In other words, the time it takes to notice that there's a hazard ahead plus the time it takes to brake to deal with it.

> #### Thinking distance
> Thinking distance is sometimes called reaction time or reaction distance. If you are driving at 30mph, your thinking distance will be 30 feet (9 metres). That means your vehicle will travel 30 feet (9 metres) before you start braking.

What is the link between stopping distance and safety margins?
• You should always leave enough space between your vehicle and the one in front. If the other driver has to slow down suddenly or stop without warning you need to be able to stop safely.

The space is your safety margin.

Safety margins for other vehicles
• Long vehicles and motorcycles need more room to stop – in other words, you must

leave a bigger safety margin when following a long vehicle or motorbike.

- When driving behind a long vehicle, pull back to increase your separation distance and your safety margin so that you get a better view of the road ahead – there could be hazards developing and if you are too close he can't see you in his rear view mirror.
- Strong winds can blow lorries and motorbikes off course. So leave a bigger safety margin.

The basic road safety rule here is: **don't get closer than the overall stopping distance.**

Thinking Distance   Braking Distance

(20 mph)
6 metres + 6 metres
= 12 metres (40 feet) or 3 car lengths

(30 mph)
9 metres + 14 metres
= 23 metres (75 feet) or 6 car lengths

(40 mph)
12 metres + 24 metres
= 36 metres (120 feet) or 9 car lengths

(50 mph)
15 metres + 38 metres
= 53 metres (175 feet) or 13 car lengths

(60 mph)
18 metres + 55 metres
= 73 metres (240 feet) or 18 car lengths

(70 mph)
21 metres + 75 metres
= 96 metres (315 feet) or 24 car lengths

Different conditions and safety margins

One or more questions in your Theory Test might be about driving in 'different conditions'.

These questions aim to make sure you know what adjustments you should make to your driving when either:

- road conditions are different from normal, for example, when parts of the road are closed off for roadworks,

or

- weather conditions affect your driving.

Safety Margins

Roadworks

You should always take extra care when you see a sign warning you that there are roadworks ahead. Remember, roadworks are a hazard and you have to anticipate them.

If you see the driver in front of you slowing down, take this as a sign that you should do the same – even if you can't see a hazard ahead. You still need to keep a safe distance from him.

Harassing the driver in front by 'tailgating' is both wrong and dangerous. So is overtaking to fill the gap.

Roadworks on motorways

It's especially important that you know what to do when you see a sign for roadworks ahead on a motorway.

- There may be a lower speed limit than normal – keep to it.
- Use your mirrors and indicators, and get into the correct lane in plenty of time.
- Don't overtake the queue and then force your way in at the last minute (this is an example of showing an inconsiderate attitude to other road users).
- Always keep a safe distance from the vehicle in front.

Weather conditions

In bad weather (often called 'adverse' weather) you need to increase your safety margins.

When it's raining you need to leave at least twice as much distance between you and the vehicle in front. When there's ice on the road, leave an even bigger gap because your stopping distance increases tenfold.

It's amazing how often drivers go too fast in bad weather. In adverse weather motorways have lower speed limits, but some drivers don't take any notice of them.

> When it's icy you should multiply your two-second gap by ten.

Questions that look alike

There are a number of questions about anti-lock brakes in this section. Lots of questions look the same. Some are easy and some are hard. Some of them appear to be the same but they are not.

The questions test two things:

- Your knowledge of the rules of the road and
- Your understanding of words to do with driving.

> **Now go to page 74 to test yourself on the questions about Safety Margins**

Section 5
Hazard Awareness

How often does a motorist protest that the accident happened before they had time to realise the person they hit was there?

Some accidents will, of course, inevitably happen, but part of your instructor's job while teaching you to drive is to help you learn to anticipate problems before they happen.

What is the difference between Hazard Awareness and Hazard Perception?

- **Hazard Awareness** and **Hazard Perception** mean the same thing.
- Hazard Perception is the name for the part of the Theory Test that uses video clips. This test is about spotting developing hazards. One of the key skills of good driving, this is called **anticipation**.
- Anticipating hazards means looking out for them in advance and taking action now.
- Hazard Awareness is about being **alert** whenever you are driving.

That is why some of the questions in this HAZARD AWARENESS section (see pages 82–100) deal with things that might make you less alert – for example:
– feeling tired
– feeling ill
– taking medicines prescribed by your doctor
– drinking alcohol.

Other questions in this section cover:
- noticing road and traffic signs and road markings

- what to do at traffic lights
- when to slow down for hazards ahead.

Taking action to avoid accidents
New drivers have a greater than average chance of being involved in accidents. Statistics show that young male drivers have the most accidents.

Why are young male drivers more at risk?
- Maybe it's because when they get their licence they want to show off to other drivers.
- Some people think that driving much too fast will earn them 'respect' from their friends.
- Some people think that they are such good drivers, the rules of the road don't apply to them.

Whatever the reason – drivers who don't watch out for hazards are at risk of being involved in an accident.

The problem has a lot to do with people's **attitude** to driving; you'll find more about the part of the Theory Test that deals with attitude on pages 19–20.

We've already said that young drivers often don't learn to anticipate hazards until they are older and more experienced.

The HP test aims to 'fill the gap' in hazard perception for young drivers and other new drivers by making sure they have some proper training to make up for their lack of experience.

This should make them safer drivers when they start out on the road alone.

Looking for clues to developing hazards

As you get more driving experience you will start to learn about the times and places where you are most likely to meet hazards.

Think about some of these examples:

Rush hour

You know that people take more risks when driving in the rush hour. Maybe they have to drop their children off at school before going to work. Maybe they are late for a business meeting. So you have to be prepared for bad driving, such as other drivers pulling out in front of you.

Dustbin day

Drivers in a hurry may get frustrated if they are held up in traffic because of a hazard such as a dustcart. They may accelerate and pull out to overtake even though they cannot see clearly ahead. You should not blindly follow the lead of another driver. Check for yourself that there are no hazards ahead.

School children

Young children are not very good at judging how far away a car is from them, and may run into the road unexpectedly. Always be on the lookout for hazards near a school entrance.

Parked cars

Imagine you are driving on a quiet one-way street with cars parked down each side. You wouldn't expect to meet any vehicles coming the other way – but what about children playing? They might run out into the road after a football. It would be difficult to see them because of the parked cars, until they were in the road in front of you.

More examples of hazards

So, what kinds of hazards are we talking about? And what should you do about them?

Road markings and road signs sometimes highlight likely hazards for you.

The list below gives some of the hazards you should look out for when driving along a busy street in town.

After each hazard there are some ideas about what you should be looking out for, and what to do next.

- You see a bus which has stopped in a lay-by ahead.
There may be some pedestrians hidden by the bus who are trying to cross the road, or the bus may signal to pull out. Be ready to slow down and stop.

- You see a white triangle painted on the road surface ahead.
This is a hazard warning sign. It tells you that there is a 'Give Way' junction just ahead. Slow down and be ready to stop.

- You see a sign for a roundabout on the road ahead.
Anticipate that other drivers may need to change lane, and be ready to leave them enough room.

• You come to some road works where the traffic is controlled by temporary traffic lights. *Watch out for drivers speeding to get through before the lights change.*

Hazards may be all around you – not just in front

• You look in your rear view mirror and see an emergency vehicle with flashing lights coming up behind you. *An emergency vehicle wants to pass, so get ready to pull over when it's safe.*

Not all hazards are on the road

• You see a small child standing with an adult near the edge of the pavement. *Check if the child is safely holding the adult's hand. Be ready to stop safely if the child suddenly steps into the road.*

• You notice dustbins or rubbish bags put out on the pavement. *The dustcart could be around the next corner, or the bin men could be crossing the road with bags of rubbish. Be ready to slow down and stop if necessary.*

Remember to listen for hazards, too.

• You hear a siren. *Look all around to find out where the emergency vehicle is. You may have to pull over to let it pass.*

You will find out more about the different types of hazards you may encounter, including what to look for when driving on narrow country roads, or in bad (adverse) weather conditions, in the Vehicle Handling section, pages 34–6.

Always expect the unexpected
Don't forget: not all hazards can be anticipated. There are bound to be some you haven't expected.

Red flashing warning lights
Level crossings, ambulance stations, fire stations and swing bridges all have red lights that flash on and off to warn you when you must stop.

Observation

Another word for taking in information through our eyes is observation.

Observation is one of the three key skills needed in hazard perception:
• observation
• anticipation
• planning.

An easy way to remember this is **O A P** for

Observe
Anticipate
Plan

Talking to yourself again?

It's a good idea to 'talk to yourself' when you're learning to drive – and even after you've passed your test. Talk about all the things you see that could be potential hazards. Your driving instructor might suggest this as a way of making you concentrate and notice hazards ahead.

Hazard Awareness

Even if you don't talk out loud, you can do a 'running commentary' in your head on everything you see around you as you drive.

For example, you might say to yourself –
'I am following a cyclist and the traffic lights ahead are red. *When the lights change I shall allow him/her plenty of time and room to move off.'*
or
'The dual carriageway ahead is starting to look very busy. There is a sign showing that the right lane is closing in 800 yards. *I must get ready to check my mirrors and if safe to do so drop back, to allow other vehicles to move into the left-hand lane ahead of me.'*

Note: Don't forget the mirrors! This way, you will notice more hazards, and you will learn to make more sense of the information that your eyes are taking in.

Scanning the road
Learner drivers tend to look straight ahead of their car and may not notice all the hazards that might be building up on both sides. You will spot more hazards when driving if you train yourself to scan the road.

- Practice looking up and ahead as far as possible.
- Use all your mirrors to look out for hazards too.
- Don't forget that you have 'blind spots' when driving – work out where they are and find safe ways of checking all round for hazards.
- Ask your driving instructor to help you with all of this.

Learn your road signs!
Notice the information in *The Highway Code* (see pages 195–290) at the bottom of the first page of traffic signs. It explains that you won't find every road sign shown here.

You can buy a copy of *Know Your Traffic Signs* from a bookshop to see some of the extra signs that are not in *The Highway Code*.

Note: In Wales, some signs have the Welsh spelling as well as the English; and in Scotland, some signs have Gaelic spelling. You'll also see some 'old-style' road signs around, which are slightly different too.

How is learning to scan the road going to help me pass my Theory Test?
- As we have said before, the idea of the Hazard Perception element of the test is to encourage you to get some real experience of driving before you take the Theory Test.
- If you meet real hazards on the road and learn how to anticipate them, you'll learn how to pass the Hazard Perception element of the test.
- In the video test you may not be able to look all around you as you would when driving a car; but the clips will be as realistic as possible in giving you a wide 'view' of the road ahead.

Observation questions

Study some of the pictures in the Hazard Awareness section on pages 82–100.

They include photographs of scenes such as:

• a cyclist at traffic lights, seen from the viewpoint of a driver in a car behind the cyclist

• what you see as a driver when you are approaching a level crossing

• what you see when coming up to a 'blind bend'

• a view of the road ahead with traffic building up where one lane is closing.

Look out for situations like these when you are out driving with your instructor, and use the practice to improve your hazard awareness.

As well as photographs, there are pictures of road and traffic signs.

What do these signs mean?

What actions should you take when you see these signs?

• If you are not sure, look them up in *The Highway Code* section pages 195–290.

• Think about why the square yellow sign with the two children is in the Vehicle Markings section and not with the rest of the road signs.

Now go to page 82 to test yourself on the questions about Hazard Awareness

Vulnerable Road Users

Section 6
Vulnerable Road Users

Today's vehicles are getting safer all the time for the driver inside the car – but not always for the pedestrian, cyclist etc outside. Many road users who are not driving cars have nothing to protect them if they are in an accident with a motor vehicle.

The questions in the VULNERABLE ROAD USERS section (see pages 101–14) deal with the following:
• why different types of road users are vulnerable
• what you as a driver must do to keep them safe.

Vulnerable road users include:
– pedestrians
– children
– elderly people
– people with disabilities
– cyclists
– motorcycle riders
– horse riders
– learner drivers and new drivers
– animals being herded along the road.

You must drive with extra care when you are near vulnerable road users.

Cyclists
Give cyclists plenty of room. Remember to **keep well back** from cyclists when you are coming up to a **junction** or a **roundabout** because you cannot be sure what they are going to do. On the roundabout they may go in any direction – left, right, or straight ahead.

They are allowed to stay in the left lane and signal right if they are going to continue round. Leave them enough room to cross in front of you if they need to. Turn to the section headed Vulnerable Road Users in the Theory Test questions (pages 101–14) to see some pictures of this. You must also give way to cyclists at toucan crossings and in cycle lanes (see the rules for cyclists in *The Highway Code*, page 205).

Look out for cyclists!
• It can be hard to see cyclists in busy town traffic.
• It can also be hard to see them coming when you are waiting to turn out at a junction. They can be hidden by other vehicles (see below).

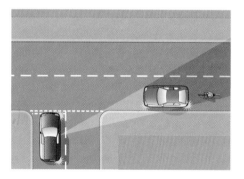

Always be on the lookout for cyclists. Especially, **check your mirror** to make sure you do not trap a cyclist on your left when you are turning left into a side road. Check your **blind spots** for cyclists, too.

Controlling your vehicle near cyclists
When you are following a cyclist, you must be able to drive **as slowly as they do**, and keep

your vehicle under control. Only overtake when you can allow them plenty of room, and it is safe to do so.

Cycle lanes

Cycle lanes are for cyclists. Car drivers should not use them.

A cycle lane is marked by a white line on the road.

A solid white line means you must not drive or park in the cycle lane during the hours it is in use.

A broken white line means you should drive or park in it only if there is no alternative. You should not park there at any time when there are waiting restrictions.

When you overtake a cyclist, a motorcyclist or a horse rider, **give them at least as much room as you would a car.**

Cyclists and motorcycle riders

Cyclists and motorcycle riders are more at risk than car drivers because:

- they are more affected by strong winds, or by turbulence caused by other vehicles
- they are more affected by an uneven road surface, and they may have to move out suddenly to avoid a pot-hole
- car drivers often cannot see them.

Pedestrians

Pedestrians most at risk include **elderly people** and **children**. Elderly people and others who cannot move easily may be slower to cross roads – you must give them plenty of time. Children don't have a sense of danger on the road; they can't tell how close a car is, or how fast it is going. They may run out into the road without looking. Or they may step out behind you when you are reversing – you may not see them because they are small.

People who are unable to see and/or hear

A blind person will usually carry a white stick to alert you to their presence.

If the stick has a red band, this means that the person is also deaf, so will have no warning of an approaching car either visually or from engine noise.

When to give way to pedestrians

At any pedestrian crossing, if a pedestrian has started to cross, wait until they have reached the other side. Do not harass them by revving your engine or edging forward.

- **On a light-controlled pedestrian crossing**

At a crossing with lights (pelican, toucan or puffin crossings), pedestrians have priority once they have started to cross even if, when on a pelican crossing, the amber lights start flashing.

- **On a zebra crossing**

Once the pedestrian has stepped on to the crossing you must stop and wait for them to cross.

Note: It is courteous to stop at a zebra crossing if a pedestrian is waiting to cross.

Vulnerable Road Users

When you take your Practical Driving Test, you must stop for any pedestrians who are waiting on the pavement at a zebra crossing – even if they haven't stepped on to the crossing yet. However, you must not wave to them to cross.

- **When they have started to cross a road that you want to turn into**

If you want to turn left into a side road and people are crossing the side road on foot, wait for them to finish crossing – people on foot have priority over car drivers.

> **DID YOU KNOW?**
> If a car hits a pedestrian at **40mph**, the pedestrian will probably be killed.
> Even at **30mph**, 50% of pedestrians hit by cars will be killed.
> At **20mph**, pedestrians have a better chance of surviving. This is why you will find 20mph limits and other things to slow traffic in some residential streets and near school entrances.

Signs that alert you to road users at risk

Look up the Traffic Signs and Vehicle Markings sections in *The Highway Code* (pages 265–9 and 273) and find the following signs:

- Pedestrians walking in the road ahead (no pavement).
- Cycle lane and pedestrian route.
- Advance warning of school crossing patrol ahead.
- School crossing patrol.
- Elderly or disabled people crossing.
- Sign on back of school bus or coach.

Other types of vulnerable road users

Be prepared to slow down for **animals, learner drivers,** and other more unusual hazards such as people walking along the road in **organised groups** (for example, on a demonstration, or a sponsored walk). There are rules in *The Highway Code* that walkers must follow (see page 198). But even if they break the rules, make sure you keep to them.

Animals

Drive slowly past horses or other animals. Allow them plenty of space on the road. Don't frighten them by sounding your horn or revving your engine.

> If you see a flock of **sheep** or a herd of **cattle** blocking the road, you must:
> - stop
> - switch off your engine
> - and wait until they have left the road.

> People riding **horses** on the road are often children, so you need to take extra care; when you see two riders abreast, it may well be that the one on the outside is shielding a less experienced rider.

Now go to page 101 to test yourself on the questions about Vulnerable Road Users

Section 7
Other Types of Vehicle

We have already come across some of the other types of vehicles that share the road with you and your car including motorbikes and bicycles. The questions in this part of the Theory Test (see pages 115–20) are mostly about long vehicles such as lorries. However, you also need to know what to do about:
– buses
– caravans
– trams
– tractors and other farm vehicles
– special vehicles for disabled drivers (powered invalid carriages)
– slow vehicles such as road gritters
– motorway repair vehicles.

Important points to remember about these types of vehicle:
• many of them can only move very slowly
• they cannot easily stop or change direction.

The driver's field of vision may be restricted – this means that car drivers have to allow them plenty of room.

Motorcycles
• Motorcycles are easily blown off course by strong winds. If you see a motorcyclist overtaking a **high-sided vehicle** such as a lorry, keep well back. The lorry may shield the motorcyclist from the wind as it is overtaking, but then a sudden gust could blow the motorcyclist off-course.
• It can be **hard to see** a motorcyclist when you are waiting at a **junction**. Always look out for them.

• If you see a motorcyclist **looking over their shoulder**, it could mean that they will **soon give a signal to turn right**. This applies to cyclists too. Keep back to give them plenty of room.
• Motorcyclists and cyclists sometimes have to **swerve to avoid hazards** such as bumps in the road, patches of ice and drain covers. As before – give them plenty of room.

Long vehicles
• Like cyclists, long vehicles coming up to roundabouts may stay in the left lane even if they intend to turn right.
This is because they need lots of room to manoeuvre. Keep well back so they have room to turn.
• Take great care when overtaking long or high-sided vehicles. Before you pull out to overtake, make sure you have a clear view of the road ahead.
• A long vehicle that needs to turn left off a major road into a minor road may prepare to do so by moving out towards the centre of the road, or by moving across to the other side.

If you're following them:
• give way, and don't try to overtake – on the right or the left
• you might need to slow down and stop while the driver of the long vehicle makes the turn.

Buses and trams
• Always give way to buses when they signal to pull out.
• Always give way to trams; they cannot steer to avoid you.

• Don't try to overtake a tram.

Trams are **quiet** vehicles – you cannot rely on engine noise to warn you that a tram is coming.

Take extra care when you see this sign, because trams are sometimes allowed to go when car drivers are not.

Tractors and slow-moving vehicles

• Always **be patient** if you are following a slow vehicle.

Drivers of slow vehicles will usually try to find a safe place to pull in to let the traffic go past. In the meantime you should keep well back, so that you can see the road ahead. Allow a safe distance in case they slow down or stop.

Slow vehicles are not allowed on motorways because they cannot keep up with the fast-moving traffic. Vehicles not allowed on motorways include:

• motorcycles under 50cc
• bicycles
• tractors and other farm vehicles
• powered invalid carriages.

For more information on Motorway Rules, see pages 36–9 of this book.

Now go to page 115 to test yourself on the questions about Other Types of Vehicle

Section 8
Vehicle Handling

The questions in this section (see pages 121–30) test how much you know about controlling your vehicle.

Your control is affected by:

• the **road surface** – is it rough or smooth? Are there any holes or bumps? Are there any 'traffic-calming measures' such as humps or chicanes?
• the **weather conditions** – you have to drive in different ways when there is fog, snow, ice or heavy rain.

Other questions in this section cover driving on country roads – on narrow and one-way roads, humpback bridges, steep hills, fords. Other questions need practical knowledge – for example, on engine braking, brake fade, and coasting your vehicle – use the **Glossary.**

This section also has some questions on overtaking and parking.

Road surface

The condition of the road surface can affect the way your vehicle handles. Your vehicle handles better on a smooth surface than on a surface that is damaged, bumpy or full of holes. If you have to drive on an uneven surface, keep your speed down so that you have full control of your vehicle, even if your steering wheel is jolted.

Take care also where there are **tramlines** on the road. The layout of the road affects the way your vehicle handles.

You may have to adjust your driving for traffic calming measures such as **traffic humps** (sometimes called 'sleeping policemen') and **chicanes**. These are double bends that have been put into the road layout to slow the traffic down. The sign before the chicane tells you who has priority.

Traffic calming measures are often used in residential areas or near school entrances to make it safer for pedestrians.

Weather conditions
Bad weather (adverse weather) such as heavy rain, ice or snow affects the way your vehicle handles. If you drive too fast in adverse weather, your tyres may lose their grip on the road when you try to brake. This means the car may skid or 'aquaplane'.

• Aquaplaning means sliding out of control on a wet surface.

Driving in snow
In snow, the best advice is do not drive at all unless you really have to make a journey. If you have to drive in snowy conditions, leave extra time for your journey and keep to the main roads. You can fit snow chains to your tyres to increase their grip in deep snow.

Driving in fog
In fog your field of vision can be down to a few metres. Your vehicle is fitted with fog lights to help you see and be seen in fog. But you must know how and when to use them. Look up the three rules about fog lights in *The Highway Code*. You'll see that the key points to remember are:

• don't dazzle other road users with your fog lights
• and switch them off as soon as you can see better (as soon as the fog starts to clear).

> **Remember the two-second rule?**
> You should double the two-second gap to four seconds when driving in rain, and increase the gap by as much as ten times when there is ice on the road.

Country driving
If you have had most of your driving lessons in a town, you need to know how to drive on narrow country roads. Some are only wide enough for one vehicle ('single-track'), and some are on very steep hills.

Your control of the gears, clutch and brakes will be important if you have to follow a tractor very slowly up a hill. On a steep downward slope you have to make sure your vehicle does not 'run away'.

On country roads you might find **humpback bridges** and **fords**. The signs below warn you of these hazards.

• Find out what you must do **first** after you have driven through a ford.

Technical knowledge

We have already mentioned engine braking. Understanding how engine braking works is part of good vehicle handling.

Note: If you press the footbrake constantly on a long hill, you may get brake fade. If you're not sure, check what that means in the **Glossary** at the back of this book.

Use the gears to control your vehicle on a downhill slope (or 'gradient'). If you put the vehicle in 'neutral', or drive with the clutch down (called coasting), your vehicle will increase speed beyond what is safe and will not be under proper control.

This sign warns you of a steep hill downwards.

- Coasting is wrong and dangerous – you should not be tempted to do it to save fuel.

Remember that if there is sudden heavy rain after a dry hot spell, the road surface can get very slippery.

> **Now go to page 121 to test yourself on the questions about Vehicle Handling**

Section 9
Motorway Rules

Learner drivers aren't allowed on motorways, so you can't get experience of what it's like to drive on them until you've passed your test. However, you do need to know all about MOTORWAY RULES before taking your Practical Test, and your Theory Test will most likely include a question about motorways (see pages 131–8).

As soon as you pass your driving test you will be legally allowed to drive on motorways. You need to know all the motorway rules in advance, so that you are confident and ready to cope with motorway driving when you pass your test.

There are some major roads and dual carriageways that learners can drive on which are very much like motorways. You may drive on some of these fast roads during your driving test, so that your examiner can see how well you cope with hazards at higher speeds.

When driving on these fast roads you need some of the same skills that you will need for motorway driving – for example, using lanes properly, knowing when it is safe to overtake, and controlling your vehicle at speed.

If you are learning to drive with a driving school, you will have the chance to book a motorway lesson with your instructor after you have passed your test. It makes sense to take up this offer before you drive on a motorway alone for the first time.

The differences between motorways and other roads

- On a motorway traffic is moving at high speed all the time.
- All lanes are in use.
- No stopping is allowed on a motorway – traffic only slows or comes to a stop because of accidents or other types of hold-up.
- Some road users are not allowed on motorways. These include:
- pedestrians, cyclists and learner drivers
- horses and other animals
- motorcycles under 50cc
- slow-moving vehicles, tractors and farm vehicles and invalid carriages.
- You always enter and leave a motorway on the left, via a slip road.
- To the left of the inside lane (left-hand lane) on a motorway is the hard shoulder. You can only drive on this in an emergency.
- Special signs and signals are used on motorways.

These include signs above the road on overhead gantries (see page 38), signs on the central reservation, and amber and red flashing lights.

Checks before your journey

Be extra careful about doing all your regular checks before you set out on a motorway journey; you cannot stop on the motorway to fix small problems, and no one wants to break down in the middle of fast traffic.

Always check:
- oil and coolant levels, screen wash container
- tyres and tyre pressures
- fuel gauge
- that all mirrors and windows are free of dirt and grease

- that the horn works.

Many of these checks are legally necessary, as well as important for your safety.

How to move on to the motorway

- Join the motorway by building up your speed on the slip road to match the speed of traffic in the left lane of the motorway.
- Use **MSM (Mirrors – Signal – Manoeuvre)** and move into the flow of traffic when it is safe to do so.

Changing lanes and overtaking

Driving on a motorway needs all the skills you have learned about **anticipation** and **forward planning**.

You should:

- make good use of all mirrors, and check your blind spots
- signal to move out in plenty of time
- look out for hazards ahead in the lane you want to move to
- not go ahead if it will force another vehicle to brake or swerve
- keep a safe distance from the vehicle in front.

Take a break

When you drive on motorways you will sometimes see signs that say 'Tiredness can kill – take a break!'

This is very good advice; motorways are monotonous – boring to drive, with long stretches of road that look the same for miles. A major cause of accidents is drivers falling asleep at the wheel. Plan your journey so that you have time to get out, stretch your legs and have a drink or snack.

The rules you need to know

- **Keep to the left-hand lane** unless you are overtaking and move back to the left lane as soon as it is safe to do so. Sometimes you need to stay in the centre lane for a time – for example, when a line of lorries is travelling up a hill in the left lane. Stay in the centre lane until you have passed the hazard, then signal left and return to the left lane.
- **NEVER reverse**
      park
      walk
      or **drive in the wrong direction** on the motorway.
- Don't **exceed the speed limit**. This is normally 70mph, but lower speed limits may be signed when the road is busy, or in bad weather.
- Keep to the correct separation distance (see Safety Margins, page 22).
- Don't **overtake on the left.**
If traffic is moving slowly in all three lanes you may find that the lane on the left is moving faster than the one to its right for a short time. Or the left lane may be signed for traffic turning off at the next junction only. But these are exceptions to the rule.
- If luggage falls from your vehicle, **do not get out to pick it up**. Stop at the next **emergency phone** and tell the police. Posts on the edge of the motorway show the way to the nearest emergency phone. You should use these phones rather than your mobile, because the emergency phone connects directly to the police and tells them exactly where you are on the motorway.
- **Don't stop on the hard shoulder except**

in an emergency. The hard shoulder is an extremely dangerous place, as many as one in eight road deaths happen there.

Traffic signs and road markings on motorways
Light signals
In *The Highway Code* you'll find the light signals only seen on motorways. Signs above the roadway, or on the central reservation, are activated as needed, to warn of accidents, lane closures or weather conditions.

Overhead gantries display arrows or red crosses showing which lanes are open or closed to traffic, and which lanes to move to when motorways merge or diverge.

They may also show temporary speed limits.

Direction signs
Direction signs on motorways are blue and those on other major roads are green – other direction signs are white with black print.

Reflective studs
It's useful to know the colours of studs on a motorway; this can help in working out which part of the road you're on if it's dark or foggy.

White studs mark lanes or the centre of the road
Red studs mark the left edge of the carriageway

Amber studs are used alongside the central reservation
Green studs mark the entry to a slip road.
Note: these markings are also found on some dual carriageways.

USING THE HARD SHOULDER
- Stop as far to the left as possible and, if you can, near an emergency phone.
- Emergency phones are situated 1 mile apart and have blue and white marker posts (left) every 100 metres. An arrow on the posts points the direction of the nearest phone.
  - If you are using a mobile phone you can identify your location from the number on the post.
- Switch on your hazard warning lights.
- Use the left-hand door to get out of the vehicle, and make sure your passengers do too.
- Get everyone away from the road – if possible, behind the barrier or up the bank.
- Leave animals in the vehicle unless they aren't safe there.
- Phone the police with full details of where you are, then go back and wait in a safe place near your vehicle.

Now go to page 131 to test yourself on the questions about Motorway Rules

Section 10
Rules of the Road

'Rules of the Road' is a good way to describe what is in *The Highway Code*.

The questions that come under this heading in the Theory Test (see pages 139–50) include several on road signs and road markings. There are lots more road sign questions in the section on Road and Traffic Signs.

Several of the topics listed in this section have already come up.

Other questions in this section cover:
- speed limits
- overtaking
- parking
- lanes and roundabouts
- clearways
- box junctions
- crossroads
- pedestrian crossings
- towing caravans and trailers.

Speed limits
Driving too fast for the road, traffic or weather conditions causes accidents.

The right speed for the road
Make sure that you keep below the speed limit shown on the signs for the road you are on.

30mph
in a built up area

50mph
on a long, twisty country road

or as low as **20mph** in a residential area with speed humps or traffic calming measures

The national speed limit for cars on a dual carriageway is **70mph**.
This is also the maximum speed for motorway driving.

National speed limit
When you leave a built up area you will usually see this sign.

- This sign tells you that the national speed limit for this type of road applies here.
- The national speed limit for cars on a normal road (single carriageway outside a built up area) is **60mph**.
- So on this road you must drive below 60mph even if it is straight and empty.

DID YOU KNOW?

Street lights usually mean that a **30mph** limit applies, unless there are signs showing other limits.

The right speed for the conditions

If it is raining or there is snow and ice on the road or if you are driving in a high wind you will have to drive more slowly than the maximum speed limit. This will keep you and other road users safe.

- Remember – you have to **double** the time you allow for stopping and braking in wet weather. Allow **even more time** in snow and ice.
- You need to be extra careful when driving in fog.

The right speed for your vehicle

Some other vehicles have lower speed limits than cars. Study the table on page 218 in *The Highway Code* at the end of this book.

Parking rules

There are some general rules about parking that all drivers should know.

- Whenever you can, you should use off-street car parks, or parking bays. These are marked out with white lines on the road.
- Never park where your vehicle could be a danger to other road users.

Special rules

Look for signs that tell you

- that you cannot park there at certain times of the day
- or that only certain people can park in that place.

Examples:
- bus lanes
- cycle lanes
- residents' parking zones
- roads edged with red or yellow lines

Orange or blue badges are given to people with disabilities. Do not park in a space reserved for a disabled driver – even if that is the only place left to park. A disabled driver may need to park there. You will break the law if you park in that space.

Parking at night
- If you park at night on a road that has a speed limit higher than 30mph, you must switch on your parking lights.

You must switch on your parking lights even if you have parked in a lay-by on this type of road.

- When parking at night, always park facing in the same direction as the traffic flow.
- If your vehicle has a trailer, you must switch on parking lights, even if the road has a 30mph speed limit.

WHERE NOT TO PARK
- On the pavement
- At a bus stop
- In front of someone's drive
- Opposite a traffic island
- Near a school entrance
- On a pedestrian crossing (or inside the zig-zag lines either side of it)
- Near a junction
- On a clearway
- On a motorway

Now go to page 139 to test yourself on the questions about Rules of the Road

Section 11
Road and Traffic Signs

When you look up the chapter on ROAD AND TRAFFIC SIGNS in the Theory Test questions (see pages 151–77) you will see that it takes up a lot of pages. This is because most of the questions have a picture of a road sign or marking. You will also see that a lot of questions ask 'What does this sign mean?'

But however differently the questions are worded – it all comes down to how well you know *The Highway Code*.

You can try to learn as much of *The Highway Code* as possible, but there are other ways you can get to know the road signs.

Be aware
As you walk or drive around, look at the road signs you see in the street, and the different markings painted on the road surface.

If you are on foot:
Look at the signs and signals that all road users must obey, whether they are in a car or walking.

For example, when you use a pedestrian crossing, check what kind of crossing it is (such as a pelican, toucan or zebra crossing).

Check whether you know the following:
- What are the rules for pedestrians and drivers coming up to the crossing?
- What kinds of crossings are controlled by traffic lights?
- What is different about a zebra crossing?

Road and Traffic Signs

During your driving lessons

If you are having a driving lesson look well ahead so that you see all the signs that tell you what to do next. Obey them in good time.

During your Driving Test

When you take your Driving Test the examiner will tell you when to move off, when to make a turn and when to carry out one of the set manoeuvres. But they will expect you to **watch out for lane markings** on the road, and **signs giving directions**, and to decide how to react to these yourself.

If you see several signs all on the same post, it can be confusing. The general rule is to **start at the top** and read down the post. The sign at the top tells you about the **first hazard** you have to look out for.

If you are a passenger in a car on a **motorway**, look at the motorway signs, because you need to know them, even though you can't drive on a motorway yet yourself.

Check that you can answer the following:

What colour are the signs at the side of the motorway?
What do the light signals above the road tell you?
What signs tell you that you are coming to an exit?

Know your shapes

Road and traffic signs come in three main shapes. Get to know them. You must learn what the signs mean.

Circles

Signs in **circles** tell you **to do** (blue) or **not do** (red) something – they **give orders**.

Triangles

Signs in **triangles** tell you of a **hazard** ahead – they **give warnings.**

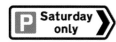

Rectangles

Signs in **rectangles** tell you about **where you are** or **where you are going** – they **give information.**

DID YOU KNOW?

There is only one sign which is **octagonal** – that is, it has eight sides. This is the sign for **STOP**. The eight-sided shape makes the sign stand out more.

Now go to page 151 to test yourself on the questions about Road and Traffic Signs

Section 12
Documents

This is quite a short section in your book of Theory Test questions (see pages 178–81). It is also different from the other sections, because it does not deal with driving skills or knowledge of *The Highway Code*.

It covers all the paperwork and the laws that you need to know about when you start learning to drive.

In this section there are questions about:
- driving licences
- insurance
- MOT certificate
- Vehicle Excise Duty (tax disc)
- Vehicle Registration Document (log book)

This section also covers:
- who can supervise a learner driver
- and changes you must tell the licensing authority about.

Driving licence
If you are learning to drive, you need a provisional licence.
- You must have a valid licence to drive legally.
- All licences now have two parts – a photo card and a paper document.
- Your signature is on both parts of the licence.
- Take good care of your provisional licence. If you lose it by mistake, you can get another one but you will have to pay a fee, and wait for the new licence to come.
- When you pass your test you can apply for a full licence.

Insurance
You must have a valid insurance certificate that covers you at least for **third party liability**. If you are learning with a driving school, you are covered by their insurance while you are in the driving school car. When you are in your own or anybody else's car, you must have insurance. Third party insurance cover usually comes as **'Third Party, Fire and Theft'. It is a basic insurance policy** that will pay for repairs to another person's car and allows you to claim on the other driver's insurance if you are in an accident that was not your fault.

If you have **comprehensive** insurance, the policy will pay for repairs to your vehicle even when the accident was your fault.

MOT certificate
Cars and motorcycles must have their first MOT test three years after they are new and first registered. After that, they must have an MOT test every year.
The MOT test checks:
- that your vehicle is roadworthy – that is, all the parts work properly and the vehicle is safe to drive
- that it keeps to the legal limits for exhaust emissions – that is, the levels of poisons in the gas that comes from the exhaust.

Documents

If your vehicle is over three years old you must not drive it without a valid MOT certificate – unless you are on your way to get an MOT and you have booked it in advance.

Vehicle Excise Duty (tax disc)

Your vehicle must have an up-to-date tax disc on the windscreen. The disc shows that you have paid Vehicle Excise Duty up to the date on the disc (you can pay for 6 or 12 months at a time). If you don't renew your tax disc within a month of the old one expiring you will be automatically fined. If you are not going to renew your tax disc (if you don't use your vehicle or keep it on a public road) you must inform the DVLA by completing a Statutory Off Road Vehicle Notification (SORN).

Vehicle Excise Duty is the tax that the government charges you to drive your vehicle on the roads. It is also sometimes called road tax. When you get your tax disc, you must show proof that your vehicle is insured, and that it has a valid MOT if required.

Vehicle Registration Document/Certificate

The Vehicle Registration Document/Certificate has all the important details about you and your vehicle, such as the make and model of the vehicle. It also has your name and address as the registered keeper of the vehicle. It is a record of the vehicle's history and is sometimes called **'the log book'**.

Changes you must tell the licensing authority about

The Driver and Vehicle Licensing Agency is known as the DVLA for short.

You must tell the DVLA
- if you are going to keep your car off road and are not renewing your tax disc
- when you buy or sell a car
- or if you change your name or address.

This is because your details go on to the **Vehicle Registration Document/Certificate** and you are legally responsible for the vehicle (car tax, parking fines etc) until you have notified the DVLA that it is off road or you have sold it.

Supervising a learner driver

As a learner driver, you cannot drive on your own. If you are not with your driving instructor, you must be supervised by a person:
- who is at least 21 years old
- and has a full licence for the kind of car you drive*
- and has had that licence for at least three years.

*Note: if a person has a licence to drive an **automatic** car only, they cannot supervise a learner in a **manual** car.

Now go to page 178 to test yourself on the questions about Documents

Section 13
Accidents

The questions in this section (see pages 182–92) are about helping anyone who is hurt in a road accident. Some people think they might do more harm than good if they try to help. But if you have some knowledge of first aid you won't panic and if you are first on the scene at accident you could even save a life.

• Look up Accidents and First Aid in *The Highway Code* at the back of this book.

The Theory Test questions in this section cover:
• what to do when warning lights come on in your vehicle
• what to do if you break down
• safety equipment to carry with you
• when to use hazard warning lights
• what to do – and what not to do – at the scene of an accident
• What to do in tunnels

Basic first aid
What to do at an accident scene
• Check that you are not putting yourself in danger before you go to help somebody else. You may need to warn other drivers of the accident.
• Check all vehicle engines are switched off.
• Make sure no one is smoking.
• Move people who are not injured to a safe place. If the accident has happened on a motorway, if possible get them away from the hard shoulder, behind the barrier or on to the bank.

• Call the emergency services. You will need to tell them exactly where you are, and how many vehicles are involved in the accident. On motorways, use the emergency phone which connects directly to the police and tells them exactly where you are.
• Do not move injured people – unless there is a risk of fire, or of an explosion.
• Give essential first aid to injured people (see below).
• Stay there until the emergency services arrive.

The ABC of first aid
This tells you what three things to check for when you go to help an injured person:
A is for Airway
B is for Breathing
C is for Circulation

Airway
If an injured person is breathing, but unconscious, if possible place them in the recovery position. If they are not breathing, first make sure there is nothing in their mouth that might be blocking the airway.

Breathing
If you have checked the airway and they are still not breathing, then give first aid as follows:
• lift their chin
• carefully tilt their head back to open their airway

- pinch their nose and blow into their mouth until their chest rises.

Repeat this every 4 seconds until the person can breathe alone, or until help arrives.

Circulation

'Circulation' here means 'bleeding'. If a person is bleeding, press firmly on the wound for up to 10 minutes, until the bleeding slows or stops. You can raise an injured arm or leg to reduce the bleeding – as long as the limb is not broken. If you carry a first aid kit use a sterile dressing over the wound.

Other ways to help:
- Do speak in a calm way to the injured person.
- Do try to keep them warm and as comfortable as possible.
- Do not give them anything to drink.
- Do not give them a cigarette.
- Don't let injured people wander into the road.

The AA's advice on safety if you break down

If you are on a non-motorway road:
- Try to get your vehicle off the main road. At least, get it right to the side of the road or on to the verge.
- If the vehicle is in a place where it might be hit by another vehicle, get any passengers out and to a safer place.
- Switch on the hazard warning lights to warn other drivers.
- If you have a red warning triangle, place it at least 45 metres behind your car to warn other traffic (but don't use it on a motorway).

- If you are a member of a motoring organisation such as the AA, call them and tell them where you are and what has happened. Wait with your vehicle until the patrol arrives.

If you are on a motorway:
- If possible, leave the motorway at the next exit. If you can't get that far, drive on to the hard shoulder. Stop far over to the left, and switch on your hazard warning lights.
- Get everyone out of the vehicle, using the nearside doors (but leave pets in the vehicle). Get them to sit on the bank, well away from the traffic.
- Use the nearest orange emergency phone to call the emergency services and tell them where you are and what has happened (for your safety, face the oncoming traffic while you are on the phone).
- Go back to your vehicle and wait on the bank near by until help arrives.
- Do not cross the motorway on foot or try to do repairs yourself – even changing a wheel. This is too dangerous on a motorway.

DID YOU KNOW?

Before driving into a tunnel you should tune into a local radio station and listen to the traffic reports incase there are any accidents or problems in the tunnel.

Now go to page 182 to test yourself on the questions about Accidents

Section 14
Vehicle Loading

This last section, called VEHICLE LOADING, is the shortest of all (see pages 193–4). It covers a mixture of the following:
- how to load your vehicle safely
- using a roof rack
- towing caravans and trailers
- child restraints and safety locks.

When you have passed your test you can tow a trailer, if the combined weight of the vehicle and trailer is less than 3,500kg. So you need to know the rules about towing.

Towing

When you get your first full driving licence, check it to see how much you are allowed to tow. Do not tow any trailer that comes to more than that weight. The weight of a trailer should be no more than 85% of the weight of the car that is to pull it. But it is best to stay well below that top weight, because towing a trailer will affect the way your vehicle handles.

When you are towing, you need to allow:
- more room when overtaking
- more time to brake and stop.

When you are turning at a roundabout or junction you will need to think about where you are on the road.

Roof racks

If you put a roof rack on your car, it will make a difference to the way your vehicle handles.

- The roof rack makes your vehicle taller, so more vulnerable to strong winds.
- You will increase your fuel consumption.
- You need to change the way you drive to allow for the extra weight.

Any load that is carried on a roof rack must be tied down securely.

To find out more, look up the parts of *The Highway Code* at the back of this book that deal with **Loads** and **Towing**.

Loading a trailer

If the weight of the load is arranged properly, this should cut down the risk of **losing control, swerving and snaking** (see below).
- Try to **spread the weight evenly** when you load your trailer. Do not put more weight towards the front, or the back, or to one side.
- It is **against the law** to have a load that is **sticking out in a dangerous way.**
- Don't forget that if you park a vehicle with a trailer overnight, it must have **lights.**

> **DID YOU KNOW?**
> A vehicle towing a trailer:
> - must **not** go over a **maximum speed limit of 60mph**
> (see table, page 218)
> - must **not** use the **right (outside) lane on a motorway.**

Snaking

'Snaking' means moving from side to side. A caravan will snake if it is not properly attached or loaded, or if the car pulling it is going too fast.

Vehicle Loading

If you are towing a caravan or trailer and it starts to snake:
- slow down – stop pressing the accelerator (do not brake suddenly)
- get back in control of the steering
- then brake gently.

The driver's responsibility for the passengers

There are also questions in the Vehicle Loading section about the safety of passengers. As the driver, you are responsible for making sure your vehicle is not overloaded – and this applies to people and animals as well as to luggage.

All passengers:
- must wear a **seat belt** (unless they have a medical certificate saying they should not wear one)
- all children under 14 must wear a seat belt or be strapped into a **child seat** or other 'restraint' suitable for their age. (See the section on Child Restraints in *The Highway Code* at the back of this book.)

Children

Children must not sit in the space behind the back seat of a hatchback car, and no passengers should sit in a caravan while it is being towed.

Pets

Pets should be kept under careful control. You might keep them and you safe with a special harness, or behind a screen in a hatchback to stop them being thrown forward in an accident.

DID YOU KNOW?

If you are going to buy a trailer, **make sure it fits your car's tow bar**. Tow bars **must** keep to EU regulations, and must have electric sockets to connect to the lights on the trailer.

When towing a heavy load, you might need to **blow your tyres up to more than the normal pressures**. Check your vehicle's handbook for advice. Remember to change back to the normal pressures when you finish your journey.

Now go to page 193 to test yourself on the questions about Vehicle Loading

Part 3

The Theory Test Questions

Contents PAGE

1 Before you make a U-turn in the road, you should

Mark one answer

- [ ] **A.** give an arm signal as well as using your indicators
- [ ] **B.** signal so that other drivers can slow down for you
- [ ] **C.** look over your shoulder for a final check
- [ ] **D.** select a higher gear than normal

See HIGHWAY CODE rule 135

2 As you approach this bridge you should

Oncoming vehicles in middle of road

Mark three answers

- [ ] **A.** move into the middle of the road to get a better view
- [ ] **B.** slow down
- [ ] **C.** get over the bridge as quickly as possible
- [ ] **D.** consider using your horn
- [ ] **E.** find another route
- [ ] **F.** beware of pedestrians

See HIGHWAY CODE rules 92, 132 & Warning signs

3 When following a large vehicle you should keep well back because

Mark one answer

- [ ] **A.** it allows you to corner more quickly
- [ ] **B.** it helps the large vehicle to stop more easily
- [ ] **C.** it allows the driver to see you in the mirrors
- [ ] **D.** it helps you to keep out of the wind

4 In which of these situations should you avoid overtaking?

Mark one answer

- [ ] **A.** Just after a bend
- [ ] **B.** In a one-way street
- [ ] **C.** On a 30mph road
- [ ] **D.** Approaching a dip in the road

See HIGHWAY CODE rule 142

5 This road marking warns

Mark one answer

- [ ] **A.** drivers to use the hard shoulder
- [ ] **B.** overtaking drivers there is a bend to the left
- [ ] **C.** overtaking drivers to move back to the left
- [ ] **D.** drivers that it is safe to overtake

See HIGHWAY CODE rule 107

6 Your mobile phone rings while you are travelling. You should

Mark one answer

- [ ] **A.** stop immediately
- [ ] **B.** answer it immediately
- [ ] **C.** pull up in a suitable place
- [ ] **D.** pull up at the nearest kerb

See HIGHWAY CODE rule 127

TIP Be aware that one in three of road accident fatalities are pedestrians or cyclists.

7 Why are these yellow lines painted across the road?

Mark one answer

- [ ] **A.** To help you choose the correct lane
- [ ] **B.** To help you keep the correct separation distance
- [ ] **C.** To make you aware of your speed
- [ ] **D.** To tell you the distance to the roundabout

8 You are approaching traffic lights that have been on green for some time. You should

Mark one answer

- [ ] **A.** accelerate hard
- [ ] **B.** maintain your speed
- [ ] **C.** be ready to stop
- [ ] **D.** brake hard

See HIGHWAY CODE rule 151 & Traffic light signals

9 Which of the following should you do before stopping?

Mark one answer

- [ ] **A.** Sound the horn
- [ ] **B.** Use the mirrors
- [ ] **C.** Select a higher gear
- [ ] **D.** Flash your headlights

See HIGHWAY CODE rule 137

10 As a driver what does the term 'Blind Spot' mean?

Mark one answer

- [ ] **A.** An area covered by your right-hand mirror
- [ ] **B.** An area not covered by your headlamps
- [ ] **C.** An area covered by your left-hand mirror
- [ ] **D.** An area not seen in your mirrors

See HIGHWAY CODE rule 135

11 Objects hanging from your interior mirror may

Mark two answers

- [ ] **A.** restrict your view
- [ ] **B.** improve your driving
- [ ] **C.** distract your attention
- [ ] **D.** help your concentration

12 Which of the following may cause loss of concentration on a long journey?

Mark four answers

- [ ] **A.** Loud music
- [ ] **B.** Arguing with a passenger
- [ ] **C.** Using a mobile phone
- [ ] **D.** Putting in a cassette tape
- [ ] **E.** Stopping regularly to rest
- [ ] **F.** Pulling up to tune the radio

See HIGHWAY CODE rules 126, 127

13 On a long motorway journey boredom can cause you to feel sleepy. You should

Mark two answers

- [ ] **A.** leave the motorway and find a safe place to stop
- [ ] **B.** keep looking around at the surrounding landscape
- [ ] **C.** drive faster to complete your journey sooner
- [ ] **D.** ensure a supply of fresh air into your vehicle
- [ ] **E.** stop on the hard shoulder for a rest

See HIGHWAY CODE rule 80

14 You are driving at dusk. You should switch your lights on

Mark two answers

- A. even when street lights are not lit
- B. so others can see you
- C. only when others have done so
- D. only when street lights are lit

See HIGHWAY CODE rules 93, 95

15 You are most likely to lose concentration when driving if you

Mark two answers

- A. use a mobile phone
- B. listen to very loud music
- C. switch on the heated rear window
- D. look at the door mirrors

See HIGHWAY CODE rules 126, 127

16 Which FOUR are most likely to cause you to lose concentration while you are driving?

Mark four answers

- A. Using a mobile phone
- B. Talking into a microphone
- C. Tuning your car radio
- D. Looking at a map
- E. Checking the mirrors
- F. Using the demisters

See HIGHWAY CODE rules 126, 127

17 You should not use a mobile phone whilst driving

Mark one answer

- A. until you are satisfied that no other traffic is near
- B. unless you are able to drive one handed
- C. because it might distract your attention from the road ahead
- D. because reception is poor when the engine is running

See HIGHWAY CODE rule 127

18 Your vehicle is fitted with a hands-free phone system. Using this equipment whilst driving

Mark one answer

- A. is quite safe as long as you slow down
- B. could distract your attention from the road
- C. is recommended by The Highway Code
- D. could be very good for road safety

See HIGHWAY CODE rule 127

19 Using a hands-free phone is likely to

Mark one answer

- A. improve your safety
- B. increase your concentration
- C. reduce your view
- D. divert your attention

See HIGHWAY CODE rule 127

20 You should ONLY use a mobile phone when

Mark one answer

- A. receiving a call
- B. suitably parked
- C. driving at less than 30mph
- D. driving an automatic vehicle

See HIGHWAY CODE rule 127

21 Using a mobile phone while you are driving

Mark one answer

- A. is acceptable in a vehicle with power steering
- B. will reduce your field of vision
- C. could distract your attention from the road
- D. will affect your vehicle's electronic systems

See HIGHWAY CODE rule 127

22 What is the safest way to use a mobile phone in your vehicle?

Mark one answer

- **A.** Use hands-free equipment
- **B.** Find a suitable place to stop
- **C.** Drive slowly on a quiet road
- **D.** Direct your call through the operator

See HIGHWAY CODE rule 127

23 You are driving on a wet road. You have to stop your vehicle in an emergency. You should

Mark one answer

- **A.** apply the handbrake and footbrake together
- **B.** keep both hands on the wheel
- **C.** select reverse gear
- **D.** give an arm signal

See HIGHWAY CODE rule 136

24 When you are moving off from behind a parked car you should

Mark three answers

- **A.** look round before you move off
- **B.** use all the mirrors on the vehicle
- **C.** look round after moving off
- **D.** use the exterior mirrors only
- **E.** give a signal if necessary
- **F.** give a signal after moving off

See HIGHWAY CODE rule 135

TIP When following long vehicles, keep well back so that you are visible in the driver's mirrors. Take a look at the markers on the sides and the end. They are there to warn you of the length of the vehicle, and sometimes overhanging loads.

25 You are travelling along this narrow country road. When passing the cyclist you should go

Mark one answer

- **A.** slowly, sounding the horn as you pass
- **B.** quickly, leaving plenty of room
- **C.** slowly, leaving plenty of room
- **D.** quickly, sounding the horn as you pass

See HIGHWAY CODE rule 139

26 Your vehicle is fitted with a hand-held telephone. To use the telephone you should

Mark one answer

- **A.** reduce your speed
- **B.** find a safe place to stop
- **C.** steer the vehicle with one hand
- **D.** be particularly careful at junctions

See HIGHWAY CODE rule 127

27 To answer a call on your mobile phone while travelling you should

Mark one answer

- **A.** reduce your speed wherever you are
- **B.** stop in a proper and convenient place
- **C.** keep the call time to a minimum
- **D.** slow down and allow others to overtake

See HIGHWAY CODE rule 127

28 Your mobile phone rings while you are on the motorway. Before answering you should

Mark one answer **NI**

- [ ] **A.** reduce your speed to 50mph
- [ ] **B.** pull up on the hard shoulder
- [ ] **C.** move into the left-hand lane
- [ ] **D.** stop in a safe place

See HIGHWAY CODE rule 127

29 You are turning right on to a dual carriageway. What should you do before emerging?

Mark one answer

- [ ] **A.** Stop, apply the handbrake and then select a low gear
- [ ] **B.** Position your vehicle well to the left of the side road
- [ ] **C.** Check that the central reserve is wide enough for your vehicle
- [ ] **D.** Make sure that you leave enough room for a following vehicle

See HIGHWAY CODE rule 149

30 You lose your way on a busy road. What is the best action to take?

Mark one answer

- [ ] **A.** Stop at traffic lights and ask pedestrians
- [ ] **B.** Shout to other drivers to ask them the way
- [ ] **C.** Turn into a side road, stop and check a map
- [ ] **D.** Check a map, and keep going with the traffic flow

See HIGHWAY CODE rules 122, 126

31 You are waiting to emerge from a junction. The screen pillar is restricting your view. What should you be particularly aware of?

Mark one answer

- [ ] **A.** Lorries
- [ ] **B.** Buses
- [ ] **C.** Motorcyclists
- [ ] **D.** Coaches

See HIGHWAY CODE rules 146, 187

32 When emerging from junctions which is most likely to obstruct your view?

Mark one answer

- [ ] **A.** Windscreen pillars
- [ ] **B.** Steering wheel
- [ ] **C.** Interior mirror
- [ ] **D.** Windscreen wipers

33 Windscreen pillars can obstruct your view. You should take particular care when

Mark one answer

- [ ] **A.** driving on a motorway
- [ ] **B.** driving on a dual carriageway
- [ ] **C.** approaching a one-way street
- [ ] **D.** approaching bends and junctions

34 You cannot see clearly behind when reversing. What should you do?

Mark one answer

- [ ] **A.** Open your window to look behind
- [ ] **B.** Open the door and look behind
- [ ] **C.** Look in the nearside mirror
- [ ] **D.** Ask someone to guide you

See HIGHWAY CODE rule 178

35 At a pelican crossing the flashing amber light means you MUST

Mark one answer
- **A.** stop and wait for the green light
- **B.** stop and wait for the red light
- **C.** give way to pedestrians waiting to cross
- **D.** give way to pedestrians already on the crossing

See HIGHWAY CODE rule 172

36 You should never wave people across at pedestrian crossings because

Mark one answer
- **A.** there may be another vehicle coming
- **B.** they may not be looking
- **C.** it is safer for you to carry on
- **D.** they may not be ready to cross

See HIGHWAY CODE rule 171

37 At a puffin crossing what colour follows the green signal?

Mark one answer
- **A.** Steady red
- **B.** Flashing amber
- **C.** Steady amber
- **D.** Flashing green

38 You could use the 'Two-Second Rule'

Mark one answer
- **A.** before restarting the engine after it has stalled
- **B.** to keep a safe gap from the vehicle in front
- **C.** before using the 'Mirror-Signal-Manoeuvre' routine
- **D.** when emerging on wet roads

See HIGHWAY CODE rule 105

39 'Tailgating' means

Mark one answer
- **A.** using the rear door of a hatchback car
- **B.** reversing into a parking space
- **C.** following another vehicle too closely
- **D.** driving with rear fog lights on

40 Following this vehicle too closely is unwise because

Mark one answer
- **A.** your brakes will overheat
- **B.** your view ahead is increased
- **C.** your engine will overheat
- **D.** your view ahead is reduced

See HIGHWAY CODE rule 197

41 You are following a vehicle on a wet road. You should leave a time gap of at least

Mark one answer
- **A.** one second
- **B.** two seconds
- **C.** three seconds
- **D.** four seconds

See HIGHWAY CODE rule 105

42 You are in a line of traffic. The driver behind you is following very closely. What action should you take?

Mark one answer
- **A.** Ignore the following driver and continue to drive within the speed limit
- **B.** Slow down, gradually increasing the gap between you and the vehicle in front
- **C.** Signal left and wave the following driver past
- **D.** Move over to a position just left of the centre line of the road

43 A long, heavily laden lorry is taking a long time to overtake you. What should you do?

Mark one answer
- [ ] **A.** Speed up
- [ ] **B.** Slow down
- [ ] **C.** Hold your speed
- [ ] **D.** Change direction

See HIGHWAY CODE rule 144

44 Which of the following vehicles will use blue flashing beacons?

Mark three answers
- [ ] **A.** Motorway maintenance
- [ ] **B.** Bomb disposal
- [ ] **C.** Blood transfusion
- [ ] **D.** Police patrol
- [ ] **E.** Breakdown recovery

45 Which THREE of these emergency services might have blue flashing beacons?

Mark three answers
- [ ] **A.** Coastguard
- [ ] **B.** Bomb disposal
- [ ] **C.** Gritting lorries
- [ ] **D.** Animal ambulances
- [ ] **E.** Mountain rescue
- [ ] **F.** Doctors' cars

46 When being followed by an ambulance showing a flashing blue beacon you should

Mark one answer
- [ ] **A.** pull over as soon as safely possible to let it pass
- [ ] **B.** accelerate hard to get away from it
- [ ] **C.** maintain your speed and course
- [ ] **D.** brake harshly and immediately stop in the road

See HIGHWAY CODE rule 194

47 What type of emergency vehicle is fitted with a green flashing beacon?

Mark one answer
- [ ] **A.** Fire engine
- [ ] **B.** Road gritter
- [ ] **C.** Ambulance
- [ ] **D.** Doctor's car

48 A flashing green beacon on a vehicle means

Mark one answer
- [ ] **A.** police on non-urgent duties
- [ ] **B.** doctor on an emergency call
- [ ] **C.** road safety patrol operating
- [ ] **D.** gritting in progress

49 A vehicle has a flashing green beacon. What does this mean?

Mark one answer
- [ ] **A.** A doctor is answering an emergency call
- [ ] **B.** The vehicle is slow moving
- [ ] **C.** It is a motorway police patrol vehicle
- [ ] **D.** A vehicle is carrying hazardous chemicals

50 Diamond-shaped signs give instructions to

Mark one answer
- [ ] **A.** tram drivers
- [ ] **B.** bus drivers
- [ ] **C.** lorry drivers
- [ ] **D.** taxi drivers

See HIGHWAY CODE rule 273

TIP *The Highway Code* advises you *not* to use your mobile if you have an accident on a motorway. Use the (free) emergency phone; it connects directly with the police, who will then be able to identify your exact location.

51 On a road where trams operate, which of these vehicles will be most at risk from the tram rails?

Mark one answer
- **A.** Cars
- **B.** Cycles
- **C.** Buses
- **D.** Lorries

See HIGHWAY CODE rule 278

52 What should you use your horn for?

Mark one answer
- **A.** To alert others to your presence
- **B.** To allow you right of way
- **C.** To greet other road users
- **D.** To signal your annoyance

See HIGHWAY CODE rule 92

53 You are in a one-way street and want to turn right. You should position yourself

Mark one answer
- **A.** in the right-hand lane
- **B.** in the left-hand lane
- **C.** in either lane, depending on the traffic
- **D.** just left of the centre line

See HIGHWAY CODE rule 121

54 You wish to turn right ahead. Why should you take up the correct position in good time?

Mark one answer
- **A.** To allow other drivers to pull out in front of you
- **B.** To give a better view into the road that you're joining
- **C.** To help other road users know what you intend to do
- **D.** To allow drivers to pass you on the right

See HIGHWAY CODE rule 85

55 At which type of crossing are cyclists allowed to ride across with pedestrians?

Mark one answer
- **A.** Toucan
- **B.** Puffin
- **C.** Pelican
- **D.** Zebra

See HIGHWAY CODE rule 65

56 A bus is stopped at a bus stop ahead of you. Its right-hand indicator is flashing. You should

Mark one answer
- **A.** flash your headlights and slow down
- **B.** slow down and give way if it is safe to do so
- **C.** sound your horn and keep going
- **D.** slow down and then sound your horn

See HIGHWAY CODE rule 198

57 You are travelling at the legal speed limit. A vehicle comes up quickly behind, flashing its headlights. You should

Mark one answer
- **A.** accelerate to make a gap behind you
- **B.** touch the brakes sharply to show your brake lights
- **C.** maintain your speed to prevent the vehicle from overtaking
- **D.** allow the vehicle to overtake

See HIGHWAY CODE rule 144

58 You should ONLY flash your headlights to other road users

Mark one answer

- [ ] **A.** to show that you are giving way
- [ ] **B.** to show that you are about to turn
- [ ] **C.** to tell them that you have right of way
- [ ] **D.** to let them know that you are there

See HIGHWAY CODE rule 90

59 You are approaching unmarked crossroads. How should you deal with this type of junction?

Mark one answer

- [ ] **A.** Accelerate and keep to the middle
- [ ] **B.** Slow down and keep to the right
- [ ] **C.** Accelerate looking to the left
- [ ] **D.** Slow down and look both ways

See HIGHWAY CODE rule 124

60 You are approaching a pelican crossing. The amber light is flashing. You MUST

Mark one answer

- [ ] **A.** give way to pedestrians who are crossing
- [ ] **B.** encourage pedestrians to cross
- [ ] **C.** not move until the green light appears
- [ ] **D.** stop even if the crossing is clear

See HIGHWAY CODE rule 172

61 At puffin crossings which light will not show to a driver?

Mark one answer

- [ ] **A.** Flashing amber
- [ ] **B.** Red
- [ ] **C.** Steady amber
- [ ] **D.** Green

See HIGHWAY CODE rule 175

62 A two-second gap between yourself and the car in front is sufficient when conditions are

Mark one answer

- [ ] **A.** wet
- [ ] **B.** good
- [ ] **C.** damp
- [ ] **D.** foggy

See HIGHWAY CODE rule 105

63 You are driving on a clear night. There is a steady stream of oncoming traffic. The national speed limit applies. Which lights should you use?

Mark one answer

- [ ] **A.** Full beam headlights
- [ ] **B.** Sidelights
- [ ] **C.** Dipped headlights
- [ ] **D.** Fog lights

See HIGHWAY CODE rules 93, 95

64 You are driving behind a large goods vehicle. It signals left but steers to the right. You should

Mark one answer

- [ ] **A.** slow down and let the vehicle turn
- [ ] **B.** drive on, keeping to the left
- [ ] **C.** overtake on the right of it
- [ ] **D.** hold your speed and sound your horn

See HIGHWAY CODE rules 146, 196

TIP Remember **O A P:**
Observe
Anticipate
Plan

65 You are driving along this road. The red van cuts in close in front of you. What should you do?

Mark one answer
- **A.** Accelerate to get closer to the red van
- **B.** Give a long blast on the horn
- **C.** Drop back to leave the correct separation distance
- **D.** Flash your headlights several times

See HIGHWAY CODE rule 144

66 You are waiting in a traffic queue at night. To avoid dazzling following drivers you should

Mark one answer
- **A.** apply the handbrake only
- **B.** apply the footbrake only
- **C.** switch off your headlights
- **D.** use both the handbrake and footbrake

See HIGHWAY CODE rule 94

67 You are driving in traffic at the speed limit for the road. The driver behind is trying to overtake. You should

Mark one answer
- **A.** move closer to the car ahead, so the driver behind has no room to overtake
- **B.** wave the driver behind to overtake when it is safe
- **C.** keep a steady course and allow the driver behind to overtake
- **D.** accelerate to get away from the driver behind

See HIGHWAY CODE rule 144

68 You are driving at night on an unlit road following a slower-moving vehicle. You should

Mark one answer
- **A.** flash your headlights
- **B.** use dipped beam headlights
- **C.** switch off your headlights
- **D.** use full beam headlights

See HIGHWAY CODE rules 94, 95

69 A bus lane on your left shows no times of operation. This means it is

BUS LANE

Mark one answer
- **A.** not in operation at all
- **B.** only in operation at peak times
- **C.** in operation 24 hours a day
- **D.** only in operation in daylight hours

See HIGHWAY CODE rule 120

70 You are driving along a country road. A horse and rider are approaching. What should you do?

Mark two answers
- **A.** Increase your speed
- **B.** Sound your horn
- **C.** Flash your headlights
- **D.** Drive slowly past
- **E.** Give plenty of room
- **F.** Rev your engine

See HIGHWAY CODE rule 191

71 A person herding sheep asks you to stop. You should

Mark one answer
- [ ] **A.** ignore them as they have no authority
- [ ] **B.** stop and switch off your engine
- [ ] **C.** continue on but drive slowly
- [ ] **D.** try and get past quickly

See HIGHWAY CODE rule 190

72 When overtaking a horse and rider you should

Mark one answer
- [ ] **A.** sound your horn as a warning
- [ ] **B.** go past as quickly as possible
- [ ] **C.** flash your headlights as a warning
- [ ] **D.** go past slowly and carefully

See HIGHWAY CODE rule 191

73 You are approaching a zebra crossing. Pedestrians are waiting to cross. You should

Mark one answer
- [ ] **A.** give way to the elderly and infirm only
- [ ] **B.** slow down and prepare to stop
- [ ] **C.** use your headlights to indicate they can cross
- [ ] **D.** wave at them to cross the road

See HIGHWAY CODE rule 171

74 You are driving a slow-moving vehicle on a narrow winding road. You should

Mark one answer
- [ ] **A.** keep well out to stop vehicles overtaking dangerously
- [ ] **B.** wave following vehicles past you if you think they can overtake quickly
- [ ] **C.** pull in safely when you can, to let following vehicles overtake
- [ ] **D.** give a left signal when it is safe for vehicles to overtake you

See HIGHWAY CODE rule 145

75 You are driving a slow-moving vehicle on a narrow road. When traffic wishes to overtake you should

Mark one answer
- [ ] **A.** take no action
- [ ] **B.** put your hazard warning lights on
- [ ] **C.** stop immediately and wave it on
- [ ] **D.** pull in safely as soon as you can do so

See HIGHWAY CODE rule 145

76 You are driving a slow-moving vehicle on a narrow winding road. In order to let other vehicles overtake you should

Mark one answer
- [ ] **A.** wave to them to pass
- [ ] **B.** pull in when you can
- [ ] **C.** show a left turn signal
- [ ] **D.** keep left and hold your speed

See HIGHWAY CODE rule 145

77 A vehicle pulls out in front of you at a junction. What should you do?

Mark one answer
- [ ] **A.** Swerve past it and sound your horn
- [ ] **B.** Flash your headlights and drive up close behind
- [ ] **C.** Slow down and be ready to stop
- [ ] **D.** Accelerate past it immediately

See HIGHWAY CODE rule 125

78 You stop for pedestrians waiting to cross at a zebra crossing. They do not start to cross. What should you do?

Mark one answer
- [ ] **A.** Be patient and wait
- [ ] **B.** Sound your horn
- [ ] **C.** Carry on
- [ ] **D.** Wave them to cross

See HIGHWAY CODE rule 171

79 You are following this lorry. You should keep well back from it to

Mark one answer

- A. give you a good view of the road ahead
- B. stop following traffic from rushing through the junction
- C. prevent traffic behind you from overtaking
- D. allow you to hurry through the traffic lights if they change

See HIGHWAY CODE rule 197

80 You are approaching a red light at a puffin crossing. Pedestrians are on the crossing. The red light will stay on until

Mark one answer

- A. you start to edge forward on to the crossing
- B. the pedestrians have reached a safe position
- C. the pedestrians are clear of the front of your vehicle
- D. a driver from the opposite direction reaches the crossing

See HIGHWAY CODE rule 175

81 Which instrument panel warning light would show that headlights are on full beam?

Mark one answer

A.

B.

C.

D.

TIP Blue flashing lights are used by ambulances, fire engines and police vehicles, as well as other emergency services Doctors on call display green flashing lights. Gritting lorries, motorway maintenance and breakdown recovery vehicles display flashing amber lights.

82 Which of these, if allowed to get low, could cause an accident?

Mark one answer

- **A.** Antifreeze level
- **B.** Brake fluid level
- **C.** Battery water level
- **D.** Radiator coolant level

See HIGHWAY CODE Annexe 6

83 Which TWO are badly affected if the tyres are under-inflated?

Mark two answers

- **A.** Braking
- **B.** Steering
- **C.** Changing gear
- **D.** Parking

See HIGHWAY CODE Annexe 6

84 Motor vehicles can harm the environment. This has resulted in

Mark three answers

- **A.** air pollution
- **B.** damage to buildings
- **C.** reduced health risks
- **D.** improved public transport
- **E.** less use of electrical vehicles
- **F.** using up natural resources

85 Excessive or uneven tyre wear can be caused by faults in which THREE?

Mark three answers

- **A.** The gearbox
- **B.** The braking system
- **C.** The accelerator
- **D.** The exhaust system
- **E.** Wheel alignment
- **F.** The suspension

See HIGHWAY CODE Annexe 6

86 You must NOT sound your horn

Mark one answer

- **A.** between 10pm and 6am in a built-up area
- **B.** at any time in a built-up area
- **C.** between 11.30pm and 7am in a built-up area
- **D.** between 11.30pm and 6am on any road

See HIGHWAY CODE rule 92

87 The pictured vehicle is 'environmentally friendly' because it

Mark three answers

- **A.** reduces noise pollution
- **B.** uses diesel fuel
- **C.** uses electricity
- **D.** uses unleaded fuel
- **E.** reduces parking spaces
- **F.** reduces town traffic

88 Supertrams or Light Rapid Transit (LRT) systems are environmentally friendly because

Mark one answer

- **A.** they use diesel power
- **B.** they use quieter roads
- **C.** they use electric power
- **D.** they do not operate during rush hour

TIP Large dogs should be in a secure area to the rear of a hatchback, with a screen to prevent them being thrown forward in the event of an accident.

89 'Red routes' in major cities have been introduced to

Mark one answer
- [ ] **A.** raise the speed limits
- [ ] **B.** help the traffic flow
- [ ] **C.** provide better parking
- [ ] **D.** allow lorries to load more freely

See HIGHWAY CODE Road markings: Along the carriageway

90 In some narrow residential streets you will find a speed limit of

Mark one answer
- [ ] **A.** 20mph
- [ ] **B.** 25mph
- [ ] **C.** 35mph
- [ ] **D.** 40mph

See HIGHWAY CODE rule 130

91 Road humps, chicanes, and narrowings are

Mark one answer
- [ ] **A.** always at major road works
- [ ] **B.** used to increase traffic speed
- [ ] **C.** at toll bridge approaches only
- [ ] **D.** traffic calming measures

See HIGHWAY CODE rule 131

92 The purpose of a catalytic converter is to reduce

Mark one answer
- [ ] **A.** fuel consumption
- [ ] **B.** the risk of fire
- [ ] **C.** toxic exhaust gases
- [ ] **D.** engine wear

93 Catalytic converters are fitted to make the

Mark one answer
- [ ] **A.** engine produce more power
- [ ] **B.** exhaust system easier to replace
- [ ] **C.** engine run quietly
- [ ] **D.** exhaust fumes cleaner

94 It is essential that tyre pressures are checked regularly. When should this be done?

Mark one answer
- [ ] **A.** After any lengthy journey
- [ ] **B.** After travelling at high speed
- [ ] **C.** When tyres are hot
- [ ] **D.** When tyres are cold

See HIGHWAY CODE Annexe 6

95 When should you NOT use your horn in a built-up area?

Mark one answer
- [ ] **A.** Between 8pm and 8am
- [ ] **B.** Between 9pm and dawn
- [ ] **C.** Between dusk and 8am
- [ ] **D.** Between 11.30pm and 7am

See HIGHWAY CODE rule 92

96 You will use more fuel if your tyres are

Mark one answer
- [ ] **A.** under-inflated
- [ ] **B.** of different makes
- [ ] **C.** over-inflated
- [ ] **D.** new and hardly used

97 How should you dispose of a used battery?

Mark two answers
- A. Take it to a local authority site
- B. Put it in the dustbin
- C. Break it up into pieces
- D. Leave it on waste land
- E. Take it to a garage
- F. Burn it on a fire

98 What is most likely to cause high fuel consumption?

Mark one answer
- A. Poor steering control
- B. Accelerating around bends
- C. Staying in high gears
- D. Harsh braking and accelerating

99 The fluid level in your battery is low. What should you top it up with?

Mark one answer
- A. Battery acid
- B. Distilled water
- C. Engine oil
- D. Engine coolant

100 You need top up your battery. What level should you fill to?

Mark one answer
- A. The top of the battery
- B. Half-way up the battery
- C. Just below the cell plates
- D. Just above the cell plates

101 You have too much oil in your engine. What could this cause?

Mark one answer
- A. Low oil pressure
- B. Engine overheating
- C. Chain wear
- D. Oil leaks

102 You are parking on a two-way road at night. The speed limit is 40mph. You should park on the

NI

Mark one answer
- A. left with parking lights on
- B. left with no lights on
- C. right with parking lights on
- D. right with dipped headlights on
See HIGHWAY CODE rule 222, 223

103 You are parked on the road at night. Where must you use parking lights?

Mark one answer
- A. Where there are continuous white lines in the middle of the road
- B. Where the speed limit exceeds 30mph
- C. Where you are facing oncoming traffic
- D. Where you are near a bus stop
See HIGHWAY CODE rule 223

104 Which FOUR of these MUST be in good working order for your car to be roadworthy?

Mark four answers
- A. Temperature gauge
- B. Speedometer
- C. Windscreen washers
- D. Windscreen wiper
- E. Oil warning light
- F. Horn
See HIGHWAY CODE Annexe 6

105 New petrol-engined cars must be fitted with catalytic converters. The reason for this is to

Mark one answer
- A. control exhaust noise levels
- B. prolong the life of the exhaust system
- C. allow the exhaust system to be recycled
- D. reduce harmful exhaust emissions

106 What can cause heavy steering?

Mark one answer

- [ ] **A.** Driving on ice
- [ ] **B.** Badly worn brakes
- [ ] **C.** Over-inflated tyres
- [ ] **D.** Under-inflated tyres

107 Driving with under-inflated tyres can affect

Mark two answers

- [ ] **A.** engine temperature
- [ ] **B.** fuel consumption
- [ ] **C.** braking
- [ ] **D.** oil pressure

108 Excessive or uneven tyre wear can be caused by faults in the

Mark two answers

- [ ] **A.** gearbox
- [ ] **B.** braking system
- [ ] **C.** suspension
- [ ] **D.** exhaust system

See HIGHWAY CODE Annexe 6

109 The main cause of brake fade is

Mark one answer

- [ ] **A.** the brakes overheating
- [ ] **B.** air in the brake fluid
- [ ] **C.** oil on the brakes
- [ ] **D.** the brakes out of adjustment

110 Your anti-lock brakes warning light stays on. You should

Mark one answer

- [ ] **A.** check the brake fluid level
- [ ] **B.** check the footbrake free play
- [ ] **C.** check that the handbrake is released
- [ ] **D.** have the brakes checked immediately

See HIGHWAY CODE Annexe 6

111 What does this instrument panel light mean when lit?

Mark one answer

- [ ] **A.** Gear lever in park
- [ ] **B.** Gear lever in neutral
- [ ] **C.** Handbrake on
- [ ] **D.** Handbrake off

112 While driving, this warning light on your dashboard comes on. It means

Mark one answer

- [ ] **A.** a fault in the braking system
- [ ] **B.** the engine oil is low
- [ ] **C.** a rear light has failed
- [ ] **D.** your seat belt is not fastened

113 It is important to wear suitable shoes when you are driving. Why is this?

Mark one answer

- [ ] **A.** To prevent wear on the pedals
- [ ] **B.** To maintain control of the pedals
- [ ] **C.** To enable you to adjust your seat
- [ ] **D.** To enable you to walk for assistance if you break down

See HIGHWAY CODE rule 73

114 A properly adjusted head restraint will

Mark one answer

- [ ] **A.** make you more comfortable
- [ ] **B.** help you to avoid neck injury
- [ ] **C.** help you to relax
- [ ] **D.** help you to maintain your driving position

See HIGHWAY CODE rule 73

115 What will reduce the risk of neck injury resulting from a collision?

Mark one answer

- [ ] **A.** An air-sprung seat
- [ ] **B.** Anti-lock brakes
- [ ] **C.** A collapsible steering wheel
- [ ] **D.** A properly adjusted head restraint

See HIGHWAY CODE rule 73

116 You are driving a friend's children home from school. They are both under 14 years old. Who is responsible for making sure they wear a seat belt?

Mark one answer

- [ ] **A.** An adult passenger
- [ ] **B.** The children
- [ ] **C.** You, the driver
- [ ] **D.** Your friend

See HIGHWAY CODE rules 75 table, 76

117 Car passengers MUST wear a seat belt if one is available, unless they are

Mark one answer

- [ ] **A.** under 14 years old
- [ ] **B.** under 1.5 metres (5 feet) in height
- [ ] **C.** sitting in the rear seat
- [ ] **D.** exempt for medical reasons

See HIGHWAY CODE rule 75 table

118 You are testing your suspension. You notice that your vehicle keeps bouncing when you press down on the front wing. What does this mean?

Mark one answer

- [ ] **A.** Worn tyres
- [ ] **B.** Tyres under-inflated
- [ ] **C.** Steering wheel not located centrally
- [ ] **D.** Worn shock absorbers

See HIGHWAY CODE Annexe 6

119 A roof rack fitted to your car will

Mark one answer

- [ ] **A.** reduce fuel consumption
- [ ] **B.** improve the road handling
- [ ] **C.** make your car go faster
- [ ] **D.** increase fuel consumption

120 It is illegal to drive with tyres that

Mark one answer

- [ ] **A.** have been bought second-hand
- [ ] **B.** have a large deep cut in the side wall
- [ ] **C.** are of different makes
- [ ] **D.** are of different tread patterns

See HIGHWAY CODE Annexe 6

121 The legal minimum depth of tread for car tyres over three quarters of the breadth is

Mark one answer

- [ ] **A.** 1mm
- [ ] **B.** 1.6mm
- [ ] **C.** 2.5mm
- [ ] **D.** 4mm

See HIGHWAY CODE Annexe 6

122 You are carrying two 13-year-old children and their parents in your car. Who is responsible for seeing that the children wear seat belts?

Mark one answer

- [ ] **A.** The children's parents
- [ ] **B.** You, the driver
- [ ] **C.** The front-seat passenger
- [ ] **D.** The children

See HIGHWAY CODE rules 75 table, 76

123 When a roof rack is not in use it should be removed. Why is this?

Mark one answer

- [ ] **A.** It will affect the suspension
- [ ] **B.** It is illegal
- [ ] **C.** It will affect your braking
- [ ] **D.** It will waste fuel

124 You have a loose filler cap on your diesel fuel tank. This will

Mark two answers

- [ ] **A.** waste fuel and money
- [ ] **B.** make roads slippery for other road users
- [ ] **C.** improve your vehicle's fuel consumption
- [ ] **D.** increase the level of exhaust emissions

125 How can you, as a driver, help the environment?

Mark three answers

- [ ] **A.** By reducing your speed
- [ ] **B.** By gentle acceleration
- [ ] **C.** By using leaded fuel
- [ ] **D.** By driving faster
- [ ] **E.** By harsh acceleration
- [ ] **F.** By servicing your vehicle properly

126 To help the environment, you can avoid wasting fuel by

Mark three answers

- [ ] **A.** having your vehicle properly serviced
- [ ] **B.** making sure your tyres are correctly inflated
- [ ] **C.** not over-revving in the lower gears
- [ ] **D.** driving at higher speeds where possible
- [ ] **E.** keeping an empty roof rack properly fitted
- [ ] **F.** servicing your vehicle less regularly

127 To reduce the volume of traffic on the roads you could

Mark three answers

- [ ] **A.** use public transport more often
- [ ] **B.** share a car when possible
- [ ] **C.** walk or cycle on short journeys
- [ ] **D.** travel by car at all times
- [ ] **E.** use a car with a smaller engine
- [ ] **F.** drive in a bus lane

128 Which THREE of the following are most likely to waste fuel?

Mark three answers

- [ ] **A.** Reducing your speed
- [ ] **B.** Carrying unnecessary weight
- [ ] **C.** Using the wrong grade of fuel
- [ ] **D.** Under-inflated tyres
- [ ] **E.** Using different brands of fuel
- [ ] **F.** A fitted, empty roof rack

129 To avoid spillage after refuelling, you should make sure that

Mark one answer

- [ ] **A.** your tank is only ¾ full
- [ ] **B.** you have used a locking filler cap
- [ ] **C.** you check your fuel gauge is working
- [ ] **D.** your filler cap is securely fastened

130 Which THREE things can you, as a road user, do to help the environment?

Mark three answers

- [ ] **A.** Cycle when possible
- [ ] **B.** Drive on under-inflated tyres
- [ ] **C.** Use the choke for as long as possible on a cold engine
- [ ] **D.** Have your vehicle properly tuned and serviced
- [ ] **E.** Watch the traffic and plan ahead
- [ ] **F.** Brake as late as possible without skidding

131 As a driver you can cause MORE damage to the environment by

Mark three answers
- [ ] **A.** choosing a fuel-efficient vehicle
- [ ] **B.** making a lot of short journeys
- [ ] **C.** driving in as high a gear as possible
- [ ] **D.** accelerating as quickly as possible
- [ ] **E.** having your vehicle regularly serviced
- [ ] **F.** using leaded fuel

132 Extra care should be taken when refuelling, because diesel fuel when spilt is

Mark one answer
- [ ] **A.** sticky
- [ ] **B.** odourless
- [ ] **C.** clear
- [ ] **D.** slippery

133 To help protect the environment you should NOT

Mark one answer
- [ ] **A.** remove your roof rack when unloaded
- [ ] **B.** use your car for very short journeys
- [ ] **C.** walk, cycle, or use public transport
- [ ] **D.** empty the boot of unnecessary weight

134 Which THREE does the law require you to keep in good condition?

Mark three answers
- [ ] **A.** Gears
- [ ] **B.** Transmission
- [ ] **C.** Headlights
- [ ] **D.** Windscreen
- [ ] **E.** Seat belts

See HIGHWAY CODE Annexe 6

135 Driving at 70mph uses more fuel than driving at 50mph by up to

Mark one answer
- [ ] **A.** 10%
- [ ] **B.** 30%
- [ ] **C.** 75%
- [ ] **D.** 100%

136 Your vehicle pulls to one side when braking. You should

Mark one answer
- [ ] **A.** change the tyres around
- [ ] **B.** consult your garage as soon as possible
- [ ] **C.** pump the pedal when braking
- [ ] **D.** use your handbrake at the same time

See HIGHWAY CODE Annexe 6

137 As a driver you can help reduce pollution levels in town centres by

Mark one answer
- [ ] **A.** driving more quickly
- [ ] **B.** using leaded fuel
- [ ] **C.** walking or cycling
- [ ] **D.** driving short journeys

138 Unbalanced wheels on a car may cause

Mark one answer
- [ ] **A.** the steering to pull to one side
- [ ] **B.** the steering to vibrate
- [ ] **C.** the brakes to fail
- [ ] **D.** the tyres to deflate

139 Turning the steering wheel while your car is stationary can cause damage to the

Mark two answers
- [ ] **A.** gearbox
- [ ] **B.** engine
- [ ] **C.** brakes
- [ ] **D.** steering
- [ ] **E.** tyres

140 How can you reduce the chances of your car being broken into when leaving it unattended?

Mark one answer

- **A.** Take all contents with you
- **B.** Park near a taxi rank
- **C.** Place any valuables on the floor
- **D.** Park near a fire station

See HIGHWAY CODE Annexe 6

141 You have to leave valuables in your car. It would be safer to

Mark one answer

- **A.** put them in a carrier bag
- **B.** park near a school entrance
- **C.** lock them out of sight
- **D.** park near a bus stop

See HIGHWAY CODE Annexe 6

142 How could you deter theft from your car when leaving it unattended?

Mark one answer

- **A.** Leave valuables in a carrier bag
- **B.** Lock valuables out of sight
- **C.** Put valuables on the seats
- **D.** Leave valuables on the floor

See HIGHWAY CODE Annexe 6

143 Which of the following may help to deter a thief from stealing your car?

Mark one answer

- **A.** Always keeping the headlights on
- **B.** Fitting reflective glass windows
- **C.** Always keeping the interior light on
- **D.** Etching the car number on the windows

See HIGHWAY CODE Annexe 6

144 How can you help to prevent your car radio being stolen?

Mark one answer

- **A.** Park in an unlit area
- **B.** Hide the radio with a blanket
- **C.** Park near a busy junction
- **D.** Install a security coded radio

145 Which of the following should not be kept in your vehicle?

Mark one answer

- **A.** A first aid kit
- **B.** A road atlas
- **C.** The tax disc
- **D.** The vehicle documents

See HIGHWAY CODE Annexe 6

146 What should you do when leaving your vehicle?

Mark one answer

- **A.** Put valuable documents under the seats
- **B.** Remove all valuables
- **C.** Cover valuables with a blanket
- **D.** Leave the interior light on

See HIGHWAY CODE Annexe 6

147 You are parking your car. You have some valuables which you are unable to take with you. What should you do?

Mark one answer

- **A.** Park near a police station
- **B.** Put them under the driver's seat
- **C.** Lock them out of sight
- **D.** Park in an unlit side road

See HIGHWAY CODE Annexe 6

148 Which of these is most likely to deter the theft of your vehicle?

Mark one answer
- A. An immobiliser
- B. Tinted windows
- C. Locking wheel nuts
- D. A sun screen

See HIGHWAY CODE Annexe 6

149 Wherever possible, which one of the following should you do when parking at night?

Mark one answer
- A. Park in a quiet car park
- B. Park in a well-lit area
- C. Park facing against the flow of traffic
- D. Park next to a busy junction

150 When parking and leaving your car you should

Mark one answer
- A. park under a shady tree
- B. remove the tax disc
- C. park in a quiet road
- D. engage the steering lock

See HIGHWAY CODE Annexe 6

151 Rear facing baby seats should NEVER be used on a seat protected with

Mark one answer
- A. an airbag
- B. seat belts
- C. head restraints
- D. seat covers

See HIGHWAY CODE rule 78

152 When leaving your vehicle parked and unattended you should

Mark one answer
- A. park near a busy junction
- B. park in a housing estate
- C. remove the key and lock it
- D. leave the left indicator on

See HIGHWAY CODE Annexe 6

153 How can you lessen the risk of your vehicle being broken into at night?

Mark one answer
- A. Leave it in a well-lit area
- B. Park in a quiet side road
- C. Don't engage the steering lock
- D. Park in a poorly lit area

154 To help keep your car secure you could join a

Mark one answer
- A. vehicle breakdown organisation
- B. vehicle watch scheme
- C. advanced drivers scheme
- D. car maintenance class

155 Which TWO of the following will improve fuel consumption?

Mark two answers
- A. Reducing your road speed
- B. Planning well ahead
- C. Late and harsh braking
- D. Driving in lower gears
- E. Short journeys with a cold engine
- F. Rapid acceleration

156 You service your own vehicle. How should you get rid of the old engine oil?

Mark one answer

- **A.** Take it to a local authority site
- **B.** Pour it down a drain
- **C.** Tip it into a hole in the ground
- **D.** Put it into your dustbin

157 On your vehicle, where would you find a catalytic converter?

Mark one answer

- **A.** In the fuel tank
- **B.** In the air filter
- **C.** On the cooling system
- **D.** On the exhaust system

158 Why do MOT tests include a strict exhaust emission test?

Mark one answer

- **A.** To recover the cost of expensive garage equipment
- **B.** To help protect the environment against pollution
- **C.** To discover which fuel supplier is used the most
- **D.** To make sure diesel and petrol engines emit the same fumes

159 To reduce the damage your vehicle causes to the environment you should

Mark three answers

- **A.** use narrow side streets
- **B.** avoid harsh acceleration
- **C.** brake in good time
- **D.** anticipate well ahead
- **E.** use busy routes

160 Your vehicle has a catalytic converter. Its purpose is to reduce

Mark one answer

- **A.** exhaust noise
- **B.** fuel consumption
- **C.** exhaust emissions
- **D.** engine noise

161 A properly serviced vehicle will give

Mark two answers

- **A.** lower insurance premiums
- **B.** you a refund on your road tax
- **C.** better fuel economy
- **D.** cleaner exhaust emissions

162 You enter a road where there are road humps. What should you do?

Mark one answer

- **A.** Maintain a reduced speed throughout
- **B.** Accelerate quickly between each one
- **C.** Always keep to the maximum legal speed
- **D.** Drive slowly at school times only

See HIGHWAY CODE rule 131

TIP Do not drive with an empty roof rack on your car. By increasing drag, the roof rack can eat up more than 10% of your total fuel consumption.

163 When should you especially check the engine oil level?

Mark one answer

- [ ] **A.** Before a long journey
- [ ] **B.** When the engine is hot
- [ ] **C.** Early in the morning
- [ ] **D.** Every 6,000 miles

164 You are having difficulty finding a parking space in a busy town. You can see there is space on the zigzag lines of a zebra crossing. Can you park there?

Mark one answer

- [ ] **A.** No, unless you stay with your car
- [ ] **B.** Yes, in order to drop off a passenger
- [ ] **C.** Yes, if you do not block people from crossing
- [ ] **D.** No, not in any circumstances

See HIGHWAY CODE rule 167

165 When leaving your car unattended for a few minutes you should

Mark one answer

- [ ] **A.** leave the engine running
- [ ] **B.** switch the engine off but leave the key in
- [ ] **C.** lock it and remove the key
- [ ] **D.** park near a traffic warden

See HIGHWAY CODE Annexe 6

166 When parking and leaving your car for a few minutes you should

Mark one answer

- [ ] **A.** leave it unlocked
- [ ] **B.** lock it and remove the key
- [ ] **C.** leave the hazard warning lights on
- [ ] **D.** leave the interior light on

See HIGHWAY CODE Annexe 6

167 When leaving your car to help keep it secure you should

Mark one answer

- [ ] **A.** leave the hazard warning lights on
- [ ] **B.** lock it and remove the key
- [ ] **C.** park on a one-way street
- [ ] **D.** park in a residential area

See HIGHWAY CODE Annexe 6

168 When leaving your vehicle where should you park if possible?

Mark one answer

- [ ] **A.** Opposite a traffic island
- [ ] **B.** In a secure car park
- [ ] **C.** On a bend
- [ ] **D.** At or near a taxi rank

See HIGHWAY CODE rules 214, 217

169 You are leaving your vehicle parked on a road. When may you leave the engine running?

Mark one answer

- [ ] **A.** If you will be parking for less than five minutes
- [ ] **B.** If the battery is flat
- [ ] **C.** When in a 20mph zone
- [ ] **D.** Never on any occasion

See HIGHWAY CODE rule 214

TIP If you have a petrol-fuelled car built after 1992, it will be fitted with a **catalytic converter**. *Catalyst* means something that enables a chemical change to take place; the catalytic converter, which is located in the car's exhaust system, converts pollutant gases into less harmful gases.

170

In which THREE places would parking your vehicle cause danger or obstruction to other road users?

Mark three answers
- A. In front of a property entrance
- B. At or near a bus stop
- C. On your driveway
- D. In a marked parking space
- E. On the approach to a level crossing

See HIGHWAY CODE rules 214, 217

TIP Driving a four-wheel drive vehicle (4WD) demands different techniques; a 4WD has a higher centre of gravity, and is more likely to topple over if you are forced to swerve or drive too fast around a tight corner. The advantage of 4WD is that it has better road holding capabilities and is excellent over rough terrain.

171

In which THREE places would parking cause an obstruction to others?

Mark three answers
- A. Near the brow of a hill
- B. In a lay-by
- C. Where the kerb is raised
- D. Where the kerb has been lowered for wheelchairs
- E. At or near a bus stop

See HIGHWAY CODE rules 217, 218

172

You are away from home and have to park your vehicle overnight. Where should you leave it?

Mark one answer
- A. Opposite another parked vehicle
- B. In a quiet road
- C. Opposite a traffic island
- D. In a secure car park

173 Braking distances on ice can be

Mark one answer

- [ ] A. twice the normal distance
- [ ] B. five times the normal distance
- [ ] C. seven times the normal distance
- [ ] D. ten times the normal distance

See HIGHWAY CODE rule 205

174 Freezing conditions will affect the distance it takes you to come to a stop. You should expect stopping distances to increase by up to

Mark one answer

- [ ] A. two times
- [ ] B. three times
- [ ] C. five times
- [ ] D. ten times

See HIGHWAY CODE rule 205

175 In very hot weather the road surface can get soft. Which TWO of the following will be affected most?

Mark two answers

- [ ] A. The suspension
- [ ] B. The grip of the tyres
- [ ] C. The braking
- [ ] D. The exhaust

See HIGHWAY CODE rule 212

176 Where are you most likely to be affected by a side wind?

Mark one answer

- [ ] A. On a narrow country lane
- [ ] B. On an open stretch of road
- [ ] C. On a busy stretch of road
- [ ] D. On a long, straight road

See HIGHWAY CODE rule 207

177 In windy conditions you need to take extra care when

Mark one answer

- [ ] A. using the brakes
- [ ] B. making a hill start
- [ ] C. turning into a narrow road
- [ ] D. passing pedal cyclists

See HIGHWAY CODE rule 207

178 What is the shortest stopping distance at 70mph?

Mark one answer

- [ ] A. 53 metres (175 feet)
- [ ] B. 60 metres (197 feet)
- [ ] C. 73 metres (240 feet)
- [ ] D. 96 metres (315 feet)

See HIGHWAY CODE rule 105 chart

179 What is the shortest overall stopping distance on a dry road from 60mph?

Mark one answer

- [ ] A. 53 metres (175 feet)
- [ ] B. 58 metres (190 feet)
- [ ] C. 73 metres (240 feet)
- [ ] D. 96 metres (315 feet)

See HIGHWAY CODE rule 105 chart

180 Your indicators may be difficult to see in bright sunlight. What should you do?

Mark one answer

- [ ] A. Put your indicator on earlier
- [ ] B. Give an arm signal as well as using your indicator
- [ ] C. Touch the brake several times to show the stop lights
- [ ] D. Turn as quickly as you can

See HIGHWAY CODE rule 85

181 In very hot weather the road surface can get soft. Which TWO of the following will be affected most?

Mark two answers

- [ ] **A.** The suspension
- [ ] **B.** The steering
- [ ] **C.** The braking
- [ ] **D.** The exhaust

See HIGHWAY CODE rule 212

182 When approaching a right-hand bend you should keep well to the left. Why is this?

Mark one answer

- [ ] **A.** To improve your view of the road
- [ ] **B.** To overcome the effect of the road's slope
- [ ] **C.** To let faster traffic from behind overtake
- [ ] **D.** To be positioned safely if you skid

See HIGHWAY CODE rule 136

183 You should not overtake when

Mark three answers

- [ ] **A.** intending to turn left shortly afterwards
- [ ] **B.** in a one-way street
- [ ] **C.** approaching a junction
- [ ] **D.** going up a long hill
- [ ] **E.** the view ahead is blocked

See HIGHWAY CODE rules 142, 143, 158

TIP Don't forget – you may have to deal with more than one hazard at a time!

184 You have just gone through deep water. To dry off the brakes you should

Mark one answer

- [ ] **A.** accelerate and keep to a high speed for a short time
- [ ] **B.** go slowly while gently applying the brakes
- [ ] **C.** avoid using the brakes at all for a few miles
- [ ] **D.** stop for at least an hour to allow them time to dry

See HIGHWAY CODE rule 101

185 You are on a fast, open road in good conditions. For safety, the distance between you and the vehicle in front should be

Mark one answer

- [ ] **A.** a two-second time gap
- [ ] **B.** one-car length
- [ ] **C.** 2 metres (6 feet 6 inches)
- [ ] **D.** two-car lengths

See HIGHWAY CODE rule 105

186 What is the most common cause of skidding?

Mark one answer

- [ ] **A.** Worn tyres
- [ ] **B.** Driver error
- [ ] **C.** Other vehicles
- [ ] **D.** Pedestrians

See HIGHWAY CODE rule 99

187 You are driving on an icy road. How can you avoid wheelspin?

Mark one answer

- [ ] **A.** Drive at a slow speed in as high a gear as possible
- [ ] **B.** Use the handbrake if the wheels start to slip
- [ ] **C.** Brake gently and repeatedly
- [ ] **D.** Drive in a low gear at all times

See HIGHWAY CODE rule 206

188 Skidding is mainly caused by

Mark one answer
- A. the weather
- B. the driver
- C. the vehicle
- D. the road

See HIGHWAY CODE rule 99

189 You are driving in freezing conditions. What should you do when approaching a sharp bend?

Mark two answers
- A. Slow down before you reach the bend
- B. Gently apply your handbrake
- C. Firmly use your footbrake
- D. Coast into the bend
- E. Avoid sudden steering movements

See HIGHWAY CODE rule 206

190 You are turning left on a slippery road. The back of your vehicle slides to the right. You should

Mark one answer
- A. brake firmly and not turn the steering wheel
- B. steer carefully to the left
- C. steer carefully to the right
- D. brake firmly and steer to the left

See HIGHWAY CODE rule 99

191 You are braking on a wet road. Your vehicle begins to skid. Your vehicle does not have anti-lock brakes. What is the FIRST thing you should do?

Mark one answer
- A. Quickly pull up the handbrake
- B. Release the footbrake fully
- C. Push harder on the brake pedal
- D. Gently use the accelerator

See HIGHWAY CODE rule 99

192 Coasting the vehicle

Mark one answer
- A. improves the driver's control
- B. makes steering easier
- C. reduces the driver's control
- D. uses more fuel

See HIGHWAY CODE rule 102

193 Before starting a journey in freezing weather you should clear ice and snow from your vehicle's

Mark four answers
- A. aerial
- B. windows
- C. bumper
- D. lights
- E. mirrors
- F. number plates

See HIGHWAY CODE rule 204

194 You are trying to move off on snow. You should use

Mark one answer
- A. the lowest gear you can
- B. the highest gear you can
- C. a high engine speed
- D. the handbrake and footbrake together

See HIGHWAY CODE rule 206

195 When driving in falling snow you should

Mark one answer
- A. brake firmly and quickly
- B. be ready to steer sharply
- C. use sidelights only
- D. brake gently in plenty of time

See HIGHWAY CODE rule 206

196 The MAIN benefit of having four-wheel drive is to improve

Mark one answer

- [ ] **A.** road holding
- [ ] **B.** fuel consumption
- [ ] **C.** stopping distances
- [ ] **D.** passenger comfort

197 You are about to go down a steep hill. To control the speed of your vehicle you should

Mark one answer

- [ ] **A.** select a high gear and use the brakes carefully
- [ ] **B.** select a high gear and use the brakes firmly
- [ ] **C.** select a low gear and use the brakes carefully
- [ ] **D.** select a low gear and avoid using the brakes

See HIGHWAY CODE rule 136

198 How can you use the engine of your vehicle as a brake?

Mark one answer

- [ ] **A.** By changing to a lower gear
- [ ] **B.** By selecting reverse gear
- [ ] **C.** By changing to a higher gear
- [ ] **D.** By selecting neutral gear

199 You wish to park facing DOWNHILL. Which TWO of the following should you do?

Mark two answers

- [ ] **A.** Turn the steering wheel towards the kerb
- [ ] **B.** Park close to the bumper of another car
- [ ] **C.** Park with two wheels on the kerb
- [ ] **D.** Put the handbrake on firmly
- [ ] **E.** Turn the steering wheel away from the kerb

See HIGHWAY CODE rule 226

200 You are driving in a built-up area. You approach a speed hump. You should

Mark one answer

- [ ] **A.** move across to the left-hand side of the road
- [ ] **B.** wait for any pedestrians to cross
- [ ] **C.** slow your vehicle right down
- [ ] **D.** stop and check both pavements

See HIGHWAY CODE rule 131

201 You are on a long, downhill slope. What should you do to help control the speed of your vehicle?

Mark one answer

- [ ] **A.** Select neutral
- [ ] **B.** Select a lower gear
- [ ] **C.** Grip the handbrake firmly
- [ ] **D.** Apply the parking brake gently

See HIGHWAY CODE rule 136

202 Your vehicle is fitted with anti-lock brakes. To stop quickly in an emergency you should

NI

Mark one answer

- [ ] **A.** brake firmly and pump the brake pedal on and off
- [ ] **B.** brake rapidly and firmly without releasing the brake pedal
- [ ] **C.** brake gently and pump the brake pedal on and off
- [ ] **D.** brake rapidly once, and immediately release the brake pedal

See HIGHWAY CODE rule 100

203 Anti-lock brakes prevent wheels from locking. This means the tyres are less likely to

Mark one answer

- [ ] **A.** aquaplane
- [ ] **B.** skid
- [ ] **C.** puncture
- [ ] **D.** wear

See HIGHWAY CODE rule 98

204 Anti-lock brakes reduce the chances of a skid occurring particularly when

Mark one answer

- [ ] **A.** driving down steep hills
- [ ] **B.** braking during normal driving
- [ ] **C.** braking in an emergency
- [ ] **D.** driving on good road surfaces

See HIGHWAY CODE rule 100

205 Anti-lock brakes are most effective when you

Mark one answer   NI

- [ ] **A.** keep pumping the footbrake to prevent skidding
- [ ] **B.** brake normally, but grip the steering wheel tightly
- [ ] **C.** brake rapidly and firmly until you have slowed down
- [ ] **D.** apply the handbrake to reduce the stopping distance

See HIGHWAY CODE rule 100

206 Your car is fitted with anti-lock brakes. You need to stop in an emergency. You should

Mark one answer   NI

- [ ] **A.** brake normally and avoid turning the steering wheel
- [ ] **B.** press the brake pedal rapidly and firmly until you have stopped
- [ ] **C.** keep pushing and releasing the footbrake quickly to prevent skidding
- [ ] **D.** apply the handbrake to reduce the stopping distance

See HIGHWAY CODE rule 100

207 Vehicles fitted with anti-lock brakes

Mark one answer

- [ ] **A.** are impossible to skid
- [ ] **B.** can be steered while you are braking
- [ ] **C.** accelerate much faster
- [ ] **D.** are not fitted with a handbrake

See HIGHWAY CODE rule 100

208 Anti-lock brakes may not work as effectively if the road surface is

Mark two answers

- [ ] **A.** dry
- [ ] **B.** loose
- [ ] **C.** wet
- [ ] **D.** good
- [ ] **E.** firm

209 Anti-lock brakes are of most use when you are

Mark one answer

- [ ] **A.** braking gently
- [ ] **B.** driving on worn tyres
- [ ] **C.** braking excessively
- [ ] **D.** driving normally

See HIGHWAY CODE rule 100

210 Driving a vehicle fitted with anti-lock brakes allows you to

Mark one answer

A. brake harder because it is impossible to skid
B. drive at higher speeds
C. steer and brake at the same time
D. pay less attention to the road ahead

See HIGHWAY CODE rule 100

211 Anti-lock brakes can greatly assist with

Mark one answer

A. a higher cruising speed
B. steering control when braking
C. control when accelerating
D. motorway driving

See HIGHWAY CODE rule 100

212 When would an anti-lock braking system start to work?

Mark one answer

A. After the parking brake has been applied
B. Whenever pressure on the brake pedal is applied
C. Just as the wheels are about to lock
D. When the normal braking system fails to operate

213 You are driving a vehicle fitted with anti-lock brakes. You need to stop in an emergency. You should apply the footbrake

Mark one answer   **NI**

A. slowly and gently
B. slowly but firmly
C. rapidly and gently
D. rapidly and firmly

See HIGHWAY CODE rule 100

214 Your vehicle has anti-lock brakes, but they may not always prevent skidding. This is most likely to happen when driving

Mark two answers

A. in foggy conditions
B. on surface water
C. on loose road surfaces
D. on dry tarmac
E. at night on unlit roads

215 Anti-lock brakes will take effect when

Mark one answer

A. you do not brake quickly enough
B. excessive brake pressure has been applied
C. you have not seen a hazard ahead
D. speeding on slippery road surfaces

216 When driving in fog, which of the following are correct?

Mark three answers

A. Use dipped headlights
B. Use headlights on full beam
C. Allow more time for your journey
D. Keep close to the car in front
E. Slow down
F. Use sidelights only

See HIGHWAY CODE rules 73, 209

TIP Never coast downhill. Keep in a low gear so that you have engine braking as well as the footbrake. The lower the gear the stronger the engine braking.

217 You are driving along a country road. You see this sign. AFTER dealing safely with the hazard you should always

Ford

Mark one answer
- **A.** check your tyre pressures
- **B.** switch on your hazard warning lights
- **C.** accelerate briskly
- **D.** test your brakes

See HIGHWAY CODE rule 101

218 You are driving in heavy rain. Your steering suddenly becomes very light. You should

Mark one answer
- **A.** steer towards the side of the road
- **B.** apply gentle acceleration
- **C.** brake firmly to reduce speed
- **D.** ease off the accelerator

See HIGHWAY CODE rule 202

219 How can you tell when you are driving over black ice?

Mark one answer
- **A.** It is easier to brake
- **B.** The noise from your tyres sounds louder
- **C.** You see black ice on the road
- **D.** Your steering feels light

See HIGHWAY CODE rule 206

220 The roads are icy. You should drive slowly

Mark one answer
- **A.** in the highest gear possible
- **B.** in the lowest gear possible
- **C.** with the handbrake partly on
- **D.** with your left foot on the brake

See HIGHWAY CODE rule 206

221 You are driving along a wet road. How can you tell if your vehicle is aquaplaning?

Mark one answer
- **A.** The engine will stall
- **B.** The engine noise will increase
- **C.** The steering will feel very heavy
- **D.** The steering will feel very light

See HIGHWAY CODE rule 202

222 How can you tell if you are driving on ice?

Mark two answers
- **A.** The tyres make a rumbling noise
- **B.** The tyres make hardly any noise
- **C.** The steering becomes heavier
- **D.** The steering becomes lighter

See HIGHWAY CODE rule 206

223 You are driving along a wet road. How can you tell if your vehicle's tyres are losing their grip on the surface?

Mark one answer
- **A.** The engine will stall
- **B.** The steering will feel very heavy
- **C.** The engine noise will increase
- **D.** The steering will feel very light

See HIGHWAY CODE rule 202

224 You are travelling at 50mph on a good, dry road. What is your shortest overall stopping distance?

Mark one answer
- **A.** 36 metres (120 feet)
- **B.** 53 metres (175 feet)
- **C.** 75 metres (245 feet)
- **D.** 96 metres (315 feet)

See HIGHWAY CODE rule 105 chart

225 Your overall stopping distance will be much longer when driving

Mark one answer
- **A.** in the rain
- **B.** in fog
- **C.** at night
- **D.** in strong winds

See HIGHWAY CODE rule 105

226 You have driven through a flood. What is the first thing you should do?

Mark one answer
- **A.** Stop and check the tyres
- **B.** Stop and dry the brakes
- **C.** Check your exhaust
- **D.** Test your brakes

See HIGHWAY CODE rule 101

227 You are on a good, dry road surface. Your vehicle has good brakes and tyres. What is the BRAKING distance at 50mph?

Mark one answer
- **A.** 38 metres (125 feet)
- **B.** 14 metres (46 feet)
- **C.** 24 metres (79 feet)
- **D.** 55 metres (180 feet)

See HIGHWAY CODE rule 105 chart

228 You are on a good, dry, road surface and your vehicle has good brakes and tyres. What is the typical overall stopping distance at 40mph?

Mark one answer
- **A.** 23 metres (75 feet)
- **B.** 36 metres (120 feet)
- **C.** 53 metres (175 feet)
- **D.** 96 metres (315 feet)

See HIGHWAY CODE rule 105 chart

TIP Remember the 'two-second rule'? Well you can 'Say it again when driving in rain!' In other words, you need to allow at least twice the distance for braking and stopping in wet weather.

229

You see this sign on the rear of a slow-moving lorry that you want to pass. It is travelling in the middle lane of a three-lane motorway. You should

Mark one answer

- [ ] **A.** cautiously approach the lorry then pass on either side
- [ ] **B.** follow the lorry until you can leave the motorway
- [ ] **C.** wait on the hard shoulder until the lorry has stopped
- [ ] **D.** approach with care and keep to the left of the lorry

See HIGHWAY CODE Road works signs

230

Where would you expect to see these markers?

Mark two answers

- [ ] **A.** On a motorway sign
- [ ] **B.** At the entrance to a narrow bridge
- [ ] **C.** On a large goods vehicle
- [ ] **D.** On a builder's skip placed on the road

See HIGHWAY CODE Vehicle markings

231

What does this signal from a police officer, mean to oncoming traffic?

Mark one answer

- [ ] **A.** Go ahead
- [ ] **B.** Stop
- [ ] **C.** Turn left
- [ ] **D.** Turn right

See HIGHWAY CODE Signals by authorised persons

232

What is the main hazard shown in this picture?

Mark one answer

- [ ] **A.** Vehicles turning right
- [ ] **B.** Vehicles doing U-turns
- [ ] **C.** The cyclist crossing the road
- [ ] **D.** Parked cars around the corner

See HIGHWAY CODE rule 146

233 Which road user has caused a hazard?

Mark one answer
- [ ] **A.** The parked car (arrowed A)
- [ ] **B.** The pedestrian waiting to cross (arrowed B)
- [ ] **C.** The moving car (arrowed C)
- [ ] **D.** The car turning (arrowed D)

See HIGHWAY CODE rule 167

234 What should the driver of the car approaching the crossing do?

Mark one answer
- [ ] **A.** Continue at the same speed
- [ ] **B.** Sound the horn
- [ ] **C.** Drive through quickly
- [ ] **D.** Slow down and get ready to stop

See HIGHWAY CODE rule 171

235 What THREE things should the driver of the grey car (arrowed) be especially aware of?

Mark three answers
- [ ] **A.** Pedestrians stepping out between cars
- [ ] **B.** Other cars behind the grey car
- [ ] **C.** Doors opening on parked cars
- [ ] **D.** The bumpy road surface
- [ ] **E.** Cars leaving parking spaces
- [ ] **F.** Empty parking spaces

See HIGHWAY CODE rule 130

236 You think the driver of the vehicle in front has forgotten to cancel the right indicator. You should

Mark one answer
- [ ] **A.** flash your lights to alert the driver
- [ ] **B.** sound your horn before overtaking
- [ ] **C.** overtake on the left if there is room
- [ ] **D.** stay behind and not overtake

See HIGHWAY CODE rules 86, 143

TIP If you are driving past parked cars, it is a good idea to leave as much space as the width of a car door – in case one opens suddenly. If you can't give that much space, slow down so that you could **stop** if necessary.

237
What is the main hazard the driver of the red car (arrowed) should be most aware of?

Mark one answer

- **A.** Glare from the sun may affect the driver's vision
- **B.** The black car may stop suddenly
- **C.** The bus may move out into the road
- **D.** Oncoming vehicles will assume the driver is turning right

See HIGHWAY CODE rule 198

238
In heavy motorway traffic you are being followed closely by the vehicle behind. How can you lower the risk of an accident?

Mark one answer

- **A.** Increase your distance from the vehicle in front
- **B.** Tap your foot on the brake pedal sharply
- **C.** Switch on your hazard lights
- **D.** Move on to the hard shoulder and stop

239
You see this sign ahead. You should expect the road to

Mark one answer

- **A.** go steeply uphill
- **B.** go steeply downhill
- **C.** bend sharply to the left
- **D.** bend sharply to the right

See HIGHWAY CODE Warning signs

240
You are approaching this cyclist. You should

Mark one answer

- **A.** overtake before the cyclist gets to the junction
- **B.** flash your headlights at the cyclist
- **C.** slow down and allow the cyclist to turn
- **D.** overtake the cyclist on the left-hand side

See HIGHWAY CODE rule 143

241 Why must you take extra care when turning right at this junction?

Mark one answer
- **A.** Road surface is poor
- **B.** Footpaths are narrow
- **C.** Road markings are faint
- **D.** There is reduced visibility

242 This yellow sign on a vehicle indicates this is

Mark one answer
- **A.** a vehicle broken down
- **B.** a school bus
- **C.** an ice-cream van
- **D.** a private ambulance

See HIGHWAY CODE Vehicle markings

243 When approaching this bridge you should give way to

Mark one answer
- **A.** bicycles
- **B.** buses
- **C.** motorcycles
- **D.** cars

See HIGHWAY CODE Warning signs

244 What type of vehicle could you expect to meet in the middle of the road?

Mark one answer
- **A.** Lorry
- **B.** Bicycle
- **C.** Car
- **D.** Motorcycle

See HIGHWAY CODE Warning signs

> **TIP** Driver sleepiness is thought to cause at least 10% of all road accidents and one in five of accidents on motorways and major roads.

245 At this blind junction you must stop

Mark one answer

- **A.** behind the line, then edge forward to see clearly
- **B.** beyond the line at a point where you can see clearly
- **C.** only if there is traffic on the main road
- **D.** only if you are turning to the right

See HIGHWAY CODE rule 147

246 A driver pulls out of a side road in front of you. You have to brake hard. You should

Mark one answer

- **A.** ignore the error and stay calm
- **B.** flash your lights to show your annoyance
- **C.** sound your horn to show your annoyance
- **D.** overtake as soon as possible

See HIGHWAY CODE rule 125

247 An elderly person's driving ability could be affected because they may be unable to

Mark one answer

- **A.** obtain car insurance
- **B.** understand road signs
- **C.** react very quickly
- **D.** give signals correctly

See HIGHWAY CODE rule 192

248 You have just passed these warning lights. What hazard would you expect to see next?

Mark one answer

- **A.** A level crossing with no barrier
- **B.** An ambulance station
- **C.** A school crossing patrol
- **D.** An opening bridge

See HIGHWAY CODE rule 184

249 Why should you be especially cautious when going past this bus?

Mark two answers

- **A.** There is traffic approaching in the distance
- **B.** The driver may open the door
- **C.** It may suddenly move off
- **D.** People may cross the road in front of it
- **E.** There are bicycles parked on the pavement

See HIGHWAY CODE rule 182

250 In areas where there are 'traffic calming' measures you should

Mark one answer

- **A.** drive at a reduced speed
- **B.** always drive at the speed limit
- **C.** position in the centre of the road
- **D.** only slow down if pedestrians are near

See HIGHWAY CODE rule 131

251 You are planning a long journey. Do you need to plan rest stops?

Mark one answer
- A. Yes, you should plan to stop every half an hour
- B. Yes, regular stops help concentration
- C. No, you will be less tired if you get there as soon as possible
- D. No, only fuel stops will be needed

See HIGHWAY CODE rule 80

252 A driver does something that upsets you. You should

Mark one answer
- A. try not to react
- B. let them know how you feel
- C. flash your headlights several times
- D. sound your horn

See HIGHWAY CODE rule 125

253 The red lights are flashing. What should you do when approaching this level crossing?

Mark one answer
- A. Go through quickly
- B. Go through carefully
- C. Stop before the barrier
- D. Switch on hazard warning lights

See HIGHWAY CODE rule 266

254 What are TWO main hazards you should be aware of when going along this street?

Mark two answers
- A. Glare from the sun
- B. Car doors opening suddenly
- C. Lack of road markings
- D. The headlights on parked cars being switched on
- E. Large goods vehicles
- F. Children running out from between vehicles

See HIGHWAY CODE rule 130

255 What is the main hazard you should be aware of when following this cyclist?

Mark one answer
- A. The cyclist may move into the left and dismount
- B. The cyclist may swerve out into the road
- C. The contents of the cyclist's carrier may fall on to the road
- D. The cyclist may wish to turn right at the end of the road

See HIGHWAY CODE rule 189

256 When approaching this hazard why should you slow down?

Mark two answers

- **A.** Because of the bend
- **B.** Because it's hard to see to the right
- **C.** Because of approaching traffic
- **D.** Because of animals crossing
- **E.** Because of the level crossing

See HIGHWAY CODE rules 104, 265 & Warning signs

257 A driver's behaviour has upset you. It may help if you

Mark one answer

- **A.** stop and take a break
- **B.** shout abusive language
- **C.** gesture to them with your hand
- **D.** follow their car, flashing the headlights

See HIGHWAY CODE rule 125

258 You are on a dual carriageway. Ahead you see a vehicle with an amber flashing light. What will this be?

Mark one answer

- **A.** An ambulance
- **B.** A fire engine
- **C.** A doctor on call
- **D.** A disabled person's vehicle

See HIGHWAY CODE rule 195

259 You are approaching crossroads. The traffic lights have failed. What should you do?

Mark one answer

- **A.** Brake and stop only for large vehicles
- **B.** Brake sharply to a stop before looking
- **C.** Be prepared to brake sharply to a stop
- **D.** Be prepared to stop for any traffic.

See HIGHWAY CODE rule 152

260 Why are destination markings painted on the road surface?

Mark one answer

- **A.** To restrict the flow of traffic
- **B.** To warn you of oncoming traffic
- **C.** To enable you to change lanes early
- **D.** To prevent you changing lanes

261 What should the driver of the red car (arrowed) do?

Mark one answer

- **A.** Wave the pedestrians who are waiting to cross
- **B.** Wait for the pedestrian in the road to cross
- **C.** Quickly drive behind the pedestrian in the road
- **D.** Tell the pedestrian in the road she should not have crossed

262 You are following a slower-moving vehicle on a narrow country road. There is a junction just ahead on the right. What should you do?

Mark one answer

- **A.** Overtake after checking your mirrors and signalling
- **B.** Stay behind until you are past the junction
- **C.** Accelerate quickly to pass before the junction
- **D.** Slow down and prepare to overtake on the left

See HIGHWAY CODE rule 143

263 What should you do as you approach this overhead bridge?

Mark one answer

- **A.** Move out to the centre of the road before going through
- **B.** Find another route, this is only for high vehicles
- **C.** Be prepared to give way to large vehicles in the middle of the road
- **D.** Move across to the right-hand side before going through

264 Why are mirrors often slightly curved (convex)?

Mark one answer

- **A.** They give a wider field of vision
- **B.** They totally cover blind spots
- **C.** They make it easier to judge the speed of following traffic
- **D.** They make following traffic look bigger

265 What does the solid white line at the side of the road indicate?

Mark one answer

- **A.** Traffic lights ahead
- **B.** Edge of the carriageway
- **C.** Footpath on the left
- **D.** Cycle path

See HIGHWAY CODE Road markings: Along the carriageway

266 You are driving towards this level crossing. What would be the first warning of an approaching train?

Mark one answer

- **A.** Both half-barriers down
- **B.** A steady amber light
- **C.** One half-barrier down
- **D.** Twin flashing red lights

See HIGHWAY CODE rule 266

TIP Leave sufficient room to allow for the mistakes of others. After all, if an accident occurs, the fact that it was not your fault will be little consolation.

267 You are driving along this motorway. It is raining. When following this lorry you should

Mark two answers
- [ ] **A.** allow at least a two-second gap
- [ ] **B.** move left and drive on the hard shoulder
- [ ] **C.** allow at least a four-second gap
- [ ] **D.** be aware of spray reducing your vision
- [ ] **E.** move right and stay in the right-hand lane

See HIGHWAY CODE rules 105, 202

268 You are behind this cyclist. When the traffic lights change, what should you do?

Mark one answer
- [ ] **A.** Try to move off before the cyclist
- [ ] **B.** Allow the cyclist time and room
- [ ] **C.** Turn right but give the cyclist room
- [ ] **D.** Tap your horn and drive through first

See HIGHWAY CODE rule 154

269 You are driving towards this left-hand bend. What dangers should you be aware of?

Mark one answer
- [ ] **A.** A vehicle overtaking you
- [ ] **B.** No white lines in the centre of the road
- [ ] **C.** No sign to warn you of the bend
- [ ] **D.** Pedestrians walking towards you

See HIGHWAY CODE rule 132

270 While driving, you see this sign ahead. You should

Mark one answer
- [ ] **A.** stop at the sign
- [ ] **B.** slow, but continue around the bend
- [ ] **C.** slow to a crawl and continue
- [ ] **D.** stop and look for open farm gates

See HIGHWAY CODE Warning signs

271 Why should the junction on the left be kept clear?

Mark one answer
- [ ] **A.** To allow vehicles to enter and emerge
- [ ] **B.** To allow the bus to reverse
- [ ] **C.** To allow vehicles to make a U-turn
- [ ] **D.** To allow vehicles to park

See HIGHWAY CODE rule 129

272 When the traffic lights change to green the white car should

Mark one answer
- [ ] **A.** wait for the cyclist to pull away
- [ ] **B.** move off quickly and turn in front of the cyclist
- [ ] **C.** move close up to the cyclist to beat the lights
- [ ] **D.** sound the horn to warn the cyclist

See HIGHWAY CODE rule 182

273 You intend to turn left at the traffic lights. Just before turning you should

Mark one answer
- [ ] **A.** check your right mirror
- [ ] **B.** move close up to the white car
- [ ] **C.** straddle the lanes
- [ ] **D.** check for bicycles on your left

See HIGHWAY CODE rule 158

274 You should reduce your speed when driving along this road because

Mark one answer
- [ ] **A.** there is a staggered junction ahead
- [ ] **B.** there is a low bridge ahead
- [ ] **C.** there is a change in the road surface
- [ ] **D.** the road ahead narrows

See HIGHWAY CODE rule 124 & Warning signs

275 You are driving at 60mph. As you approach this hazard you should

Mark one answer

- A. maintain your speed
- B. reduce your speed
- C. take the next right turn
- D. take the next left turn

See HIGHWAY CODE rule 124 & Warning signs

276 The traffic ahead of you in the left lane is slowing. You should

Mark two answers

- A. be wary of cars on your right cutting in
- B. accelerate past the vehicles in the left lane
- C. pull up on the left-hand verge
- D. move across and continue in the right-hand lane
- E. slow down keeping a safe separation distance

See HIGHWAY CODE rules 144, 263

277 What might you expect to happen in this situation?

Mark one answer

- A. Traffic will move into the right-hand lane
- B. Traffic speed will increase
- C. Traffic will move into the left-hand lane
- D. Traffic will not need to change position

See HIGHWAY CODE Road works signs

278 You are driving on a road with several lanes. You see these signs above the lanes. What do they mean?

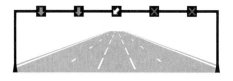

Mark one answer

- A. The two right lanes are open
- B. The two left lanes are open
- C. Traffic in the left lanes should stop
- D. Traffic in the right lanes should stop

See HIGHWAY CODE rule 232 & Lane control signals

279 As a provisional licence holder, you must not drive a motor car

Mark two answers **NI**

- A. at more than 50mph
- B. on your own
- C. on the motorway
- D. under the age of 18 years of age at night
- E. with passengers in the rear seats

See HIGHWAY CODE rule 227 & Annexe 3

280 After passing your driving test, you suffer from ill health. This affects your driving. You MUST

Mark one answer

- A. inform your local police station
- B. get on as best you can
- C. not inform anyone as you hold a full licence
- D. inform the licensing authority

See HIGHWAY CODE rule 79

281 You are invited to a pub lunch. You know that you will have to drive in the evening. What is your best course of action?

Mark one answer

- A. Avoid mixing your alcoholic drinks
- B. Not drink any alcohol at all
- C. Have some milk before drinking alcohol
- D. Eat a hot meal with your alcoholic drinks

See HIGHWAY CODE rule 83

282 You have been convicted of driving whilst unfit through drink or drugs. You will find this is likely to cause the cost of one of the following to rise considerably. Which one?

Mark one answer

- A. Road fund licence
- B. Insurance premiums
- C. Vehicle test certificate
- D. Driving licence

See HIGHWAY CODE Annexe 5

283 What advice should you give to a driver who has had a few alcoholic drinks at a party?

Mark one answer

- A. Have a strong cup of coffee and then drive home
- B. Drive home carefully and slowly
- C. Go home by public transport
- D. Wait a short while and then drive home

See HIGHWAY CODE rule 83

284 You have been taking medicine for a few days which made you feel drowsy. Today you feel better but still need to take the medicine. You should only drive

Mark one answer

- A. if your journey is necessary
- B. at night on quiet roads
- C. if someone goes with you
- D. after checking with your doctor

See HIGHWAY CODE rule 84

285
You are about to return home from holiday when you become ill. A doctor prescribes drugs which are likely to affect your driving. You should

Mark one answer

- A. drive only if someone is with you
- B. avoid driving on motorways
- C. not drive yourself
- D. never drive at more than 30mph

See HIGHWAY CODE rule 84

286
During periods of illness your ability to drive may be impaired. You MUST

Mark two answers

- A. see your doctor each time before you drive
- B. only take smaller doses of any medicines
- C. be medically fit to drive
- D. not drive after taking certain medicines
- E. take all your medicines with you when you drive

See HIGHWAY CODE rule 84

287
You feel drowsy when driving. You should

Mark two answers

- A. stop and rest as soon as possible
- B. turn the heater up to keep you warm and comfortable
- C. make sure you have a good supply of fresh air
- D. continue with your journey but drive more slowly
- E. close the car windows to help you concentrate

See HIGHWAY CODE rule 80

288
You are driving along a motorway and become tired. You should

Mark two answers

- A. stop at the next service area and rest
- B. leave the motorway at the next exit and rest
- C. increase your speed and turn up the radio volume
- D. close all your windows and set heating to warm
- E. pull up on the hard shoulder and change drivers

See HIGHWAY CODE rule 80

289
You are taking drugs that are likely to affect your driving. What should you do?

Mark one answer

- A. Seek medical advice before driving
- B. Limit your driving to essential journeys
- C. Only drive if accompanied by a full licence-holder
- D. Drive only for short distances

See HIGHWAY CODE rule 84

290
You are about to drive home. You feel very tired and have a severe headache. You should

Mark one answer

- A. wait until you are fit and well before driving
- B. drive home, but take a tablet for headaches
- C. drive home if you can stay awake for the journey
- D. wait for a short time, then drive home slowly

See HIGHWAY CODE rule 80

291
If you are feeling tired it is best to stop as soon as you can. Until then you should

Mark one answer
- **A.** increase your speed to find a stopping place quickly
- **B.** ensure a supply of fresh air
- **C.** gently tap the steering wheel
- **D.** keep changing speed to improve concentration

See HIGHWAY CODE rule 80

292
If your motorway journey seems boring and you feel drowsy whilst driving you should

Mark one answer
- **A.** open a window and drive to the next service area
- **B.** stop on the hard shoulder for a sleep
- **C.** speed up to arrive at your destination sooner
- **D.** slow down and let other drivers overtake

See HIGHWAY CODE rule 80

293
Driving long distances can be tiring. You can prevent this by

Mark three answers
- **A.** stopping every so often for a walk
- **B.** opening a window for some fresh air
- **C.** ensuring plenty of refreshment breaks
- **D.** completing the journey without stopping
- **E.** eating a large meal before driving

See HIGHWAY CODE rule 80

TIP The reason motorcyclists have their headlamps on in daylight is to make them more visible to other road users.

294
You go to a social event and need to drive a short time after. What precaution should you take?

Mark one answer
- **A.** Avoid drinking alcohol on an empty stomach
- **B.** Drink plenty of coffee after drinking alcohol
- **C.** Avoid drinking alcohol completely
- **D.** Drink plenty of milk before drinking alcohol

See HIGHWAY CODE rule 83

295
You take some cough medicine given to you by a friend. What should you do before driving?

Mark one answer
- **A.** Ask your friend if taking the medicine affected their driving
- **B.** Drink some strong coffee one hour before driving
- **C.** Check the label to see if the medicine will affect your driving
- **D.** Drive a short distance to see if the medicine is affecting your driving

See HIGHWAY CODE rule 84

296
You take the wrong route and find you are on a one-way street. You should

Mark one answer
- **A.** reverse out of the road
- **B.** turn round in a side road
- **C.** continue to the end of the road
- **D.** reverse into a driveway

See HIGHWAY CODE rule 121

297 Which THREE are likely to make you lose concentration while driving?

Mark three answers

- [ ] **A.** Looking at road maps
- [ ] **B.** Listening to loud music
- [ ] **C.** Using your windscreen washers
- [ ] **D.** Looking in your wing mirror
- [ ] **E.** Using a mobile phone

See HIGHWAY CODE rules 126, 127

298 You are driving along this road. The driver on the left is reversing from a driveway. You should

Mark one answer

- [ ] **A.** move to the opposite side of the road
- [ ] **B.** drive through as you have priority
- [ ] **C.** sound your horn and be prepared to stop
- [ ] **D.** speed up and drive through quickly

See HIGHWAY CODE rule 92

299 You have been involved in an argument before starting your journey. This has made you feel angry. You should

Mark one answer

- [ ] **A.** start to drive, but open a window
- [ ] **B.** drive slower than normal and turn your radio on
- [ ] **C.** have an alcoholic drink to help you relax before driving
- [ ] **D.** calm down before you start to drive

See HIGHWAY CODE rule 126

300 You start to feel tired while driving. What should you do?

Mark one answer

- [ ] **A.** Increase your speed slightly
- [ ] **B.** Decrease your speed slightly
- [ ] **C.** Find a less busy route
- [ ] **D.** Pull over at a safe place to rest

See HIGHWAY CODE rule 80

301 You are driving on this dual carriageway. Why may you need to slow down?

Mark one answer

- [ ] **A.** There is a broken white line in the centre
- [ ] **B.** There are solid white lines either side
- [ ] **C.** There are road works ahead of you
- [ ] **D.** There are no footpaths

See HIGHWAY CODE Road works signs

TIP It is tragic but true that people have been killed or seriously injured when struck by a vehicle being driven slowly in reverse gear. Young children, elderly and disabled people are especially vulnerable, often because they may not be aware of any danger. If in doubt get out and check!

302 You have just been overtaken by this motorcyclist who is cutting in sharply. You should

Mark one answer

- [ ] **A.** sound the horn
- [ ] **B.** brake firmly
- [ ] **C.** keep a safe gap
- [ ] **D.** flash your lights

See HIGHWAY CODE rule 144

303 You are about to drive home. You cannot find the glasses you need to wear. You should

Mark one answer

- [ ] **A.** drive home slowly, keeping to quiet roads
- [ ] **B.** borrow a friend's glasses and use those
- [ ] **C.** drive home at night, so that the lights will help you
- [ ] **D.** find a way of getting home without driving

See HIGHWAY CODE rule 81

304 Which THREE result from drinking alcohol?

Mark three answers

- [ ] **A.** Less control
- [ ] **B.** A false sense of confidence
- [ ] **C.** Faster reactions
- [ ] **D.** Poor judgement of speed
- [ ] **E.** Greater awareness of danger

See HIGHWAY CODE rule 83

305 Which THREE of these are likely effects of drinking alcohol?

Mark three answers

- [ ] **A.** Reduced co-ordination
- [ ] **B.** Increased confidence
- [ ] **C.** Poor judgement
- [ ] **D.** Increased concentration
- [ ] **E.** Faster reactions
- [ ] **F.** Colour blindness

See HIGHWAY CODE rule 83

306 How does alcohol affect you?

Mark one answer

- [ ] **A.** It speeds up your reactions
- [ ] **B.** It increases your awareness
- [ ] **C.** It improves your co-ordination
- [ ] **D.** It reduces your concentration

See HIGHWAY CODE rule 83

307 Your doctor has given you a course of medicine. Why should you ask how it will affect you?

Mark one answer

- [ ] **A.** Drugs make you a better driver by quickening your reactions
- [ ] **B.** You will have to let your insurance company know about the medicine
- [ ] **C.** Some types of medicine can cause your reactions to slow down
- [ ] **D.** The medicine you take may affect your hearing

See HIGHWAY CODE rule 84

308 You are not sure if your cough medicine will affect you. What TWO things could you do?

Mark two answers
- [ ] **A.** Ask your doctor
- [ ] **B.** Check the medicine label
- [ ] **C.** Drive if you feel alright
- [ ] **D.** Ask a friend or relative for advice

See HIGHWAY CODE rule 84

309 You are on a motorway. You feel tired. You should

Mark one answer
- [ ] **A.** carry on but go slowly
- [ ] **B.** leave the motorway at the next exit
- [ ] **C.** complete your journey as quickly as possible
- [ ] **D.** stop on the hard shoulder

See HIGHWAY CODE rule 80

310 You find that you need glasses to read vehicle number plates at the required distance. When MUST you wear them?

Mark one answer
- [ ] **A.** Only in bad weather conditions
- [ ] **B.** At all times when driving
- [ ] **C.** Only when you think it necessary
- [ ] **D.** Only in bad light or at night time

See HIGHWAY CODE rule 81

311 Which TWO things would help to keep you alert during a long journey?

Mark two answers
- [ ] **A.** Finishing your journey as fast as you can
- [ ] **B.** Keeping off the motorways and using country roads
- [ ] **C.** Making sure that you get plenty of fresh air
- [ ] **D.** Making regular stops for refreshments

See HIGHWAY CODE rule 80

312 Which of the following types of glasses should NOT be worn when driving at night?

Mark one answer
- [ ] **A.** Half-moon
- [ ] **B.** Round
- [ ] **C.** Bi-focal
- [ ] **D.** Tinted

See HIGHWAY CODE rule 82

313 Drinking any amount of alcohol is likely to

Mark three answers
- [ ] **A.** slow down your reactions to hazards
- [ ] **B.** increase the speed of your reactions
- [ ] **C.** worsen your judgement of speed
- [ ] **D.** improve your awareness of danger
- [ ] **E.** give a false sense of confidence

See HIGHWAY CODE rule 83

314 What else can seriously affect your concentration, other than alcoholic drinks?

Mark three answers
- [ ] **A.** Drugs
- [ ] **B.** Tiredness
- [ ] **C.** Tinted windows
- [ ] **D.** Contact lenses
- [ ] **E.** Loud music

See HIGHWAY CODE rules 80, 84, 126

315 As a driver you find that your eyesight has become very poor. Your optician says they cannot help you. The law says that you should tell

Mark one answer
- [ ] **A.** the licensing authority
- [ ] **B.** your own doctor
- [ ] **C.** the local police station
- [ ] **D.** another optician

See HIGHWAY CODE rule 79

316 For which of these may you use hazard warning lights?

Mark one answer

- A. When driving on a motorway to warn traffic behind of a hazard ahead
- B. When you are double-parked on a two-way road
- C. When your direction indicators are not working
- D. When warning oncoming traffic that you intend to stop

See HIGHWAY CODE rule 96

317 When should you use hazard warning lights?

Mark one answer

- A. When you are double-parked on a two-way road
- B. When your direction indicators are not working
- C. When warning oncoming traffic that you intend to stop
- D. When your vehicle has broken down and is causing an obstruction

See HIGHWAY CODE rule 248

TIP A blind person will usually carry a **white stick** to alert you to their presence. If the stick has a **red band**, this means that the person is also deaf, so will have no warning of an approaching car either visually or from engine noise.

318 You want to turn left at this junction. The view of the main road is restricted. What should you do?

Mark one answer

- A. Stay well back and wait to see if something comes
- B. Build up your speed so that you can emerge quickly
- C. Stop and apply the handbrake even if the road is clear
- D. Approach slowly and edge out until you can see more clearly

319 You are driving on a motorway. The traffic ahead is braking sharply because of an accident. How could you warn following traffic?

Mark one answer

- A. Briefly use the hazard warning lights
- B. Switch on the hazard warning lights continuously
- C. Briefly use the rear fog lights
- D. Switch on the headlamps continuously

See HIGHWAY CODE rule 96

320 When may you use hazard warning lights?

Mark one answer

- A. To park alongside another car
- B. To park on double yellow lines
- C. When you are being towed
- D. When you have broken down

See HIGHWAY CODE rule 248

321 Hazard warning lights should be used when vehicles are

Mark one answer

- A. broken down and causing an obstruction
- B. faulty and moving slowly
- C. being towed along a road
- D. reversing into a side road

See HIGHWAY CODE rule 248

322 When driving a car fitted with automatic transmission what would you use 'kick down' for?

Mark one answer

- A. Cruise control
- B. Quick acceleration
- C. Slow braking
- D. Fuel economy

TIP Research shows that male drivers (aged 18–30) are more at risk of falling asleep at the wheel than other drivers. They may keep late hours and be lacking in sleep; they tend to drive fast and be over-confident of their ability; and they are less likely to stop and take a break.

323 Which sign means that there may be people walking along the road?

Mark one answer

A.

B.

C.

D.

See HIGHWAY CODE Traffic signs

324 You are turning left at a junction. Pedestrians have started to cross the road. You should

Mark one answer

A. go on, giving them plenty of room

B. stop and wave at them to cross

C. blow your horn and proceed

D. give way to them

See HIGHWAY CODE rule 146

325 You are turning left from a main road into a side road. People are already crossing the road into which you are turning. You should

Mark one answer

A. continue, as it is your right of way

B. signal to them to continue crossing

C. wait and allow them to cross

D. sound your horn to warn them of your presence

See HIGHWAY CODE rule 146

326 You are at a road junction, turning into a minor road. There are pedestrians crossing the minor road. You should

Mark one answer

A. stop and wave the pedestrians across

B. sound your horn to let the pedestrians know that you are there

C. give way to the pedestrians who are already crossing

D. carry on; the pedestrians should give way to you

See HIGHWAY CODE rule 146

327 You are turning left into a side road. What hazards should you be especially aware of?

Mark one answer
- A. One-way street
- B. Pedestrians
- C. Traffic congestion
- D. Parked vehicles

See HIGHWAY CODE rule 146

328 You intend to turn right into a side road. Just before turning you should check for motorcyclists who might be

Mark one answer
- A. overtaking on your left
- B. following you closely
- C. emerging from the side road
- D. overtaking on your right

See HIGHWAY CODE rule 156

329 A toucan crossing is different from other crossings because

Mark one answer
- A. moped riders can use it
- B. it is controlled by a traffic warden
- C. it is controlled by two flashing lights
- D. cyclists can use it

See HIGHWAY CODE rule 65

330 At toucan crossings

Mark two answers
- A. there is no flashing amber light
- B. cyclists are not permitted
- C. there is a continuously flashing amber beacon
- D. pedestrians and cyclists may cross
- E. you only stop if someone is waiting to cross

See HIGHWAY CODE rules 65, 175

331 What does this sign tell you?

Mark one answer
- A. No cycling
- B. Cycle route ahead
- C. Route for cycles only
- D. End of cycle route

See HIGHWAY CODE Warning signs

332 How will a school crossing patrol signal you to stop?

Mark one answer
- A. By pointing to children on the opposite pavement
- B. By displaying a red light
- C. By displaying a stop sign
- D. By giving you an arm signal

See HIGHWAY CODE rule 186 & Signs giving orders

333 Where would you see this sign?

Mark one answer
- A. In the window of a car taking children to school
- B. At the side of the road
- C. At playground areas
- D. On the rear of a school bus or coach

See HIGHWAY CODE Vehicle markings

334 Which sign tells you that pedestrians may be walking in the road as there is no pavement?

Mark one answer

A. B.

C. D.

See HIGHWAY CODE Warning signs

335 What does this sign mean?

Mark one answer

A. No route for pedestrians and cyclists
B. A route for pedestrians only
C. A route for cyclists only
D. A route for pedestrians and cyclists

336 You see a pedestrian with a white stick and red band. This means that the person is

Mark one answer

A. physically disabled
B. deaf only
C. blind only
D. deaf and blind

See HIGHWAY CODE rule 183

337 What action would you take when elderly people are crossing the road?

Mark one answer

A. Wave them across so they know that you have seen them
B. Be patient and allow them to cross in their own time
C. Rev the engine to let them know that you are waiting
D. Tap the horn in case they are hard of hearing

See HIGHWAY CODE rule 183

338 You see two elderly pedestrians about to cross the road ahead. You should

Mark one answer

A. expect them to wait for you to pass
B. speed up to get past them quickly
C. stop and wave them across the road
D. be careful, they may misjudge your speed

See HIGHWAY CODE rule 183

339 What does this sign mean?

Mark one answer

A. Contraflow pedal cycle lane
B. With-flow pedal cycle lane
C. Pedal cycles and buses only
D. No pedal cycles or buses

See HIGHWAY CODE Signs giving orders

340
You are coming up to a roundabout. A cyclist is signalling to turn right. What should you do?

Mark one answer
- [ ] A. Overtake on the right
- [ ] B. Give a horn warning
- [ ] C. Signal the cyclist to move across
- [ ] D. Give the cyclist plenty of room

See HIGHWAY CODE rule 163

341
You are approaching this roundabout and see the cyclist signal right. Why is the cyclist keeping to the left?

Mark one answer
- [ ] A. It is a quicker route for the cyclist
- [ ] B. The cyclist is going to turn left instead
- [ ] C. The cyclist thinks *The Highway Code* does not apply to bicycles
- [ ] D. The cyclist is slower and more vulnerable

See HIGHWAY CODE rule 62

342
When you are overtaking a cyclist you should leave as much room as you would give to a car. What is the main reason for this?

Mark one answer
- [ ] A. The cyclist might change lanes
- [ ] B. The cyclist might get off the bike
- [ ] C. The cyclist might swerve
- [ ] D. The cyclist might have to make a right turn

See HIGHWAY CODE rules 139, 189

343
Which TWO should you allow extra room when overtaking?

Mark two answers
- [ ] A. Motorcycles
- [ ] B. Tractors
- [ ] C. Bicycles
- [ ] D. Road-sweeping vehicles

See HIGHWAY CODE rules 139, 189

344
Why should you look particularly for motorcyclists and cyclists at junctions?

Mark one answer
- [ ] A. They may want to turn into the side road
- [ ] B. They may slow down to let you turn
- [ ] C. They are harder to see
- [ ] D. They might not see you turn

See HIGHWAY CODE rule 187

345
You are waiting to come out of a side road. Why should you watch carefully for motorcycles?

Mark one answer
- [ ] A. Motorcycles are usually faster than cars
- [ ] B. Police patrols often use motorcycles
- [ ] C. Motorcycles are small and hard to see
- [ ] D. Motorcycles have right of way

See HIGHWAY CODE rule 187

346
In daylight, an approaching motorcyclist is using a dipped headlight. Why?

Mark one answer
- [ ] A. So that the rider can be seen more easily
- [ ] B. To stop the battery overcharging
- [ ] C. To improve the rider's vision
- [ ] D. The rider is inviting you to proceed

See HIGHWAY CODE rule 69

347 Motorcyclists should wear bright clothing mainly because

Mark one answer
- A. they must do so by law
- B. it helps keep them cool in summer
- C. the colours are popular
- D. drivers often do not see them

See HIGHWAY CODE rule 69

348 There is a slow-moving motorcyclist ahead of you. You are unsure what the rider is going to do. You should

Mark one answer
- A. pass on the left
- B. pass on the right
- C. stay behind
- D. move closer

349 Motorcyclists will often look round over their right shoulder just before turning right. This is because

Mark one answer
- A. they need to listen for following traffic
- B. motorcycles do not have mirrors
- C. looking around helps them balance as they turn
- D. they need to check for traffic in their blind area

See HIGHWAY CODE rules 71, 137

350 At road junctions which of the following are most vulnerable?

Mark three answers
- A. Cyclists
- B. Motorcyclists
- C. Pedestrians
- D. Car drivers
- E. Lorry drivers

See HIGHWAY CODE rule 146

351 Motorcyclists are particularly vulnerable

Mark one answer
- A. when moving off
- B. on dual carriageways
- C. when approaching junctions
- D. on motorways

See HIGHWAY CODE rules 146, 187

352 An injured motorcyclist is lying unconscious in the road. You should

Mark one answer
- A. remove the safety helmet
- B. seek medical assistance
- C. move the person off the road
- D. remove the leather jacket

See HIGHWAY CODE rule 257

353 You notice horse riders in front. What should you do FIRST?

Mark one answer
- A. Pull out to the middle of the road
- B. Be prepared to slow down
- C. Accelerate around them
- D. Signal right

See HIGHWAY CODE rule 190

354
You are approaching a roundabout. There are horses just ahead of you. You should

Mark two answers
- A. be prepared to stop
- B. treat them like any other vehicle
- C. give them plenty of room
- D. accelerate past as quickly as possible
- E. sound your horn as a warning

See HIGHWAY CODE rules 190, 191

355
Which THREE should you do when passing sheep on a road?

Mark three answers
- A. Allow plenty of room
- B. Go very slowly
- C. Pass quickly but quietly
- D. Be ready to stop
- E. Briefly sound your horn

See HIGHWAY CODE rule 190

356
At night you see a pedestrian wearing reflective clothing and carrying a bright red light. What does this mean?

Mark one answer
- A. You are approaching road works
- B. You are approaching an organised walk
- C. You are approaching a slow-moving vehicle
- D. You are approaching an accident black spot

See HIGHWAY CODE rule 5

357
As you approach a pelican crossing the lights change to green. Elderly people are half-way across. You should

Mark one answer
- A. wave them to cross as quickly as they can
- B. rev your engine to make them hurry
- C. flash your lights in case they have not heard you
- D. wait because they will take longer to cross

See HIGHWAY CODE rule 174

358
There are flashing amber lights under a school warning sign. What action should you take?

Mark one answer
- A. Reduce speed until you are clear of the area
- B. Keep up your speed and sound the horn
- C. Increase your speed to clear the area quickly
- D. Wait at the lights until they change to green

See HIGHWAY CODE rule 184

359
Which of the following types of crossing can detect when people are on them?

Mark one answer
- A. Pelican
- B. Toucan
- C. Zebra
- D. Puffin

TIP It's the motorist's responsibility to look out for hazards and give pedestrians plenty of room.

360 You are approaching this crossing. You should

Mark one answer
- A. prepare to slow down and stop
- B. stop and wave the pedestrians across
- C. speed up and pass by quickly
- D. drive on unless the pedestrians step out

See HIGHWAY CODE rule 171

361 You see a pedestrian with a dog. The dog has a bright orange lead and collar. This especially warns you that the pedestrian is

Mark one answer
- A. elderly
- B. dog training
- C. colour blind
- D. deaf

362 These road markings must be kept clear to allow

SCHOOL KEEP CLEAR

Mark one answer
- A. schoolchildren to be dropped off
- B. for teachers to park
- C. schoolchildren to be picked up
- D. a clear view of the crossing area

See HIGHWAY CODE Other road markings

363 You must not stop on these road markings because you may obstruct

Mark one answer
- A. children's view of the crossing area
- B. teachers' access to the school
- C. delivery vehicles' access to the school
- D. emergency vehicles' access to the school

See HIGHWAY CODE Other road markings

364 The left-hand pavement is closed due to street repairs. What should you do?

Mark one answer
- A. Watch out for pedestrians walking in the road
- B. Use your right-hand mirror more often
- C. Speed up to get past the road works quicker
- D. Position close to the left-hand kerb

See HIGHWAY CODE rule 182

365 Where would you see this sign?

Mark one answer
- A. Near a school crossing
- B. At a playground entrance
- C. On a school bus
- D. At a 'pedestrians only' area

See HIGHWAY CODE Vehicle markings

366 You are following a motorcyclist on an uneven road. You should

Mark one answer

- [ ] **A.** allow less room so you can be seen in their mirrors
- [ ] **B.** overtake immediately
- [ ] **C.** allow extra room in case they swerve to avoid pot-holes
- [ ] **D.** allow the same room as normal because road surfaces do not affect motorcyclists

See HIGHWAY CODE rule 189

367 You are following two cyclists. They approach a roundabout in the left-hand lane. In which direction should you expect the cyclists to go?

Mark one answer

- [ ] **A.** Left
- [ ] **B.** Right
- [ ] **C.** Any direction
- [ ] **D.** Straight ahead

See HIGHWAY CODE rules 62, 163

368 You are travelling behind a moped. You want to turn left just ahead. You should

Mark one answer

- [ ] **A.** overtake the moped before the junction
- [ ] **B.** pull alongside the moped and stay level until just before the junction
- [ ] **C.** sound your horn as a warning and pull in front of the moped
- [ ] **D.** stay behind until the moped has passed the junction

See HIGHWAY CODE rule 158

369 Which THREE of the following are hazards motorcyclists present in queues of traffic?

Mark three answers

- [ ] **A.** Cutting in just in front of you
- [ ] **B.** Riding in single file
- [ ] **C.** Passing very close to you
- [ ] **D.** Riding with their headlight on dipped beam
- [ ] **E.** Filtering between the lanes

370 You see a horse rider as you approach a roundabout. They are signalling right but keeping well to the left. You should

Mark one answer

- [ ] **A.** proceed as normal
- [ ] **B.** keep close to them
- [ ] **C.** cut in front of them
- [ ] **D.** stay well back

See HIGHWAY CODE rule 163

371 How would you react to drivers who appear to be inexperienced?

Mark one answer

- [ ] **A.** Sound your horn to warn them of your presence
- [ ] **B.** Be patient and prepare for them to react more slowly
- [ ] **C.** Flash your headlights to indicate that it is safe for them to proceed
- [ ] **D.** Overtake them as soon as possible

See HIGHWAY CODE rule 193

372 You are following a learner driver who stalls at a junction. You should

Mark one answer

- [ ] **A.** be patient as you expect them to make mistakes
- [ ] **B.** stay very close behind and flash your headlights
- [ ] **C.** start to rev your engine if they take too long to restart
- [ ] **D.** immediately steer around them and drive on

See HIGHWAY CODE rule 193

373 You are on a country road. What should you expect to see coming towards you on YOUR side of the road?

Mark one answer

- [ ] **A.** Motorcycles
- [ ] **B.** Bicycles
- [ ] **C.** Pedestrians
- [ ] **D.** Horse riders

See HIGHWAY CODE rule 132

374 You are turning left into a side road. Pedestrians are crossing the road near the junction. You must

Mark one answer

- [ ] **A.** wave them on
- [ ] **B.** sound your horn
- [ ] **C.** switch on your hazard lights
- [ ] **D.** wait for them to cross

See HIGHWAY CODE rule 146

375 You are following a car driven by an elderly driver. You should

Mark one answer

- [ ] **A.** expect the driver to drive badly
- [ ] **B.** flash your lights and overtake
- [ ] **C.** be aware that the driver's reactions may not be as fast as yours
- [ ] **D.** stay very close behind but be careful

See HIGHWAY CODE rule 192

376 You are following a cyclist. You wish to turn left just ahead. You should

Mark one answer

- [ ] **A.** overtake the cyclist before the junction
- [ ] **B.** pull alongside the cyclist and stay level until after the junction
- [ ] **C.** hold back until the cyclist has passed the junction
- [ ] **D.** go around the cyclist on the junction

See HIGHWAY CODE rule 158

377 A horse rider is in the left-hand lane approaching a roundabout. You should expect the rider to

Mark one answer

- [ ] **A.** go in any direction
- [ ] **B.** turn right
- [ ] **C.** turn left
- [ ] **D.** go ahead

See HIGHWAY CODE rules 41, 163

378 You have just passed your test. How can you decrease your risk of accidents on the motorway?

Mark one answer

- A. By keeping up with the car in front
- B. By never going over 40mph
- C. By staying only in the left-hand lane
- D. By taking further training

379 Powered vehicles used by disabled people are small and hard to see. How do they give early warning when on a dual carriageway?

Mark one answer

- A. They will have a flashing red light
- B. They will have a flashing green light
- C. They will have a flashing blue light
- D. They will have a flashing amber light

See HIGHWAY CODE rule 195

380 You should never attempt to overtake a cyclist

Mark one answer

- A. just before you turn left
- B. on a left-hand bend
- C. on a one-way street
- D. on a dual carriageway

See HIGHWAY CODE rule 158

381 Ahead of you there is a moving vehicle with a flashing amber beacon. This means it is

Mark one answer

- A. slow moving
- B. broken down
- C. a doctor's car
- D. a school crossing patrol

See HIGHWAY CODE rule 200

382 You want to reverse into a side road. You are not sure that the area behind your car is clear. What should you do?

Mark one answer

- A. Look through the rear window only
- B. Get out and check
- C. Check the mirrors only
- D. Carry on, assuming it is clear

383 You are about to reverse into a side road. A pedestrian wishes to cross behind you. You should

Mark one answer

- A. wave to the pedestrian to stop
- B. give way to the pedestrian
- C. wave to the pedestrian to cross
- D. reverse before the pedestrian starts to cross

See HIGHWAY CODE rule 182

384 Who is especially in danger of not being seen as you reverse your car?

Mark one answer

- A. Motorcyclists
- B. Car drivers
- C. Cyclists
- D. Children

See HIGHWAY CODE rule 178

385 You are reversing around a corner when you notice a pedestrian walking behind you. What should you do?

Mark one answer

- A. Slow down and wave the pedestrian across
- B. Continue reversing and steer round the pedestrian
- C. Stop and give way
- D. Continue reversing and sound your horn

See HIGHWAY CODE rule 182

386 You want to turn right from a junction but your view is restricted by parked vehicles. What should you do?

Mark one answer
- [ ] **A.** Move out quickly, but be prepared to stop
- [ ] **B.** Sound your horn and pull out if there is no reply
- [ ] **C.** Stop, then move slowly forward until you have a clear view
- [ ] **D.** Stop, get out and look along the main road to check

387 You are at the front of a queue of traffic waiting to turn right into a side road. Why is it important to check your right mirror just before turning?

Mark one answer
- [ ] **A.** To look for pedestrians about to cross
- [ ] **B.** To check for overtaking vehicles
- [ ] **C.** To make sure the side road is clear
- [ ] **D.** To check for emerging traffic

See HIGHWAY CODE rule 156

388 What must a driver do at a pelican crossing when the amber light is flashing?

Mark one answer
- [ ] **A.** Signal the pedestrian to cross
- [ ] **B.** Always wait for the green light before proceeding
- [ ] **C.** Give way to any pedestrians on the crossing
- [ ] **D.** Wait for the red-and-amber light before proceeding

See HIGHWAY CODE rule 172

389 You have stopped at a pelican crossing. A disabled person is crossing slowly in front of you. The lights have now changed to green. You should

Mark two answers
- [ ] **A.** allow the person to cross
- [ ] **B.** drive in front of the person
- [ ] **C.** drive behind the person
- [ ] **D.** sound your horn
- [ ] **E.** be patient
- [ ] **F.** edge forward slowly

See HIGHWAY CODE rule 174

390 You are driving past parked cars. You notice a wheel of a bicycle sticking out between them. What should you do?

Mark one answer
- [ ] **A.** Accelerate past quickly and sound your horn
- [ ] **B.** Slow down and wave the cyclist across
- [ ] **C.** Brake sharply and flash your headlights
- [ ] **D.** Slow down and be prepared to stop for a cyclist

See HIGHWAY CODE rule 130

TIP **Pass Plus** is a scheme set up in 1995 by the Driving Standards Agency and the Department of the Environment, Transport and the Regions. Planned in consultation with driving instructors and the insurance industry, it's aimed at encouraging people to go on training to *improve* their standard of driving during the first year after they pass their test.

391
You are driving past a line of parked cars. You notice a ball bouncing out into the road ahead. What should you do?

Mark one answer
- **A.** Continue driving at the same speed and sound your horn
- **B.** Continue driving at the same speed and flash your headlights
- **C.** Slow down and be prepared to stop for children
- **D.** Stop and wave the children across to fetch their ball

See HIGHWAY CODE rule 130

392
You want to turn right from a main road into a side road. Just before turning you should

Mark one answer
- **A.** cancel your right-turn signal
- **B.** select first gear
- **C.** check for traffic overtaking on your right
- **D.** stop and set the handbrake

See HIGHWAY CODE rule 156

393
You are driving in slow-moving queues of traffic. Just before changing lane you should

Mark one answer
- **A.** sound the horn
- **B.** look for motorcyclists filtering through the traffic
- **C.** give a 'slowing down' arm signal
- **D.** change down to first gear

See HIGHWAY CODE rules 112, 187

394
You are driving in town. There is a bus at the bus stop on the other side of the road. Why should you be careful?

Mark one answer
- **A.** The bus may have broken down
- **B.** Pedestrians may come from behind the bus
- **C.** The bus may move off suddenly
- **D.** The bus may remain stationary

See HIGHWAY CODE rules 182, 198

395
How should you overtake horse riders?

Mark one answer
- **A.** Drive up close and overtake as soon as possible
- **B.** Speed is not important but allow plenty of room
- **C.** Use your horn just once to warn them
- **D.** Drive slowly and leave plenty of room

See HIGHWAY CODE rules 190, 191

396
A friend wants to teach you to drive a car. They MUST

Mark one answer
- **A.** be over 21 and have held a full licence for at least two years
- **B.** be over 18 and hold an advanced driver's certificate
- **C.** be over 18 and have fully comprehensive insurance
- **D.** be over 21 and have held a full licence for at least three years

See HIGHWAY CODE Annexe 3

397
You are dazzled at night by a vehicle behind you. You should

Mark one answer
- **A.** set your mirror to anti-dazzle
- **B.** set your mirror to dazzle the other driver
- **C.** brake sharply to a stop
- **D.** switch your rear lights on and off

398 You have a collision whilst your car is moving. What is the first thing you must do?

Mark one answer
- A. Stop only if there are injured people
- B. Call the emergency services
- C. Stop at the scene of the accident
- D. Call your insurance company

See HIGHWAY CODE rule 260

399 Yellow zigzag lines on the road outside schools mean

|Λ–SCHOOL KEEP CLEAR–Λ|

Mark one answer
- A. sound your horn to alert other road users
- B. stop to allow children to cross
- C. you must not wait or park on these lines
- D. you must not drive over these lines

See HIGHWAY CODE Other road markings

400 What do these road markings outside a school mean?

|Λ–SCHOOL KEEP CLEAR–Λ|

Mark one answer
- A. You may park here if you are a teacher
- B. Sound your horn before parking
- C. When parking use your hazard warning lights
- D. You must not wait or park your vehicle here

See HIGHWAY CODE Other road markings

401 You are driving on a main road. You intend to turn right into a side road. Just before turning you should

Mark one answer
- A. adjust your interior mirror
- B. flash your headlamps
- C. steer over to the left
- D. check for traffic overtaking on your right

See HIGHWAY CODE rule 156

402 Why should you allow extra room when overtaking a motorcyclist on a windy day?

Mark one answer
- A. The rider may turn off suddenly to get out of the wind
- B. The rider may be blown across in front of you
- C. The rider may stop suddenly
- D. The rider may be travelling faster than normal

See HIGHWAY CODE rule 207

403 Which age group of drivers is most likely to be involved in a road accident?

Mark one answer
- A. 36 to 45-year-olds
- B. 55-year-olds and over
- C. 46 to 55-year-olds
- D. 17 to 25-year-olds

TIP Remember: part of learning to drive safely is being able to control the car at very slow speeds, as when following a cyclist.

404

You are driving towards a zebra crossing. Waiting to cross is a person in a wheelchair. You should

Mark one answer
- [ ] **A.** continue on your way
- [ ] **B.** wave to the person to cross
- [ ] **C.** wave to the person to wait
- [ ] **D.** be prepared to stop

See HIGHWAY CODE rule 171

405

Where in particular should you look out for motorcyclists?

Mark one answer
- [ ] **A.** In a filling station
- [ ] **B.** At a road junction
- [ ] **C.** Near a service area
- [ ] **D.** When entering a car park

See HIGHWAY CODE rule 187

406

Where should you take particular care to look out for motorcyclists and cyclists?

Mark one answer
- [ ] **A.** On dual carriageways
- [ ] **B.** At junctions
- [ ] **C.** At zebra crossings
- [ ] **D.** On one-way streets

See HIGHWAY CODE rule 187

407

The road outside this school is marked with yellow zigzag lines. What do these lines mean?

Mark one answer
- [ ] **A.** You may park on the lines when dropping off schoolchildren
- [ ] **B.** You may park on the lines when picking schoolchildren up
- [ ] **C.** You must not wait or park your vehicle here at all
- [ ] **D.** You must stay with your vehicle if you park here

See HIGHWAY CODE Other road markings

> **TIP** By far the greatest number of accidents occurs within 18 metres (20 yards) of a junction. T-junctions and staggered junctions have proved to be more dangerous than roundabouts, or even crossroads.

408

The road is wet. Why might a motorcyclist steer round drain covers on a bend?

Mark one answer

- [ ] **A.** To avoid puncturing the tyres on the edge of the drain covers
- [ ] **B.** To prevent the motorcycle sliding on the metal drain covers
- [ ] **C.** To help judge the bend using the drain covers as marker points
- [ ] **D.** To avoid splashing pedestrians on the pavement

See HIGHWAY CODE rule 189

409

You are about to overtake a slow-moving motorcyclist. Which one of these signs would make you take special care?

Mark one answer

- [ ] **A.**
- [ ] **B.**
- [ ] **C.**
- [ ] **D.**

See HIGHWAY CODE Traffic signs & rules 207, 208

410

You are waiting to emerge left from a minor road. A large vehicle is approaching from the right. You have time to turn, but you should wait. Why?

Mark one answer

- [ ] **A.** The large vehicle can easily hide an overtaking vehicle
- [ ] **B.** The large vehicle can turn suddenly
- [ ] **C.** The large vehicle is difficult to steer in a straight line
- [ ] **D.** The large vehicle can easily hide vehicles from the left

See HIGHWAY CODE rule 187

411

You are following a long vehicle. It approaches a crossroads and signals left, but moves out to the right. You should

Mark one answer

- [ ] **A.** get closer in order to pass it quickly
- [ ] **B.** stay well back and give it room
- [ ] **C.** assume the signal is wrong and it is really turning right
- [ ] **D.** overtake as it starts to slow down

See HIGHWAY CODE rule 196

TIP If you cannot see the side mirrors of the long vehicle ahead, the driver is unaware you are there. Keep well back.

412

You are following a long vehicle approaching a crossroads. The driver signals right but moves close to the left-hand kerb. What should you do?

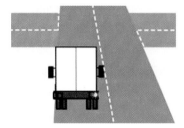

Mark one answer
- **A.** Warn the driver of the wrong signal
- **B.** Wait behind the long vehicle
- **C.** Report the driver to the police
- **D.** Overtake on the right-hand side

See HIGHWAY CODE rule 196

413

You are approaching a mini-roundabout. The long vehicle in front is signalling left but positioned over to the right. You should

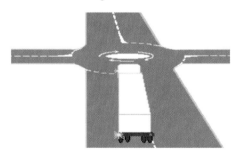

Mark one answer
- **A.** sound your horn
- **B.** overtake on the left
- **C.** follow the same course as the lorry
- **D.** keep well back

See HIGHWAY CODE rule 163

414

Before overtaking a large vehicle you should keep well back. Why is this?

Mark one answer
- **A.** To give acceleration space to overtake quickly on blind bends
- **B.** To get the best view of the road ahead
- **C.** To leave a gap in case the vehicle stops and rolls back
- **D.** To offer other drivers a safe gap if they want to overtake you

See HIGHWAY CODE rule 140

415

Why is passing a lorry more risky than passing a car?

Mark one answer
- **A.** Lorries are longer than cars
- **B.** Lorries may suddenly pull up
- **C.** The brakes of lorries are not as good
- **D.** Lorries climb hills more slowly

See HIGHWAY CODE rule 140

416

You are travelling behind a bus that pulls up at a bus stop. What should you do?

Mark two answers
- **A.** Accelerate past the bus sounding your horn
- **B.** Watch carefully for pedestrians
- **C.** Be ready to give way to the bus
- **D.** Pull in closely behind the bus

See HIGHWAY CODE rule 198

TIP Watch carefully for speed limits marked on the road – not just on traffic signs.

417
When you approach a bus signalling to move off from a bus stop you should

Mark one answer
- [ ] **A.** get past before it moves
- [ ] **B.** allow it to pull away, if it is safe to do so
- [ ] **C.** flash your headlights as you approach
- [ ] **D.** signal left and wave the bus on

See HIGHWAY CODE rule 198

418
Which of these vehicles is LEAST likely to be affected by crosswinds?

Mark one answer
- [ ] **A.** Cyclists
- [ ] **B.** Motorcyclists
- [ ] **C.** High-sided vehicles
- [ ] **D.** Cars

See HIGHWAY CODE rules 207, 208

419
You are following a large lorry on a wet road. Spray makes it difficult to see. You should

Mark one answer
- [ ] **A.** drop back until you can see better
- [ ] **B.** put your headlights on full beam
- [ ] **C.** keep close to the lorry, away from the spray
- [ ] **D.** speed up and overtake quickly

See HIGHWAY CODE rule 202

420
Some two-way roads are divided into three lanes. Why are these particularly dangerous?

Mark one answer
- [ ] **A.** Traffic in both directions can use the middle lane to overtake
- [ ] **B.** Traffic can travel faster in poor weather conditions
- [ ] **C.** Traffic can overtake on the left
- [ ] **D.** Traffic uses the middle lane for emergencies only

See HIGHWAY CODE rule 114

421
What should you do as you approach this lorry?

Mark one answer
- [ ] **A.** Slow down and be prepared to wait
- [ ] **B.** Make the lorry wait for you
- [ ] **C.** Flash your lights at the lorry
- [ ] **D.** Move to the right-hand side of the road

See HIGHWAY CODE rules 146, 196

TIP Box junctions were introduced to prevent blockages at crossroads and other junctions. The rule is: do not enter the box unless your exit is clear. Usually you will not stop in the yellow box unless, while your exit route is clear, you are caused to wait by oncoming traffic.

422
You are following a large articulated vehicle. It is going to turn left into a narrow road. What action should you take?

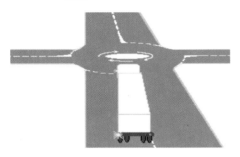

Mark one answer
- **A.** Move out and overtake on the right
- **B.** Pass on the left as the vehicle moves out
- **C.** Be prepared to stop behind
- **D.** Overtake quickly before the lorry moves out

See HIGHWAY CODE rules 163, 196

423
You keep well back while waiting to overtake a large vehicle. A car fills the gap. You should

Mark one answer
- **A.** sound your horn
- **B.** drop back further
- **C.** flash your headlights
- **D.** start to overtake

See HIGHWAY CODE rule 144

TIP Many drivers 'tailgate' in fog because the rear lights ahead give them a false sense of security. In fact, you should leave a much greater separation distance from the vehicle in front in any kind of adverse weather.

424
At a junction you see this signal. It means

Mark one answer
- **A.** cars must stop
- **B.** trams must stop
- **C.** both trams and cars must stop
- **D.** both trams and cars can continue

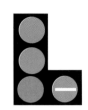

See HIGHWAY CODE rule 274

425
You are following a large vehicle approaching crossroads. The driver signals to turn left. What should you do?

Mark one answer
- **A.** Overtake if you can leave plenty of room
- **B.** Overtake only if there are no oncoming vehicles
- **C.** Do not overtake until the vehicle begins to turn
- **D.** Do not overtake when at or approaching a junction

See HIGHWAY CODE rules 163, 196

426
You are following a long lorry. The driver signals to turn left into a narrow road. What should you do?

Mark one answer
- **A.** Overtake on the left before the lorry reaches the junction
- **B.** Overtake on the right as soon as the lorry slows down
- **C.** Do not overtake unless you can see there is no oncoming traffic
- **D.** Do not overtake, stay well back and be prepared to stop

See HIGHWAY CODE rules 146, 196

427 You wish to overtake a long, slow-moving vehicle on a busy road. You should

Mark one answer

- A. follow it closely and keep moving out to see the road ahead
- B. flash your headlights for the oncoming traffic to give way
- C. stay behind until the driver waves you past
- D. keep well back until you can see that it is clear

See HIGHWAY CODE rule 140

428 It is very windy. You are behind a motorcyclist who is overtaking a high-sided vehicle. What should you do?

Mark one answer

- A. Overtake the motorcyclist immediately
- B. Keep well back
- C. Stay level with the motorcyclist
- D. Keep close to the motorcyclist

See HIGHWAY CODE rule 208

429 It is very windy. You are about to overtake a motorcyclist. You should

Mark one answer

- A. overtake slowly
- B. allow extra room
- C. sound your horn
- D. keep close as you pass

See HIGHWAY CODE rule 207

430 You are towing a caravan. Which is the safest type of rear view mirror to use?

Mark one answer

- A. Interior wide-angle-view mirror
- B. Extended-arm side mirrors
- C. Ordinary door mirrors
- D. Ordinary interior mirror

431 You are driving downhill. There is a car parked on the other side of the road. Large, slow lorries are coming towards you. You should

Mark one answer

- A. keep going because you have the right of way
- B. slow down and give way
- C. speed up and get past quickly
- D. pull over on the right behind the parked car

See HIGHWAY CODE rule 196

432 You are driving in town. Ahead of you a bus is at a bus stop. Which TWO of the following should you do?

Mark two answers

- A. Be prepared to give way if the bus suddenly moves off
- B. Continue at the same speed but sound your horn as a warning
- C. Watch carefully for the sudden appearance of pedestrians
- D. Pass the bus as quickly as you possibly can

See HIGHWAY CODE rules 182, 198

433 You are driving in heavy traffic on a wet road. Spray makes it difficult to be seen. You should use your

Mark two answers

- A. full beam headlights
- B. rear fog lights if visibility is less than 100 metres (328 feet)
- C. rear fog lights if visibility is more than 100 metres (328 feet)
- D. dipped headlights
- E. sidelights only

See HIGHWAY CODE rule 201

434 You are driving along this road. What should you be prepared to do?

Mark one answer

- **A.** Sound your horn and continue
- **B.** Slow down and give way
- **C.** Report the driver to the police
- **D.** Squeeze through the gap

See HIGHWAY CODE rules 146, 196

435 You are on a wet motorway with surface spray. You should use

Mark one answer

- **A.** hazard flashers
- **B.** dipped headlights
- **C.** rear fog lights
- **D.** sidelights

See HIGHWAY CODE rule 201

436 As a driver why should you be more careful where trams operate?

Mark one answer

- **A.** Because they do not have a horn
- **B.** Because they do not stop for cars
- **C.** Because they do not have lights
- **D.** Because they cannot steer to avoid you

See HIGHWAY CODE rule 199

TIP If there's been a sudden downpour there may be water covering the road surface, making it difficult to control the car; and excessive speed may result in **aquaplaning**. It is rather like skidding, but on water, because the tyres cannot grip effectively. If you find yourself aquaplaning, take your foot off the accelerator and slow down gently. And keep a safe distance from the vehicle in front.

437
You are following a vehicle at a safe distance on a wet road. Another driver overtakes you and pulls into the gap you have left. What should you do?

Mark one answer

- **A.** Flash your headlights as a warning
- **B.** Try to overtake safely as soon as you can
- **C.** Drop back to regain a safe distance
- **D.** Stay close to the other vehicle until it moves on

See HIGHWAY CODE rules 144, 202

438
In which THREE of these situations may you overtake another vehicle on the left?

Mark three answers

- **A.** When you are in a one-way street
- **B.** When approaching a motorway slip road where you will be turning off
- **C.** When the vehicle in front is signalling to turn right
- **D.** When a slower vehicle is travelling in the right-hand lane of a dual carriageway
- **E.** In slow-moving traffic queues when traffic in the right-hand lane is moving more slowly

See HIGHWAY CODE rules 121, 139

439
You are travelling in very heavy rain. Your overall stopping distance is likely to be

Mark one answer

- **A.** doubled
- **B.** halved
- **C.** up to ten times greater
- **D.** no different

See HIGHWAY CODE rule 202

440
Which TWO of the following are correct? When overtaking at night you should

Mark two answers

- **A.** wait until a bend so that you can see the oncoming headlights
- **B.** sound your horn twice before moving out
- **C.** be careful because you can see less
- **D.** beware of bends in the road ahead
- **E.** put headlights on full beam

See HIGHWAY CODE rules 139, 142

441
When may you wait in a box junction?

Mark one answer

- **A.** When you are stationary in a queue of traffic
- **B.** When approaching a pelican crossing
- **C.** When approaching a zebra crossing
- **D.** When oncoming traffic prevents you turning right

See HIGHWAY CODE rule 150

442 Which of these plates normally appear with this road sign?

Mark one answer

A.
Humps for ½ mile

B.
Hump Bridge

C.
Low Bridge

D.
Soft Verge

See HIGHWAY CODE Traffic signs

443 Areas reserved for trams may have

Mark three answers

A. metal studs around them
B. white line markings
C. zigzag markings
D. a different coloured surface
E. yellow hatch markings
F. a different surface texture

See HIGHWAY CODE rule 273

444 Traffic calming measures are used to

Mark one answer

A. stop road rage
B. help overtaking
C. slow traffic down
D. help parking

See HIGHWAY CODE rule 131

445 Why should you always reduce your speed when travelling in fog?

Mark one answer

A. Because the brakes do not work as well
B. Because you could be dazzled by other people's fog lights
C. Because the engine is colder
D. Because it is more difficult to see events ahead

See HIGHWAY CODE rule 210

446 You are on a motorway in fog. The left-hand edge of the motorway can be identified by reflective studs. What colour are they?

Mark one answer

A. Green
B. Amber
C. Red
D. White

See HIGHWAY CODE rule 111

447 A rumble device is designed to

Mark two answers

A. give directions
B. prevent cattle escaping
C. alert you to low tyre pressure
D. alert you to a hazard
E. encourage you to reduce speed

448 You are on a narrow road at night. A slower-moving vehicle ahead has been signalling right for some time. What should you do?

Mark one answer
- [ ] **A.** Overtake on the left
- [ ] **B.** Flash your headlights before overtaking
- [ ] **C.** Signal right and sound your horn
- [ ] **D.** Wait for the signal to be cancelled before overtaking

See HIGHWAY CODE rule 143

449 Why should you test your brakes after this hazard?

![Ford](triangular warning sign reading "Ford")

Mark one answer
- [ ] **A.** Because you will be on a slippery road
- [ ] **B.** Because your brakes will be soaking wet
- [ ] **C.** Because you will have gone down a long hill
- [ ] **D.** Because you will have just crossed a long bridge

See HIGHWAY CODE rule 101

450 You have to make a journey in foggy conditions. You should

Mark one answer
- [ ] **A.** follow other vehicles' tail-lights closely
- [ ] **B.** avoid using dipped headlights
- [ ] **C.** leave plenty of time for your journey
- [ ] **D.** keep two seconds behind other vehicles

See HIGHWAY CODE rule 73

451 You are overtaking a car at night. You must be sure that

Mark one answer
- [ ] **A.** you flash your headlights before overtaking
- [ ] **B.** you select a higher gear
- [ ] **C.** you have switched your lights to full beam before overtaking
- [ ] **D.** you do not dazzle other road users

See HIGHWAY CODE rule 95

452 You see a vehicle coming towards you on a single track road. You should

Mark one answer
- [ ] **A.** go back to the main road
- [ ] **B.** do an emergency stop
- [ ] **C.** stop at a passing place
- [ ] **D.** put on your hazard warning lights

See HIGHWAY CODE rule 133

453 You are on a road which has speed humps. A driver in front is travelling slower than you. You should

Mark one answer
- [ ] **A.** sound your horn
- [ ] **B.** overtake as soon as you can
- [ ] **C.** flash your headlights
- [ ] **D.** slow down and stay behind

See HIGHWAY CODE rule 131

454 You are following other vehicles in fog with your lights on. How else can you reduce the chances of being involved in an accident?

Mark one answer

- **A.** Keep close to the vehicle in front
- **B.** Use your main beam instead of dipped headlights
- **C.** Keep together with the faster vehicles
- **D.** Reduce your speed and increase the gap

See HIGHWAY CODE rule 210

455 You see these markings on the road. Why are they there?

Mark one answer

- **A.** To show a safe distance between vehicles
- **B.** To keep the area clear of traffic
- **C.** To make you aware of your speed
- **D.** To warn you to change direction

456 When MUST you use dipped headlights during the day?

Mark one answer

- **A.** All the time
- **B.** Along narrow streets
- **C.** In poor visibility
- **D.** When parking

See HIGHWAY CODE rule 93

457 What are TWO main reasons why coasting downhill is wrong?

Mark two answers

- **A.** Fuel consumption will be higher
- **B.** The vehicle will pick up speed
- **C.** It puts more wear and tear on the tyres
- **D.** You have less braking and steering control
- **E.** It damages the engine

See HIGHWAY CODE rule 102

458 Hills can affect the performance of your vehicle. Which TWO apply when driving up steep hills?

Mark two answers

- **A.** Higher gears will pull better
- **B.** You will slow down sooner
- **C.** Overtaking will be easier
- **D.** The engine will work harder
- **E.** The steering will feel heavier

459 Why is coasting wrong?

Mark one answer

- **A.** It will cause the car to skid
- **B.** It will make the engine stall
- **C.** The engine will run faster
- **D.** There is no engine braking

See HIGHWAY CODE rule 102

460 You are driving on the motorway in windy conditions. When passing high-sided vehicles you should

Mark one answer

- **A.** increase your speed
- **B.** be wary of a sudden gust
- **C.** drive alongside very closely
- **D.** expect normal conditions

See HIGHWAY CODE rules 207, 208

461 To correct a rear wheel skid you should

Mark one answer
- A. not steer at all
- B. steer away from it
- C. steer into it
- D. apply your handbrake

See HIGHWAY CODE rule 99

462 You have to make a journey in fog. What are the TWO most important things you should do before you set out?

Mark two answers
- A. Top up the radiator with antifreeze
- B. Make sure that you have a warning triangle in the vehicle
- C. Check that your lights are working
- D. Check the battery
- E. Make sure that the windows are clean

See HIGHWAY CODE rule 210

463 You are driving in fog. Why should you keep well back from the vehicle in front?

Mark one answer
- A. In case it changes direction suddenly
- B. In case its fog lights dazzle you
- C. In case it stops suddenly
- D. In case its brake lights dazzle you

See HIGHWAY CODE rule 210

464 You should switch your rear fog lights on when visibility drops below

Mark one answer
- A. your overall stopping distance
- B. ten car lengths
- C. 200 metres (656 feet)
- D. 100 metres (328 feet)

See HIGHWAY CODE rule 201

465 Whilst driving, the fog clears and you can see more clearly. You must remember to

Mark one answer
- A. switch off the fog lights
- B. reduce your speed
- C. switch off the demister
- D. close any open windows

See HIGHWAY CODE rules 201, 211

466 You have to park on the road in fog. You should

Mark one answer
- A. leave sidelights on
- B. leave dipped headlights and fog lights on
- C. leave dipped headlights on
- D. leave main beam headlights on

See HIGHWAY CODE rule 225

467 On a foggy day you unavoidably have to park your car on the road. You should

Mark one answer
- A. leave your headlights on
- B. leave your fog lights on
- C. leave your sidelights on
- D. leave your hazard lights on

See HIGHWAY CODE rule 225

468 You are travelling at night. You are dazzled by headlights coming towards you. You should

Mark one answer
- A. pull down your sun visor
- B. slow down or stop
- C. switch on your main beam headlights
- D. put your hand over your eyes

See HIGHWAY CODE rule 95

469 Which of the following may apply when dealing with this hazard?

Mark four answers

- [ ] **A.** It could be more difficult in winter
- [ ] **B.** Use a low gear and drive slowly
- [ ] **C.** Use a high gear to prevent wheelspin
- [ ] **D.** Test your brakes afterwards
- [ ] **E.** Always switch on fog lamps
- [ ] **F.** There may be a depth gauge

See HIGHWAY CODE rule 101

470 Front fog lights may be used ONLY if

Mark one answer

- [ ] **A.** visibility is seriously reduced
- [ ] **B.** they are fitted above the bumper
- [ ] **C.** they are not as bright as the headlights
- [ ] **D.** an audible warning device is used

See HIGHWAY CODE rules 201, 211

471 Front fog lights may be used ONLY if

Mark one answer

- [ ] **A.** your headlights are not working
- [ ] **B.** they are operated with rear fog lights
- [ ] **C.** they were fitted by the vehicle manufacturer
- [ ] **D.** visibility is seriously reduced

See HIGHWAY CODE rules 201, 211

472 You are driving with your front fog lights switched on. Earlier fog has now cleared. What should you do?

Mark one answer

- [ ] **A.** Leave them on if other drivers have their lights on
- [ ] **B.** Switch them off as long as visibility remains good
- [ ] **C.** Flash them to warn oncoming traffic that it is foggy
- [ ] **D.** Drive with them on instead of your headlights

See HIGHWAY CODE rules 201, 211

473 Front fog lights should be used ONLY when

Mark one answer

- [ ] **A.** travelling in very light rain
- [ ] **B.** visibility is seriously reduced
- [ ] **C.** daylight is fading
- [ ] **D.** driving after midnight

See HIGHWAY CODE rules 201, 211

474 Why is it dangerous to leave rear fog lights on when they are not needed?

NI

Mark two answers

- [ ] **A.** Brake lights are less clear
- [ ] **B.** Following drivers can be dazzled
- [ ] **C.** Electrical systems could be overloaded
- [ ] **D.** Direction indicators may not work properly
- [ ] **E.** The battery could fail

See HIGHWAY CODE rule 211

475

You are driving on a clear dry night with your rear fog lights switched on. This may

Mark two answers **NI**

- A. reduce glare from the road surface
- B. make other drivers think you are braking
- C. give a better view of the road ahead
- D. dazzle following drivers
- E. help your indicators to be seen more clearly

See HIGHWAY CODE rule 211

476

You have just driven out of fog. Visibility is now good. You MUST

Mark one answer

- A. switch off all your fog lights
- B. keep your rear fog lights on
- C. keep your front fog lights on
- D. leave fog lights on in case fog returns

See HIGHWAY CODE rules 201, 211

477

You forget to switch off your rear fog lights when the fog has cleared. This may

Mark three answers **NI**

- A. dazzle other road users
- B. reduce battery life
- C. cause brake lights to be less clear
- D. be breaking the law
- E. seriously affect engine power

See HIGHWAY CODE rule 211

478

You have been driving in thick fog which has now cleared. You must switch OFF your rear fog lights because

Mark one answer **NI**

- A. they use a lot of power from the battery
- B. they make your brake lights less clear
- C. they will cause dazzle in your rear-view mirrors
- D. they may not be properly adjusted

See HIGHWAY CODE rule 211

479

Front fog lights should be used

Mark one answer

- A. when visibility is reduced to 100 metres (328 feet)
- B. as a warning to oncoming traffic
- C. when driving during the hours of darkness
- D. in any conditions and at any time

See HIGHWAY CODE rule 201

480

Using rear fog lights in clear daylight will

Mark one answer

- A. be useful when towing a trailer
- B. give extra protection
- C. dazzle other drivers
- D. make following drivers keep back

See HIGHWAY CODE rule 211

481

Using front fog lights in clear daylight will

Mark one answer

- A. flatten the battery
- B. dazzle other drivers
- C. improve your visibility
- D. increase your awareness

See HIGHWAY CODE rule 211

482

You may use front fog lights with headlights ONLY when visibility is reduced to less than

Mark one answer

- A. 100 metres (328 feet)
- B. 200 metres (656 feet)
- C. 300 metres (984 feet)
- D. 400 metres (1,312 feet)

See HIGHWAY CODE rule 201

483 You may drive with front fog lights switched on

N 512 CTW

Mark one answer

- A. when visibility is less than 100 metres (328 feet)
- B. at any time to be noticed
- C. instead of headlights on high-speed roads
- D. when dazzled by the lights of oncoming vehicles

See HIGHWAY CODE rule 201

484 Chains can be fitted to your wheels to help prevent

Mark one answer

- A. damage to the road surface
- B. wear to the tyres
- C. skidding in deep snow
- D. the brakes locking

485 Pressing the clutch pedal down or rolling in neutral for too long while driving will

Mark one answer

- A. use more fuel
- B. cause the engine to overheat
- C. reduce your control
- D. improve tyre wear

See HIGHWAY CODE rule 102

486 How can you use the engine of your vehicle to control your speed?

Mark one answer

- A. By changing to a lower gear
- B. By selecting reverse gear
- C. By changing to a higher gear
- D. By selecting neutral

See HIGHWAY CODE rule 136

487 You are driving down a steep hill. Why could keeping the clutch down or selecting neutral for too long be dangerous?

Mark one answer

- A. Fuel consumption will be higher
- B. Your vehicle will pick up speed
- C. It will damage the engine
- D. It will wear tyres out more quickly

See HIGHWAY CODE rule 102

488 Why could keeping the clutch down or selecting neutral for long periods of time be dangerous?

Mark one answer

- A. Fuel spillage will occur
- B. Engine damage may be caused
- C. You will have less steering and braking control
- D. It will wear tyres out more quickly

See HIGHWAY CODE rule 102

489

You are driving on an icy road. What distance should you drive from the car in front?

Mark one answer

- [ ] A. four times the normal distance
- [ ] B. six times the normal distance
- [ ] C. eight times the normal distance
- [ ] D. ten times the normal distance

See HIGHWAY CODE rule 205

490

You are on a well-lit motorway at night. You must

Mark one answer

- [ ] A. use only your sidelights
- [ ] B. always use your headlights
- [ ] C. always use rear fog lights
- [ ] D. use headlights only in bad weather

See HIGHWAY CODE rule 93

491

You are on a motorway at night with other vehicles just ahead of you. Which lights should you have on?

Mark one answer

- [ ] A. Front fog lights
- [ ] B. Main beam headlights
- [ ] C. Sidelights only
- [ ] D. Dipped headlights

See HIGHWAY CODE rule 93

492

Which THREE of the following will affect your stopping distance?

Mark three answers

- [ ] A. How fast you are going
- [ ] B. The tyres on your vehicle
- [ ] C. The time of day
- [ ] D. The weather
- [ ] E. The street lighting

See HIGHWAY CODE rule 105

493

You are on a motorway at night. You MUST have your headlights switched on unless

`NI`

Mark one answer

- [ ] A. there are vehicles close in front of you
- [ ] B. you are travelling below 50mph
- [ ] C. the motorway is lit
- [ ] D. your vehicle is broken down on the hard shoulder

See HIGHWAY CODE rule 248

494

You will feel the effects of engine braking when you

Mark one answer

- [ ] A. only use the handbrake
- [ ] B. only use neutral
- [ ] C. change to a lower gear
- [ ] D. change to a higher gear

495

Daytime visibility is poor but not seriously reduced. You should switch on

Mark one answer

- [ ] A. headlights and fog lights
- [ ] B. front fog lights
- [ ] C. dipped headlights
- [ ] D. rear fog lights

See HIGHWAY CODE rule 95

496

Why are vehicles fitted with rear fog lights?

Mark one answer

- [ ] A. To be seen when driving at high speed
- [ ] B. To use if broken down in a dangerous position
- [ ] C. To make them more visible in thick fog
- [ ] D. To warn drivers following closely to drop back

497 While you are driving in fog, it becomes necessary to use front fog lights. You should

Mark one answer

- A. only turn them on in heavy traffic conditions
- B. remember not to use them on motorways
- C. only use them on dual carriageways
- D. remember to switch them off as visibility improves

See HIGHWAY CODE rules 201, 211

498 When snow is falling heavily you should

Mark one answer

- A. only drive with your hazard lights on
- B. not drive unless you have a mobile phone
- C. only drive when your journey is short
- D. not drive unless it is essential

See HIGHWAY CODE rule 203

499 You are driving down a long steep hill. You suddenly notice your brakes are not working as well as normal. What is the usual cause of this?

Mark one answer

- A. The brakes overheating
- B. Air in the brake fluid
- C. Oil on the brakes
- D. Badly adjusted brakes

TIP If you are being tailgated, gradually slow down to increase the gap between your vehicle and the one in front, allowing at least double the distance of the two-second rule. If you need to brake, allow for the following driver by braking early and gently, keeping an eye on the mirror. This is called **braking for two** – that is, for yourself and the tailgater.

500 Which FOUR of these must NOT use motorways?

Mark four answers

- [ ] **A.** Learner car drivers
- [ ] **B.** Motorcycles over 50cc
- [ ] **C.** Double-decker buses
- [ ] **D.** Farm tractors
- [ ] **E.** Horse riders
- [ ] **F.** Cyclists

See HIGHWAY CODE rule 227

501 Which FOUR of these must NOT use motorways?

Mark four answers

- [ ] **A.** Learner car drivers
- [ ] **B.** Motorcycles over 50cc
- [ ] **C.** Double-deck buses
- [ ] **D.** Farm tractors
- [ ] **E.** Learner motorcyclists
- [ ] **F.** Cyclists

See HIGHWAY CODE rule 227

502 Immediately after joining a motorway you should normally

Mark one answer

- [ ] **A.** try to overtake
- [ ] **B.** re-adjust your mirrors
- [ ] **C.** position your vehicle in the centre lane
- [ ] **D.** keep in the left lane

See HIGHWAY CODE rule 233

503 When joining a motorway you must always

Mark one answer

- [ ] **A.** use the hard shoulder
- [ ] **B.** stop at the end of the acceleration lane
- [ ] **C.** come to a stop before joining the motorway
- [ ] **D.** give way to traffic already on the motorway

See HIGHWAY CODE rule 233

504 What is the national speed limit for cars and motorcycles in the centre lane of a three-lane motorway?

Mark one answer

- [ ] **A.** 40mph
- [ ] **B.** 50mph
- [ ] **C.** 60mph
- [ ] **D.** 70mph

See HIGHWAY CODE rules 103 table, 235

505 What is the national speed limit on motorways for cars and motorcycles?

Mark one answer

- [ ] **A.** 30mph
- [ ] **B.** 50mph
- [ ] **C.** 60mph
- [ ] **D.** 70mph

See HIGHWAY CODE rules 103 table, 235

506 The left-hand lane on a three-lane motorway is for use by

Mark one answer

- [ ] **A.** any vehicle
- [ ] **B.** large vehicles only
- [ ] **C.** emergency vehicles only
- [ ] **D.** slow vehicles only

See HIGHWAY CODE rule 238

507 What is the right-hand lane used for on a three-lane motorway?

Mark one answer

- [ ] **A.** Emergency vehicles only
- [ ] **B.** Overtaking
- [ ] **C.** Vehicles towing trailers
- [ ] **D.** Coaches only

See HIGHWAY CODE rule 238

508 Which of these IS NOT allowed to travel in the right-hand lane of a three-lane motorway?

Mark one answer
- [ ] **A.** A small delivery van
- [ ] **B.** A motorcycle
- [ ] **C.** A vehicle towing a trailer
- [ ] **D.** A motorcycle and sidecar

See HIGHWAY CODE rule 239

509 You are travelling on a motorway. You decide you need a rest. You should

Mark two answers
- [ ] **A.** stop on the hard shoulder
- [ ] **B.** go to a service area
- [ ] **C.** park on the slip road
- [ ] **D.** park on the central reservation
- [ ] **E.** leave at the next exit

See HIGHWAY CODE rule 80

510 You break down on a motorway. You need to call for help. Why may it be better to use an emergency roadside telephone rather than a mobile phone?

NI

Mark one answer
- [ ] **A.** It connects you to a local garage
- [ ] **B.** Using a mobile phone will distract other drivers
- [ ] **C.** It allows easy location by the emergency services
- [ ] **D.** Mobile phones do not work on motorways

See HIGHWAY CODE rule 249

511 What should you use the hard shoulder of a motorway for?

Mark one answer
- [ ] **A.** Stopping in an emergency
- [ ] **B.** Leaving the motorway
- [ ] **C.** Stopping when you are tired
- [ ] **D.** Joining the motorway

See HIGHWAY CODE rule 249

512 After a breakdown you need to rejoin the main carriageway of a motorway from the hard shoulder. You should

Mark one answer
- [ ] **A.** move out on to the carriageway then build up your speed
- [ ] **B.** move out on to the carriageway using your hazard lights
- [ ] **C.** gain speed on the hard shoulder before moving out on to the carriageway
- [ ] **D.** wait on the hard shoulder until someone flashes their headlights at you

See HIGHWAY CODE rule 250

513 A crawler lane on a motorway is found

Mark one answer
- [ ] **A.** on a steep gradient
- [ ] **B.** before a service area
- [ ] **C.** before a junction
- [ ] **D.** along the hard shoulder

See HIGHWAY CODE rule 118

514
You are driving on a motorway. There are red flashing lights above every lane. You must

Mark one answer
- **A.** pull on to the hard shoulder
- **B.** slow down and watch for further signals
- **C.** leave at the next exit
- **D.** stop and wait

See HIGHWAY CODE rule 232

515
You are driving in the right-hand lane on a motorway. You see these overhead signs. This means

Mark one answer
- **A.** move to the left and reduce your speed to 50mph
- **B.** there are road works 50 metres (55 yards) ahead
- **C.** use the hard shoulder until you have passed the hazard
- **D.** leave the motorway at the next exit

See HIGHWAY CODE Motorway signals

516
What do these motorway signs show?

Mark one answer
- **A.** They are countdown markers to a bridge
- **B.** They are distance markers to the next telephone
- **C.** They are countdown markers to the next exit
- **D.** They warn of a police control ahead

See HIGHWAY CODE Information signs

517
On a motorway the amber reflective studs can be found between

Mark one answer
- **A.** the hard shoulder and the carriageway
- **B.** the acceleration lane and the carriageway
- **C.** the central reservation and the carriageway
- **D.** each pair of the lanes

See HIGHWAY CODE rule 111

518
What colour are the reflective studs between the lanes on a motorway?

Mark one answer
- **A.** Green
- **B.** Amber
- **C.** White
- **D.** Red

See HIGHWAY CODE rule 111

519
What colour are the reflective studs between a motorway and its slip road?

Mark one answer
- **A.** Amber
- **B.** White
- **C.** Green
- **D.** Red

See HIGHWAY CODE rule 111

520
You are allowed to stop on a motorway when you

Mark one answer
- **A.** need to walk and get fresh air
- **B.** wish to pick up hitch-hikers
- **C.** are told to do so by flashing red lights
- **D.** need to use a mobile telephone

See HIGHWAY CODE rules 232, 244

521 You have broken down on a motorway. To find the nearest emergency telephone you should always walk

Mark one answer
- [ ] **A.** with the traffic flow
- [ ] **B.** facing oncoming traffic
- [ ] **C.** in the direction shown on the marker posts
- [ ] **D.** in the direction of the nearest exit

See HIGHWAY CODE rule 249

522 You are travelling along the left lane of a three-lane motorway. Traffic is joining from a slip road. You should

Mark one answer
- [ ] **A.** race the other vehicles
- [ ] **B.** move to another lane
- [ ] **C.** maintain a steady speed
- [ ] **D.** switch on your hazard flashers

523 You are joining a motorway. Why is it important to make full use of the slip road?

Mark one answer
- [ ] **A.** Because there is space available to turn round if you need to
- [ ] **B.** To allow you direct access to the overtaking lanes
- [ ] **C.** To build up a speed similar to traffic on the motorway
- [ ] **D.** Because you can continue on the hard shoulder

See HIGHWAY CODE rule 233

TIP Never underestimate how dangerous the hard shoulder can be. As many as one in eight road deaths happen there.

524 How should you use the emergency telephone on a motorway?

Mark one answer
- [ ] **A.** Stay close to the carriageway
- [ ] **B.** Face the oncoming traffic
- [ ] **C.** Keep your back to the traffic
- [ ] **D.** Stand on the hard shoulder

525 You are on a motorway. What colour are the reflective studs on the left of the carriageway?

Mark one answer
- [ ] **A.** Green
- [ ] **B.** Red
- [ ] **C.** White
- [ ] **D.** Amber

See HIGHWAY CODE rule 111

526 On a three-lane motorway which lane should you normally use?

Mark one answer
- [ ] **A.** Left
- [ ] **B.** Right
- [ ] **C.** Centre
- [ ] **D.** Either the right or centre

See HIGHWAY CODE rule 238

527 A basic rule when on motorways is

Mark one answer
- [ ] **A.** use the lane that has least traffic
- [ ] **B.** keep to the left lane unless overtaking
- [ ] **C.** overtake on the side that is clearest
- [ ] **D.** try to keep above 50mph to prevent congestion

See HIGHWAY CODE rule 238

528 When going through a contraflow system on a motorway you should

Mark one answer

- A. ensure that you do not exceed 30mph
- B. keep a good distance from the vehicle ahead
- C. switch lanes to keep the traffic flowing
- D. stay close to the vehicle ahead to reduce queues

See HIGHWAY CODE rule 264

529 You are on a three-lane motorway. There are red reflective studs on your left and white ones to your right. Where are you?

Mark one answer

- A. In the right-hand lane
- B. In the middle lane
- C. On the hard shoulder
- D. In the left-hand lane

See HIGHWAY CODE rule 111

530 When may you stop on a motorway?

Mark three answers

- A. If you have to read a map
- B. When you are tired and need a rest
- C. If red lights show above every lane
- D. When told to by the police
- E. If your mobile phone rings
- F. In an emergency or a breakdown

See HIGHWAY CODE rule 244

531 You are approaching road works on a motorway. What should you do?

Mark one answer

- A. Speed up to clear the area quickly
- B. Always use the hard shoulder
- C. Obey all speed limits
- D. Stay very close to the vehicle in front

See HIGHWAY CODE rule 262

532 On motorways you should never overtake on the left UNLESS

Mark one answer

- A. you can see well ahead that the hard shoulder is clear
- B. the traffic in the right-hand lane is signalling right
- C. you warn drivers behind by signalling left
- D. there is a queue of slow-moving traffic to your right that is moving slower than you are

See HIGHWAY CODE rule 242

533 You are towing a trailer on a motorway. What is your maximum speed limit?

Mark one answer

- A. 40mph
- B. 50mph
- C. 60mph
- D. 70mph

See HIGHWAY CODE rule 103 table

534 The left-hand lane of a motorway should be used for

Mark one answer

A. breakdowns and emergencies only
B. overtaking slower traffic in the other lanes
C. slow vehicles only
D. normal driving

See HIGHWAY CODE rule 238

535 You are driving on a motorway. You have to slow down quickly due to a hazard. You should

Mark one answer

A. switch on your hazard lights
B. switch on your headlights
C. sound your horn
D. flash your headlights

See HIGHWAY CODE rule 96

536 You get a puncture on the motorway. You manage to get your vehicle on to the hard shoulder. You should

Mark one answer

A. change the wheel yourself immediately
B. use the emergency telephone and call for assistance
C. try to wave down another vehicle for help
D. only change the wheel if you have a passenger to help you

See HIGHWAY CODE rule 249

537 You are driving on a motorway. By mistake, you go past the exit that you wanted to take. You should

Mark one answer

A. carefully reverse on the hard shoulder
B. carry on to the next exit
C. carefully reverse in the left-hand lane
D. make a U-turn at the next gap in the central reservation

See HIGHWAY CODE rule 237

538 Your vehicle breaks down on the hard shoulder of a motorway. You decide to use your mobile phone to call for help. You should

NI

Mark one answer

A. stand at the rear of the vehicle while making the call
B. try to repair the vehicle yourself
C. get out of the vehicle by the right-hand door
D. check your location from the marker posts on the left

See HIGHWAY CODE rules 249, 257

539 You are driving a car on a motorway. Unless signs show otherwise you must NOT exceed

Mark one answer

A. 50mph
B. 60mph
C. 70mph
D. 80mph

See HIGHWAY CODE rule 103 table

540
You are on a three-lane motorway towing a trailer. You may use the right-hand lane when

Mark one answer **NI**

- A. there are lane closures
- B. there is slow-moving traffic
- C. you can maintain a high speed
- D. large vehicles are in the left and centre lanes

See HIGHWAY CODE rule 263

541
You are on a motorway. There is a contraflow system ahead. What would you expect to find?

Mark one answer

- A. Temporary traffic lights
- B. Lower speed limits
- C. Wider lanes than normal
- D. Speed humps

See HIGHWAY CODE rule 264

542
You are driving at 70mph on a three-lane motorway. There is no traffic ahead. Which lane should you use?

Mark one answer

- A. Any lane
- B. Middle lane
- C. Right lane
- D. Left lane

See HIGHWAY CODE rule 238

543
Your vehicle has broken down on a motorway. You are not able to stop on the hard shoulder. What should you do?

Mark one answer

- A. Switch on your hazard warning lights
- B. Stop following traffic and ask for help
- C. Attempt to repair your vehicle quickly
- D. Stand behind your vehicle to warn others

See HIGHWAY CODE rule 248

544
Why is it particularly important to carry out a check on your vehicle before making a long motorway journey?

Mark one answer

- A. You will have to do more harsh braking on motorways
- B. Motorway service stations do not deal with breakdowns
- C. The road surface will wear down the tyres faster
- D. Continuous high speeds may increase the risk of your vehicle breaking down

545
For what reason may you use the right-hand lane of a motorway?

Mark one answer

- A. For keeping out of the way of lorries
- B. For driving at more than 70mph
- C. For turning right
- D. For overtaking other vehicles

See HIGHWAY CODE rule 238

546 On a motorway you may ONLY stop on the hard shoulder

Mark one answer

- [ ] **A.** in an emergency
- [ ] **B.** if you feel tired and need to rest
- [ ] **C.** if you accidentally go past the exit that you wanted to take
- [ ] **D.** to pick up a hitch-hiker

See HIGHWAY CODE rule 244

547 You are driving on a motorway. The car ahead shows its hazard lights for a short time. This tells you that

Mark one answer

- [ ] **A.** the driver wants you to overtake
- [ ] **B.** the other car is going to change lanes
- [ ] **C.** traffic ahead is slowing or stopping suddenly
- [ ] **D.** there is a police speed check ahead

See HIGHWAY CODE rule 96

548 The emergency telephones on a motorway are connected to the

Mark one answer

- [ ] **A.** ambulance service
- [ ] **B.** police control
- [ ] **C.** fire brigade
- [ ] **D.** breakdown service

See HIGHWAY CODE rule 249

549 You are intending to leave the motorway at the next exit. Before you reach the exit you should normally position your vehicle

Mark one answer

- [ ] **A.** in the middle lane
- [ ] **B.** in the left-hand lane
- [ ] **C.** on the hard shoulder
- [ ] **D.** in any lane

See HIGHWAY CODE rule 246

550 As a provisional licence holder you should not drive a car

Mark one answer

- [ ] **A.** over 30mph
- [ ] **B.** at night
- [ ] **C.** on the motorway
- [ ] **D.** with passengers in rear seats

See HIGHWAY CODE rule 227

TIP The first motorway sign-board, a mile before the exit, will only provide the road numbers and sometimes major town names. The half-mile sign gives major town names. Make sure you know in advance which junction number you're looking for.

551 What is the meaning of this sign?

Mark one answer
- [ ] **A.** Local speed limit applies
- [ ] **B.** No waiting on the carriageway
- [ ] **C.** National speed limit applies
- [ ] **D.** No entry to vehicular traffic

See HIGHWAY CODE Signs giving orders

552 What is the national speed limit on a single carriageway road for cars and motorcycles?

Mark one answer
- [ ] **A.** 70mph
- [ ] **B.** 60mph
- [ ] **C.** 50mph
- [ ] **D.** 30mph

See HIGHWAY CODE rule 103 table

553 What is the national speed limit for cars and motorcycles on a dual carriageway?

Mark one answer
- [ ] **A.** 30mph
- [ ] **B.** 50mph
- [ ] **C.** 60mph
- [ ] **D.** 70mph

See HIGHWAY CODE rule 103 table

554 There are no speed limit signs on the road. How is a 30mph limit indicated?

Mark one answer
- [ ] **A.** By hazard warning lines
- [ ] **B.** By street lighting
- [ ] **C.** By pedestrian islands
- [ ] **D.** By double or single yellow lines

See HIGHWAY CODE rule 103

555 Where you see street lights but no speed limit signs the limit is usually

Mark one answer
- [ ] **A.** 30mph
- [ ] **B.** 40mph
- [ ] **C.** 50mph
- [ ] **D.** 60mph

See HIGHWAY CODE rule 103

556 What does this sign mean?

Mark one answer
- [ ] **A.** Minimum speed 30mph
- [ ] **B.** End of maximum speed
- [ ] **C.** End of minimum speed
- [ ] **D.** Maximum speed 30mph

See HIGHWAY CODE Signs giving orders

557 There is a tractor ahead of you. You wish to overtake but you are NOT sure if it is safe to do so. You should

Mark one answer
- [ ] **A.** follow another overtaking vehicle through
- [ ] **B.** sound your horn to the slow vehicle to pull over
- [ ] **C.** speed through but flash your lights to oncoming traffic
- [ ] **D.** not overtake if you are in doubt

See HIGHWAY CODE rule 139

TIP When judging the probable actions of another vehicle at a junction, check for clues such as the position on the road of the other vehicle and the angle of the wheels.

558 Which three of the following are most likely to take an unusual course at roundabouts?

Mark three answers
- [ ] **A.** Horse riders
- [ ] **B.** Milk floats
- [ ] **C.** Delivery vans
- [ ] **D.** Long vehicles
- [ ] **E.** Estate cars
- [ ] **F.** Cyclists

See HIGHWAY CODE rule 163

559 In which FOUR places must you NOT park or wait?

Mark four answers
- [ ] **A.** On a dual carriageway
- [ ] **B.** At a bus stop
- [ ] **C.** On the slope of a hill
- [ ] **D.** Opposite a traffic island
- [ ] **E.** In front of someone else's drive
- [ ] **F.** On the brow of a hill

See HIGHWAY CODE rule 217

560 In which TWO places must you NOT park?

Mark two answers
- [ ] **A.** Near a school entrance
- [ ] **B.** Near a police station
- [ ] **C.** In a side road
- [ ] **D.** At a bus stop
- [ ] **E.** In a one-way street

See HIGHWAY CODE rule 217

561 On a clearway you must not stop

Mark one answer
- [ ] **A.** at any time
- [ ] **B.** when it is busy
- [ ] **C.** in the rush hour
- [ ] **D.** during daylight hours

See HIGHWAY CODE rule 215

562 What is the meaning of this sign?

Mark one answer
- [ ] **A.** No entry
- [ ] **B.** Waiting restrictions
- [ ] **C.** National speed limit
- [ ] **D.** School crossing patrol

See HIGHWAY CODE Signs giving orders

563 You can park on the right-hand side of a road at night

Mark one answer
- [ ] **A.** in a one-way street
- [ ] **B.** with your sidelights on
- [ ] **C.** more than 10 metres (32 feet) from a junction
- [ ] **D.** under a lamppost

See HIGHWAY CODE rule 222

564 On a three-lane dual carriageway the right-hand lane can be used for

Mark one answer
- [ ] **A.** overtaking only, never turning right
- [ ] **B.** overtaking or turning right
- [ ] **C.** fast-moving traffic only
- [ ] **D.** turning right only, never overtaking

See HIGHWAY CODE rules 116, 117

565 You are approaching a busy junction. There are several lanes with road markings. At the last moment you realise that you are in the wrong lane. You should

Mark one answer

- [ ] **A.** continue in that lane
- [ ] **B.** force your way across
- [ ] **C.** stop until the area has cleared
- [ ] **D.** use clear arm signals to cut across

566 Where may you overtake on a one-way street?

Mark one answer

- [ ] **A.** Only on the left-hand side
- [ ] **B.** Overtaking is not allowed
- [ ] **C.** Only on the right-hand side
- [ ] **D.** Either on the right or the left

See HIGHWAY CODE rules 121, 139

567 When going straight ahead at a roundabout you should

Mark one answer

- [ ] **A.** indicate left before leaving the roundabout
- [ ] **B.** not indicate at any time
- [ ] **C.** indicate right when approaching the roundabout
- [ ] **D.** indicate left when approaching the roundabout

See HIGHWAY CODE rule 162

568 Which vehicle might have to use a different course to normal at roundabouts?

Mark one answer

- [ ] **A.** Sports car
- [ ] **B.** Van
- [ ] **C.** Estate car
- [ ] **D.** Long vehicle

See HIGHWAY CODE rule 163

569 You are going straight ahead at a roundabout. How should you signal?

Mark one answer

- [ ] **A.** Signal right on the approach and then left to leave the roundabout
- [ ] **B.** Signal left as you leave the roundabout
- [ ] **C.** Signal left on the approach to the roundabout and keep the signal on until you leave
- [ ] **D.** Signal left just after you pass the exit before the one you will take

See HIGHWAY CODE rule 162

570 You may only enter a box junction when

Mark one answer

- [ ] **A.** there are less than two vehicles in front of you
- [ ] **B.** the traffic lights show green
- [ ] **C.** your exit road is clear
- [ ] **D.** you need to turn left

See HIGHWAY CODE rule 150

TIP In your driving test, where there are lanes the examiner will check your position on the road; it's important not to be straddling two lanes at a time.

571 You may wait in a yellow box junction when

Mark one answer

- A. oncoming traffic is preventing you from turning right
- B. you are in a queue of traffic turning left
- C. you are in a queue of traffic to go ahead
- D. you are on a roundabout

See HIGHWAY CODE rule 150

572 You MUST stop when signalled to do so by which THREE of these?

Mark three answers

- A. A police officer
- B. A pedestrian
- C. A school crossing patrol
- D. A bus driver
- E. A red traffic light

See HIGHWAY CODE rule 87, 88

TIP Did you know that you are allowed to have your seat belt unfastened when you are reversing? It's the only time you can do so when driving.

573 You will see these markers when approaching

Mark one answer

- A. the end of a motorway
- B. a concealed level crossing
- C. a concealed speed limit sign
- D. the end of a dual carriageway

574 Someone is waiting to cross at a zebra crossing. They are standing on the pavement. You should normally

Mark one answer

- A. go on quickly before they step on to the crossing
- B. stop before you reach the zigzag lines and let them cross
- C. stop, let them cross, wait patiently
- D. ignore them as they are still on the pavement

See HIGHWAY CODE rule 171

575 At toucan crossings, apart from pedestrians you should be aware of

Mark one answer

- A. emergency vehicles emerging
- B. buses pulling out
- C. trams crossing in front
- D. cyclists riding across

See HIGHWAY CODE rule 65

576 Who can use a toucan crossing?

Mark two answers
- [ ] **A.** Trains
- [ ] **B.** Cyclists
- [ ] **C.** Buses
- [ ] **D.** Pedestrians
- [ ] **E.** Trams

See HIGHWAY CODE rule 65

577 At a pelican crossing, what does a flashing amber light mean?

Mark one answer
- [ ] **A.** You must not move off until the lights stop flashing
- [ ] **B.** You must give way to pedestrians still on the crossing
- [ ] **C.** You can move off, even if pedestrians are still on the crossing
- [ ] **D.** You must stop because the lights are about to change to red

See HIGHWAY CODE rule 172

578 You are waiting at a pelican crossing. The red light changes to flashing amber. This means you must

Mark one answer
- [ ] **A.** wait for pedestrians on the crossing to clear
- [ ] **B.** move off immediately without any hesitation
- [ ] **C.** wait for the green light before moving off
- [ ] **D.** get ready and go when the continuous amber light shows

See HIGHWAY CODE rule 172

579 You are travelling on a well-lit road at night in a built-up area. By using dipped headlights you will be able to

Mark one answer
- [ ] **A.** see further along the road
- [ ] **B.** go at a much faster speed
- [ ] **C.** switch to main beam quickly
- [ ] **D.** be easily seen by others

See HIGHWAY CODE rule 95

580 When can you park on the left opposite these road markings?

Mark one answer
- [ ] **A.** If the line nearest to you is broken
- [ ] **B.** When there are no yellow lines
- [ ] **C.** To pick up or set down passengers
- [ ] **D.** During daylight hours only

See HIGHWAY CODE rule 215

581 You are intending to turn right at a crossroads. An oncoming driver is also turning right. It will normally be safer to

Mark one answer
- [ ] **A.** keep the other vehicle to your RIGHT and turn behind it (offside to offside)
- [ ] **B.** keep the other vehicle to your LEFT and turn in front of it (nearside to nearside)
- [ ] **C.** carry on and turn at the next junction instead
- [ ] **D.** hold back and wait for the other driver to turn first

See HIGHWAY CODE rule 157

582 You are on a road that has no traffic signs. There are street lights. What is the speed limit?

Mark one answer
- [ ] **A.** 20mph
- [ ] **B.** 30mph
- [ ] **C.** 40mph
- [ ] **D.** 60mph

See HIGHWAY CODE rule 103

583 You are going along a street with parked vehicles on the left-hand side. For which THREE reasons should you keep your speed down?

Mark three answers

- [ ] **A.** So that oncoming traffic can see you more clearly
- [ ] **B.** You may set off car alarms
- [ ] **C.** Vehicles may be pulling out
- [ ] **D.** Drivers' doors may open
- [ ] **E.** Children may run out from between the vehicles

See HIGHWAY CODE rule 130

584 You meet an obstruction on your side of the road. You should

Mark one answer

- [ ] **A.** carry on, you have priority
- [ ] **B.** give way to oncoming traffic
- [ ] **C.** wave oncoming vehicles through
- [ ] **D.** accelerate to get past first

See HIGHWAY CODE rule 139

585 You are on a two-lane dual carriageway. For which TWO of the following would you use the right-hand lane?

Mark two answers

- [ ] **A.** Turning right
- [ ] **B.** Normal progress
- [ ] **C.** Staying at the minimum allowed speed
- [ ] **D.** Constant high speed
- [ ] **E.** Overtaking slower traffic
- [ ] **F.** Mending punctures

See HIGHWAY CODE rule 116

586 Who has priority at an unmarked crossroads?

Mark one answer

- [ ] **A.** The larger vehicle
- [ ] **B.** No one has priority
- [ ] **C.** The faster vehicle
- [ ] **D.** The smaller vehicle

See HIGHWAY CODE rule 124

587 What is the nearest you may park to a junction?

Mark one answer **NI**

- [ ] **A.** 10 metres (32 feet)
- [ ] **B.** 12 metres (39 feet)
- [ ] **C.** 15 metres (49 feet)
- [ ] **D.** 20 metres (66 feet)

See HIGHWAY CODE rule 217

588 In which THREE places must you NOT park?

Mark three answers **NI**

- [ ] **A.** Near the brow of a hill
- [ ] **B.** At or near a bus stop
- [ ] **C.** Where there is no pavement
- [ ] **D.** Within 10 metres (32 feet) of a junction
- [ ] **E.** On a 40mph road

See HIGHWAY CODE rule 217

589 You are waiting at a level crossing. A train has passed but the lights keep flashing. You must

Mark one answer

- [ ] **A.** carry on waiting
- [ ] **B.** phone the signal operator
- [ ] **C.** edge over the stop line and look for trains
- [ ] **D.** park and investigate

See HIGHWAY CODE rule 266

590 You park overnight on a road with a 40mph speed limit. You should park

Mark one answer

- A. facing the traffic
- B. with parking lights on
- C. with dipped headlights on
- D. near a street light

See HIGHWAY CODE rule 223

591 The dual carriageway you are turning right on to has a very narrow central reserve. What should you do?

Mark one answer

- A. Proceed to the central reserve and wait
- B. Wait until the road is clear in both directions
- C. Stop in the first lane so that other vehicles give way
- D. Emerge slightly to show your intentions

See HIGHWAY CODE rule 149

592 At a crossroads there are no signs or road markings. Two vehicles approach. Which has priority?

Mark one answer

- A. Neither of the vehicles
- B. The vehicle travelling the fastest
- C. Oncoming vehicles turning right
- D. Vehicles approaching from the right

See HIGHWAY CODE rule 124

593 What does this sign tell you?

Mark one answer

- A. That it is a no-through road
- B. End of traffic calming zone
- C. Free parking zone ends
- D. No waiting zone ends

See HIGHWAY CODE Signs giving orders

594 You are entering an area of road works. There is a temporary speed limit displayed. You should

Mark one answer

- A. not exceed the speed limit
- B. obey the limit only during rush hour
- C. ignore the displayed limit
- D. obey the limit except at night

See HIGHWAY CODE rule 262

595 You may drive over a footpath

Mark one answer

- A. to overtake slow-moving traffic
- B. when the pavement is very wide
- C. if no pedestrians are near
- D. to get into a property

See HIGHWAY CODE rule 123

596

A single-carriageway road has this sign. What is the maximum permitted speed for a car towing a trailer?

Mark one answer

- [ ] **A.** 30mph
- [ ] **B.** 40mph
- [ ] **C.** 50mph
- [ ] **D.** 60mph

See HIGHWAY CODE rule 103 table

597

You are towing a small caravan on a dual carriageway. You must not exceed

Mark one answer

- [ ] **A.** 50mph
- [ ] **B.** 40mph
- [ ] **C.** 70mph
- [ ] **D.** 60mph

See HIGHWAY CODE rule 103 table

598

You want to park and you see this sign. On the days and times shown you should

Meter ZONE

No loading

Mon - Fri
8.30 am - 6.30 pm
Saturday
8.30 am - 1.30 pm

Mark one answer

- [ ] **A.** park in a bay and not pay
- [ ] **B.** park on yellow lines and pay
- [ ] **C.** park on yellow lines and not pay
- [ ] **D.** park in a bay and pay

See HIGHWAY CODE rule 219 & Information signs

599

As a car driver which THREE lanes are you NOT normally allowed to use?

Mark three answers

- [ ] **A.** Crawler lane
- [ ] **B.** Bus lane
- [ ] **C.** Overtaking lane
- [ ] **D.** Acceleration lane
- [ ] **E.** Cycle lane
- [ ] **F.** Tram lane

See HIGHWAY CODE rule 119, 120

600

You are driving along a road that has a cycle lane. The lane is marked by a solid white line. This means that during its period of operation

Mark one answer

- [ ] **A.** the lane may be used for parking your car
- [ ] **B.** you may drive in that lane at any time
- [ ] **C.** the lane may be used when necessary
- [ ] **D.** you must not drive in that lane

See HIGHWAY CODE rule 119

601

A cycle lane is marked by a solid white line. You must not drive or park in it

Mark one answer

- [ ] **A.** at any time
- [ ] **B.** during the rush hour
- [ ] **C.** if a cyclist is using it
- [ ] **D.** during its period of operation

See HIGHWAY CODE rule 119

602

While driving, you intend to turn left into a minor road. On the approach you should

Mark one answer

- [ ] **A.** keep just left of the middle of the road
- [ ] **B.** keep in the middle of the road
- [ ] **C.** swing out wide just before turning
- [ ] **D.** keep well to the left of the road

See HIGHWAY CODE rule 159

603 You are waiting at a level crossing. The red warning lights continue to flash after a train has passed by. What should you do?

Mark one answer
- **A.** Get out and investigate
- **B.** Telephone the signal operator
- **C.** Continue to wait
- **D.** Drive across carefully

See HIGHWAY CODE rule 266

604 You are driving over a level crossing. The warning lights come on and a bell rings. What should you do?

Mark one answer
- **A.** Get everyone out of the vehicle immediately
- **B.** Stop and reverse back to clear the crossing
- **C.** Keep going and clear the crossing
- **D.** Stop immediately and use your hazard warning lights

See HIGHWAY CODE rule 266

605 You are on a busy main road and find that you are travelling in the wrong direction. What should you do?

Mark one answer
- **A.** Turn into a side road on the right and reverse into the main road
- **B.** Make a U-turn in the main road
- **C.** Make a 'three-point' turn in the main road
- **D.** Turn round in a side road

See HIGHWAY CODE rule 176

606 You may remove your seat belt when carrying out a manoeuvre that involves

Mark one answer
- **A.** reversing
- **B.** a hill start
- **C.** an emergency stop
- **D.** driving slowly

607 You must not reverse

Mark one answer
- **A.** for longer than necessary
- **B.** for more than a car's length
- **C.** into a side road
- **D.** in a built-up area

See HIGHWAY CODE rule 179

608 You are parked in a busy high street. What is the safest way to turn your vehicle around to go the opposite way?

Mark one answer
- **A.** Find a quiet side road to turn round in
- **B.** Drive into a side road and reverse into the main road
- **C.** Get someone to stop the traffic
- **D.** Do a U-turn

See HIGHWAY CODE rule 176

609 When you are NOT sure that it is safe to reverse your vehicle you should

Mark one answer
- [ ] **A.** use your horn
- [ ] **B.** rev your engine
- [ ] **C.** get out and check
- [ ] **D.** reverse slowly

610 When may you reverse from a side road into a main road?

Mark one answer
- [ ] **A.** Only if both roads are clear of traffic
- [ ] **B.** Not at any time
- [ ] **C.** At any time
- [ ] **D.** Only if the main road is clear of traffic

See HIGHWAY CODE rule 177

611 You want to turn right at a box junction. There is oncoming traffic. You should

Mark one answer
- [ ] **A.** wait in the box junction if your exit is clear
- [ ] **B.** wait before the junction until it is clear of all traffic
- [ ] **C.** drive on, you cannot turn right at a box junction
- [ ] **D.** drive slowly into the box junction when signalled by oncoming traffic

See HIGHWAY CODE rule 150

612 You are reversing your vehicle into a side road. When would the greatest hazard to passing traffic occur?

Mark one answer
- [ ] **A.** After you've completed the manoeuvre
- [ ] **B.** Just before you actually begin to manoeuvre
- [ ] **C.** After you've entered the side road
- [ ] **D.** When the front of your vehicle swings out

See HIGHWAY CODE rule 178

613 You are driving on a road that has a cycle lane. The lane is marked by a broken white line. This means that

Mark two answers
- [ ] **A.** you should not drive in the lane unless it is unavoidable
- [ ] **B.** you should not park in the lane unless it is unavoidable
- [ ] **C.** you can drive in the lane at any time
- [ ] **D.** the lane must be used by motorcyclists in heavy traffic

See HIGHWAY CODE rule 119

614 Where is the safest place to park your vehicle at night?

Mark one answer
- [ ] **A.** In a garage
- [ ] **B.** On a busy road
- [ ] **C.** In a quiet car park
- [ ] **D.** Near a red route

615 To help keep your vehicle secure at night where should you park?

Mark one answer
- [ ] **A.** Near a police station
- [ ] **B.** In a quiet road
- [ ] **C.** On a red route
- [ ] **D.** In a well-lit area

616

You are in the right-hand lane of a dual carriageway. You see signs showing that the right lane is closed 800 yards ahead. You should

GET IN LANE

↑ ↑ ▬
| | |

800 yards

Mark one answer

- **A.** keep in that lane until you reach the queue
- **B.** move to the left immediately
- **C.** wait and see which lane is moving faster
- **D.** move to the left in good time

See HIGHWAY CODE rule 262

617

You are driving on an urban clearway. You may stop only to

Mark one answer

- **A.** set down and pick up passengers
- **B.** use a mobile telephone
- **C.** ask for directions
- **D.** load or unload goods

See HIGHWAY CODE rule 215

618

You are looking for somewhere to park your vehicle. The area is full EXCEPT for spaces marked 'disabled use'. You can

Mark one answer

- **A.** use these spaces when elsewhere is full
- **B.** park if you stay with your vehicle
- **C.** use these spaces, disabled or not
- **D.** not park there unless permitted

See HIGHWAY CODE rule 216

619

Your vehicle is parked on the road at night. When must you use sidelights?

Mark one answer

- **A.** Where there are continuous white lines in the middle of the road
- **B.** Where the speed limit exceeds 30mph
- **C.** Where you are facing oncoming traffic
- **D.** Where you are near a bus stop

See HIGHWAY CODE rule 223

620

On which THREE occasions MUST you stop your vehicle?

Mark three answers

- **A.** When involved in an accident
- **B.** At a red traffic light
- **C.** When signalled to do so by a police officer
- **D.** At a junction with double broken white lines
- **E.** At a pelican crossing when the amber light is flashing and no pedestrians are crossing

See HIGHWAY CODE rules 87, 88, 260

621

You are on a road that is only wide enough for one vehicle. There is a car coming towards you. What should you do?

Mark one answer

- **A.** Pull into a passing place on your right
- **B.** Force the other driver to reverse
- **C.** Pull into a passing place if your vehicle is wider
- **D.** Pull into a passing place on your left

See HIGHWAY CODE rule 133

622 What MUST you have to park in a disabled space?

Mark one answer

- [ ] **A.** An orange or blue badge
- [ ] **B.** A wheelchair
- [ ] **C.** An advanced driver certificate
- [ ] **D.** A modified vehicle

See HIGHWAY CODE rule 216

DISABLED

623 You are driving at night with full beam headlights on. A vehicle is overtaking you. You should dip your lights

Mark one answer

- [ ] **A.** some time after the vehicle has passed you
- [ ] **B.** before the vehicle starts to pass you
- [ ] **C.** only if the other driver dips their headlights
- [ ] **D.** as soon as the vehicle passes you

See HIGHWAY CODE rule 94

TIP You can recognise a car driven by someone who is disabled because they display a **Blue Card** (formerly an Orange Badge). This gives them the right to park in a space with disabilities.

624 When may you drive a motor car in this bus lane?

local

**Mon - Fri
7 - 10 am
4.00 - 6.30 pm**

Mark one answer

- [ ] **A.** Outside its hours of operation
- [ ] **B.** To get to the front of a traffic queue
- [ ] **C.** You may not use it at any time
- [ ] **D.** To overtake slow-moving traffic

See HIGHWAY CODE rule 120

625 Signals are normally given by direction indicators and

Mark one answer

- [ ] **A.** brake lights
- [ ] **B.** sidelights
- [ ] **C.** fog lights
- [ ] **D.** interior lights

See HIGHWAY CODE Signals to other users

626 You MUST obey signs giving orders. These signs are mostly in

Mark one answer
- **A.** green rectangles
- **B.** red triangles
- **C.** blue rectangles
- **D.** red circles

See HIGHWAY CODE Traffic signs

627 Traffic signs giving orders are generally which shape?

Mark one answer

- **A.**
- **B.**
- **C.**
- **D.**

See HIGHWAY CODE Traffic signs

628 Which type of sign tells you NOT to do something?

Mark one answer
- **A.**
- **B.**
- **C.**
- **D.**

See HIGHWAY CODE Traffic signs

629 What does this sign mean?

Mark one answer
- **A.** Maximum speed limit with traffic calming
- **B.** Minimum speed limit with traffic calming
- **C.** '20 cars only' parking zone
- **D.** Only 20 cars allowed at any one time

20 ZONE
symbol
Place Name

See HIGHWAY CODE Signs giving orders

630 Which sign means no motor vehicles are allowed?

Mark one answer
- **A.**
- **B.**
- **C.**
- **D.**

See HIGHWAY CODE Signs giving orders

631 Which of these signs means no motor vehicles?

Mark one answer
- **A.**
- **B.**
- **C.**
- **D.**

See HIGHWAY CODE Signs giving orders

632 What does this sign mean?

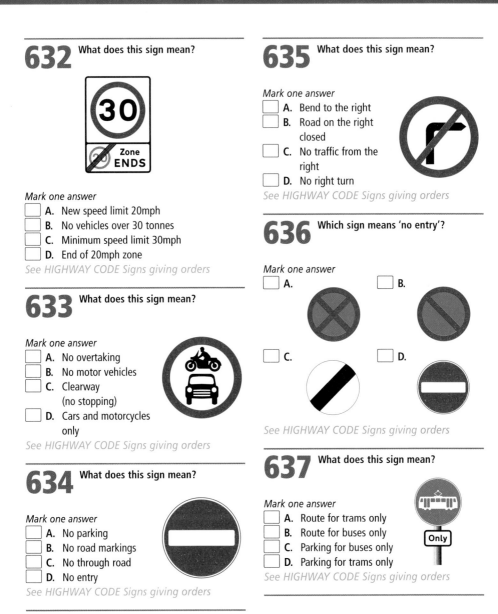

Mark one answer
- A. New speed limit 20mph
- B. No vehicles over 30 tonnes
- C. Minimum speed limit 30mph
- D. End of 20mph zone

See HIGHWAY CODE Signs giving orders

633 What does this sign mean?

Mark one answer
- A. No overtaking
- B. No motor vehicles
- C. Clearway (no stopping)
- D. Cars and motorcycles only

See HIGHWAY CODE Signs giving orders

634 What does this sign mean?

Mark one answer
- A. No parking
- B. No road markings
- C. No through road
- D. No entry

See HIGHWAY CODE Signs giving orders

635 What does this sign mean?

Mark one answer
- A. Bend to the right
- B. Road on the right closed
- C. No traffic from the right
- D. No right turn

See HIGHWAY CODE Signs giving orders

636 Which sign means 'no entry'?

Mark one answer
- A.
- B.
- C.
- D.

See HIGHWAY CODE Signs giving orders

637 What does this sign mean?

Mark one answer
- A. Route for trams only
- B. Route for buses only
- C. Parking for buses only
- D. Parking for trams only

See HIGHWAY CODE Signs giving orders

638 Which type of vehicle does this sign apply to?

Mark one answer

- **A.** Wide vehicles
- **B.** Long vehicles
- **C.** High vehicles
- **D.** Heavy vehicles

See HIGHWAY CODE Signs giving orders

639 Which sign means NO motor vehicles allowed?

Mark one answer

- **A.**
- **B.**
- **C.**
- **D.**

See HIGHWAY CODE Signs giving orders

640 What does this sign mean?

Mark one answer

- **A.** You have priority
- **B.** No motor vehicles
- **C.** Two-way traffic
- **D.** No overtaking

See HIGHWAY CODE Signs giving orders

641 What does this sign mean?

Mark one answer

- **A.** Keep in one lane
- **B.** Give way to oncoming traffic
- **C.** Do not overtake
- **D.** Form two lanes

See HIGHWAY CODE Signs giving orders

642 Which sign means no overtaking?

Mark one answer

- **A.**
- **B.**
- **C.**
- **D.**

See HIGHWAY CODE Traffic signs

643 What does this sign mean?

Mark one answer

- **A.** Waiting restrictions apply
- **B.** Waiting permitted
- **C.** National speed limit applies
- **D.** Clearway (no stopping)

See HIGHWAY CODE Signs giving orders

644 What does this sign mean?

Mark one answer
- [ ] **A.** End of restricted speed area
- [ ] **B.** End of restricted parking area
- [ ] **C.** End of clearway
- [ ] **D.** End of cycle route

See HIGHWAY CODE Information signs

645 Which sign means 'no stopping'?

Mark one answer
- [ ] **A.**
- [ ] **B.**
- [ ] **C.**
- [ ] **D.**

See HIGHWAY CODE Signs giving orders

646 What does this sign mean?

Mark one answer
- [ ] **A.** Roundabout
- [ ] **B.** Crossroads
- [ ] **C.** No stopping
- [ ] **D.** No entry

See HIGHWAY CODE Signs giving orders

TIP Remember that where there are street lamps spaced less than 185 metres (202 yards) apart, a 30mph speed limit applies unless signs on the posts state otherwise.

647 You see this sign ahead. It means

Mark one answer
- [ ] **A.** national speed limit applies
- [ ] **B.** waiting restrictions apply
- [ ] **C.** no stopping
- [ ] **D.** no entry

See HIGHWAY CODE Signs giving orders

648 What does this sign mean?

Mark one answer
- [ ] **A.** Distance to parking place ahead
- [ ] **B.** Distance to public telephone ahead
- [ ] **C.** Distance to public house ahead
- [ ] **D.** Distance to passing place ahead

649 What does this sign mean?

Mark one answer
- [ ] **A.** Vehicles may not park on the verge or footway
- [ ] **B.** Vehicles may park on the left-hand side of the road only
- [ ] **C.** Vehicles may park fully on the verge or footway
- [ ] **D.** Vehicles may park on the right-hand side of the road only

650 What does this traffic sign mean?

Mark one answer
- A. No overtaking allowed
- B. Give priority to oncoming traffic
- C. Two-way traffic
- D. One-way traffic only

See HIGHWAY CODE Signs giving orders

651 What is the meaning of this traffic sign?

Mark one answer
- A. End of two-way road
- B. Give priority to vehicles coming towards you
- C. You have priority over vehicles coming towards you
- D. Bus lane ahead

See HIGHWAY CODE Information signs

652 What MUST you do when you see this sign?

Mark one answer
- A. Stop, ONLY if traffic is approaching
- B. Stop, even if the road is clear
- C. Stop, ONLY if children are waiting to cross
- D. Stop, ONLY if a red light is showing

See HIGHWAY CODE Signs giving orders

653 What does this sign mean?

Mark one answer
- A. No overtaking
- B. You are entering a one-way street
- C. Two-way traffic ahead
- D. You have priority over vehicles from the opposite direction

See HIGHWAY CODE Information signs

654 What shape is a STOP sign at a junction?

Mark one answer
- A.
- B.
- C.
- D.

See HIGHWAY CODE Traffic signs

655 At a junction you see this sign partly covered by snow. What does it mean?

Mark one answer
- A. Crossroads
- B. Give way
- C. Stop
- D. Turn right

See HIGHWAY CODE Signs giving orders

656 Which shape is used for a GIVE WAY sign?

Mark one answer

A. △

B. ○

C. ⬣

D. ▽

See HIGHWAY CODE Traffic signs

657 What does this sign mean?

Mark one answer

A. Service area 30 miles ahead

B. Maximum speed 30mph

C. Minimum speed 30mph

D. Lay-by 30 miles ahead

See HIGHWAY CODE Signs giving orders

658 Which of these signs means turn left ahead?

Mark one answer

A.

B.

C.

D.

See HIGHWAY CODE Signs giving orders

659 What does this sign mean?

Mark one answer

A. Buses turning

B. Ring road

C. Mini-roundabout

D. Keep right

See HIGHWAY CODE Signs giving orders

660 What does this sign mean?

Mark one answer

A. Give way to oncoming vehicles

B. Approaching traffic passes you on both sides

C. Turn off at the next available junction

D. Pass either side to get to the same destination

See HIGHWAY CODE Signs giving orders

661 What does this sign mean?

Mark one answer

A. Route for trams

B. Give way to trams

C. Route for buses

D. Give way to buses

See HIGHWAY CODE Signs giving orders

662 What does a circular traffic sign with a blue background do?

Mark one answer

- [ ] **A.** Give warning of a motorway ahead
- [ ] **B.** Give directions to a car park
- [ ] **C.** Give motorway information
- [ ] **D.** Give an instruction

See HIGHWAY CODE Traffic signs

663 Which of these signs means that you are entering a one-way street?

Mark one answer

- [ ] **A.**
- [ ] **B.**
- [ ] **C.**
- [ ] **D.**

See HIGHWAY CODE Traffic signs

664 Where would you see a contraflow bus and cycle lane?

Mark one answer

- [ ] **A.** On a dual carriageway
- [ ] **B.** On a roundabout
- [ ] **C.** On an urban motorway
- [ ] **D.** On a one-way street

See HIGHWAY CODE rule 121

665 What does this sign mean?

Mark one answer

- [ ] **A.** Bus station on the right
- [ ] **B.** Contraflow bus lane
- [ ] **C.** With-flow bus lane
- [ ] **D.** Give way to buses

See HIGHWAY CODE Signs giving orders

666 What does this sign mean?

Mark one answer

- [ ] **A.** With-flow bus and cycle lane
- [ ] **B.** Contraflow bus and cycle lane
- [ ] **C.** No buses and cycles allowed
- [ ] **D.** No waiting for buses and cycles

667 What does a sign with a brown background show?

Mark one answer

- [ ] **A.** Tourist directions
- [ ] **B.** Primary roads
- [ ] **C.** Motorway routes
- [ ] **D.** Minor routes

668 This sign means

Mark one answer
- **A.** tourist attraction
- **B.** beware of trains
- **C.** level crossing
- **D.** beware of trams

669 What are triangular signs for?

Mark one answer
- **A.** To give warnings
- **B.** To give information
- **C.** To give orders
- **D.** To give directions

See HIGHWAY CODE Traffic signs

670 What does this sign mean?

Mark one answer
- **A.** Turn left ahead
- **B.** T-junction
- **C.** No through road
- **D.** Give way

See HIGHWAY CODE Warning signs

671 What does this sign mean?

Mark one answer
- **A.** Multi-exit roundabout
- **B.** Risk of ice
- **C.** Six roads converge
- **D.** Place of historical interest

See HIGHWAY CODE Warning signs

672 What does this sign mean?

Mark one answer
- **A.** Crossroads
- **B.** Level crossing with gate
- **C.** Level crossing without gate
- **D.** Ahead only

See HIGHWAY CODE Warning signs

673 What does this sign mean?

Mark one answer
- **A.** Ring road
- **B.** Mini-roundabout
- **C.** No vehicles
- **D.** Roundabout

See HIGHWAY CODE Warning signs

674 Which FOUR of these would be indicated by a triangular road sign?

Mark four answers
- [ ] **A.** Road narrows
- [ ] **B.** Ahead only
- [ ] **C.** Low bridge
- [ ] **D.** Minimum speed
- [ ] **E.** Children crossing
- [ ] **F.** T-junction

See HIGHWAY CODE Warning signs

675 What does this sign mean?

Mark one answer
- [ ] **A.** Cyclists must dismount
- [ ] **B.** Cycles are not allowed
- [ ] **C.** Cycle route ahead
- [ ] **D.** Cycle in single file

See HIGHWAY CODE Warning signs

676 Which sign means that pedestrians may be walking along the road?

Mark one answer
- [ ] **A.**
- [ ] **B.**
- [ ] **C.**
- [ ] **D.**

See HIGHWAY CODE Warning signs

677 Which of these signs warn you of a pedestrian crossing?

Mark one answer
- [ ] **A.**
- [ ] **B.**
- [ ] **C.**
- [ ] **D.**

See HIGHWAY CODE Warning signs

678 What does this sign mean?

Mark one answer
- [ ] **A.** No footpath ahead
- [ ] **B.** Pedestrians only ahead
- [ ] **C.** Pedestrian crossing ahead
- [ ] **D.** School crossing ahead

See HIGHWAY CODE Warning signs

679 What does this sign mean?

Mark one answer
- [ ] **A.** School crossing patrol
- [ ] **B.** No pedestrians allowed
- [ ] **C.** Pedestrian zone – no vehicles
- [ ] **D.** Pedestrian crossing ahead

See HIGHWAY CODE Warning signs

680 Which of these signs means there is a double bend ahead?

Mark one answer

☐ A.

☐ B.

☐ C.

☐ D.

See HIGHWAY CODE Warning signs

681 What does this sign mean?

Mark one answer

☐ A. Wait at the barriers
☐ B. Wait at the crossroads
☐ C. Give way to trams
☐ D. Give way to farm vehicles

682 What does this sign mean?

Mark one answer

☐ A. Humpback bridge
☐ B. Humps in the road
☐ C. Entrance to tunnel
☐ D. Soft verges

See HIGHWAY CODE Warning signs

683 What does this sign mean?

Mark one answer

☐ A. Low bridge ahead
☐ B. Tunnel ahead
☐ C. Ancient monument ahead
☐ D. Accident black spot ahead

See HIGHWAY CODE Warning signs

684 What does this sign mean?

Mark one answer

☐ A. Two-way traffic straight ahead
☐ B. Two-way traffic crossing a one-way street
☐ C. Two-way traffic over a bridge
☐ D. Two-way traffic crosses a two-way road

See HIGHWAY CODE Warning signs

685 Which sign means 'two-way traffic crosses a one-way road'?

Mark one answer

☐ A.

☐ B.

☐ C.

☐ D.

See HIGHWAY CODE Traffic signs

686 Which of these signs means the end of a dual carriageway?

Mark one answer

- [ ] A.
- [ ] B.
- [ ] C.
- [ ] D.

See HIGHWAY CODE Warning signs

687 What does this sign mean?

Mark one answer

- [ ] A. End of dual carriageway
- [ ] B. Tall bridge
- [ ] C. Road narrows
- [ ] D. End of narrow bridge

See HIGHWAY CODE Warning signs

688 What does this sign mean?

Mark one answer

- [ ] A. Two-way traffic ahead across a one-way street
- [ ] B. Traffic approaching you has priority
- [ ] C. Two-way traffic straight ahead
- [ ] D. Motorway contraflow system ahead

See HIGHWAY CODE Warning signs

689 What does this sign mean?

Mark one answer

- [ ] A. Crosswinds
- [ ] B. Road noise
- [ ] C. Airport
- [ ] D. Adverse camber

See HIGHWAY CODE Warning signs

690 What does this traffic sign mean?

Mark one answer

- [ ] A. Slippery road ahead
- [ ] B. Tyres liable to punctures ahead
- [ ] C. Danger ahead
- [ ] D. Service area ahead

See HIGHWAY CODE Warning signs

691 You are about to overtake when you see this sign. You should

Mark one answer

- [ ] A. overtake the other driver as quickly as possible
- [ ] B. move to the right to get a better view
- [ ] C. switch your headlights on before overtaking
- [ ] D. hold back until you can see clearly ahead

Hidden dip

See HIGHWAY CODE Warning signs

692 What does this sign mean?

Mark one answer
- [ ] **A.** Level crossing with gate or barrier
- [ ] **B.** Gated road ahead
- [ ] **C.** Level crossing without gate or barrier
- [ ] **D.** Cattle grid ahead

See HIGHWAY CODE Warning signs

693 What does this sign mean?

Mark one answer
- [ ] **A.** No trams ahead
- [ ] **B.** Oncoming trams
- [ ] **C.** Trams crossing ahead
- [ ] **D.** Trams only

See HIGHWAY CODE Warning signs

694 What does this sign mean?

Mark one answer
- [ ] **A.** Adverse camber
- [ ] **B.** Steep hill downwards
- [ ] **C.** Uneven road
- [ ] **D.** Steep hill upwards

See HIGHWAY CODE Warning signs

695 What does this sign mean?

Mark one answer
- [ ] **A.** Uneven road surface
- [ ] **B.** Bridge over the road
- [ ] **C.** Road ahead ends
- [ ] **D.** Water across the road

See HIGHWAY CODE Warning signs

696 What does this sign mean?

Mark one answer
- [ ] **A.** Humpback bridge
- [ ] **B.** Traffic calming hump
- [ ] **C.** Low bridge
- [ ] **D.** Uneven road

See HIGHWAY CODE Warning signs

697 What does this sign mean?

Mark one answer
- [ ] **A.** Turn left for parking area
- [ ] **B.** No through road on the left
- [ ] **C.** No entry for traffic turning left
- [ ] **D.** Turn left for ferry terminal

698 What does this sign mean?

Mark one answer
- A. T-junction
- B. No through road
- C. Telephone box ahead
- D. Toilet ahead

See HIGHWAY CODE Information signs

699 Which sign means 'no through road'?

Mark one answer
- A.
- B.
- C.
- D.

See HIGHWAY CODE Information signs

700 Which of the following signs informs you that you are coming to a No Through Road?

Mark one answer
- A.
- B.
- C.
- D.

See HIGHWAY CODE Information signs

701 What does this sign mean?

Mark one answer
- A. Direction to park and ride car park
- B. No parking for buses or coaches
- C. Directions to bus and coach park
- D. Parking area for cars and coaches

702 You are driving through a tunnel and you see this sign. What does it mean?

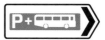

Mark one answer
- A. Direction to emergency pedestrian exit
- B. Beware of pedestrians, no footpath ahead
- C. No access for pedestrians
- D. Beware of pedestrians crossing ahead

703 Which is the sign for a ring road?

Mark one answer
- A.
- B.
- C.
- D.

704 What does this sign mean?

Mark one answer

- A. Route for lorries
- B. Ring road
- C. Rest area
- D. Roundabout

705 What does this sign mean?

Mark one answer

- A. Hilly road
- B. Humps in road
- C. Holiday route
- D. Hospital route

See HIGHWAY CODE Direction signs

706 What does this sign mean?

Mark one answer

- A. The right-hand lane ahead is narrow
- B. Right-hand lane for buses only
- C. Right-hand lane for turning right
- D. The right-hand lane is closed

See HIGHWAY CODE Road works signs

707 What does this sign mean?

Mark one answer

- A. Change to the left lane
- B. Leave at the next exit
- C. Contraflow system
- D. One-way street

See HIGHWAY CODE Road works signs

708 To avoid an accident when entering a contraflow system, you should

Mark three answers

- A. reduce speed in good time
- B. switch lanes any time to make progress
- C. choose an appropriate lane early
- D. keep the correct separation distance
- E. increase speed to pass through quickly
- F. follow other motorists closely to avoid long queues

See HIGHWAY CODE rules 262, 264

709 What does this sign mean?

Mark one answer

- A. Leave motorway at next exit
- B. Lane for heavy and slow vehicles
- C. All lorries use the hard shoulder
- D. Rest area for lorries

See HIGHWAY CODE rule 118

710

You are approaching a red traffic light. The signal will change from red to

Mark one answer

- [ ] **A.** red and amber, then green
- [ ] **B.** green, then amber
- [ ] **C.** amber, then green
- [ ] **D.** green and amber, then green

See HIGHWAY CODE Traffic light signals

711

A red traffic light means

Mark one answer

- [ ] **A.** you should stop unless turning left
- [ ] **B.** stop, if you are able to brake safely
- [ ] **C.** you must stop and wait behind the stop line
- [ ] **D.** proceed with caution

See HIGHWAY CODE Traffic light signals

712

At traffic lights, amber on its own means

Mark one answer

- [ ] **A.** prepare to go
- [ ] **B.** go if the way is clear
- [ ] **C.** go if no pedestrians are crossing
- [ ] **D.** stop at the stop line

See HIGHWAY CODE Traffic light signals

713

You are approaching traffic lights. Red and amber are showing. This means

Mark one answer

- [ ] **A.** pass the lights if the road is clear
- [ ] **B.** there is a fault with the lights – take care
- [ ] **C.** wait for the green light before you pass the lights
- [ ] **D.** the lights are about to change to red

See HIGHWAY CODE Traffic light signals

714

You are at a junction controlled by traffic lights. When should you NOT proceed at green?

Mark one answer

- [ ] **A.** When pedestrians are waiting to cross
- [ ] **B.** When your exit from the junction is blocked
- [ ] **C.** When you think the lights may be about to change
- [ ] **D.** When you intend to turn right

See HIGHWAY CODE rule 152

715

You are in the left-hand lane at traffic lights. You are waiting to turn left. At which of these traffic lights must you NOT move on?

Mark one answer

- [ ] **A.**
- [ ] **B.**
- [ ] **C.**
- [ ] **D.**

See HIGHWAY CODE Traffic light signals

716 What does this sign mean?

Mark one answer

- [ ] **A.** Traffic lights out of order
- [ ] **B.** Amber signal out of order
- [ ] **C.** Temporary traffic lights ahead
- [ ] **D.** New traffic lights ahead

717 When traffic lights are out of order, who has priority?

Mark one answer

- [ ] **A.** Traffic going straight on
- [ ] **B.** Traffic turning right
- [ ] **C.** Nobody
- [ ] **D.** Traffic turning left

See HIGHWAY CODE rule 152

718 These flashing red lights mean STOP. In which THREE of the following places could you find them?

Mark three answers

- [ ] **A.** Pelican crossings
- [ ] **B.** Lifting bridges
- [ ] **C.** Zebra crossings
- [ ] **D.** Level crossings
- [ ] **E.** Motorway exits
- [ ] **F.** Fire stations

See HIGHWAY CODE rules 266 & Flashing red lights

719 What do these zigzag lines at pedestrian crossings mean?

Mark one answer

- [ ] **A.** No parking at any time
- [ ] **B.** Parking allowed only for a short time
- [ ] **C.** Slow down to 20mph
- [ ] **D.** Sounding horns is not allowed

See HIGHWAY CODE rule 167

720 When may you cross a double solid white line in the middle of the road?

Mark one answer

- [ ] **A.** To pass traffic that is queuing back at a junction
- [ ] **B.** To pass a car signalling to turn left ahead
- [ ] **C.** To pass a road maintenance vehicle travelling at 10mph or less
- [ ] **D.** To pass a vehicle that is towing a trailer

See HIGHWAY CODE rule 108

721 What does this road marking mean?

Mark one answer

- **A.** Do not cross the line
- **B.** No stopping allowed
- **C.** You are approaching a hazard
- **D.** No overtaking allowed

See HIGHWAY CODE rule 106 & Road markings: Along the carriageway

722 This marking appears on the road just before a

Mark one answer

- **A.** no entry sign
- **B.** give way sign
- **C.** stop sign
- **D.** no through road sign

See HIGHWAY CODE rule 148 & Other road markings

723 Where would you see this road marking?

Mark one answer

- **A.** At traffic lights
- **B.** On road humps
- **C.** Near a level crossing
- **D.** At a box junction

724 Which is a hazard warning line?

Mark one answer

- [ ] **A.**

- [ ] **B.**

- [ ] **C.**

- [ ] **D.**

See HIGHWAY CODE rule 106 & Road markings

725 At this junction there is a stop sign with a solid white line on the road surface. Why is there a stop sign here?

Mark one answer

- **A.** Speed on the major road is de-restricted
- **B.** It is a busy junction
- **C.** Visibility along the major road is restricted
- **D.** There are hazard warning lines in the centre of the road

726 You see this line across the road at the entrance to a roundabout. What does it mean?

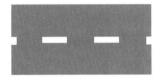

Mark one answer
- [ ] **A.** Give way to traffic from the right
- [ ] **B.** Traffic from the left has right of way
- [ ] **C.** You have right of way
- [ ] **D.** Stop at the line

See HIGHWAY CODE rule 161 & Road markings: Across the carriageway

727 Where would you find this road marking?

Mark one answer
- [ ] **A.** At a railway crossing
- [ ] **B.** At a junction
- [ ] **C.** On a motorway
- [ ] **D.** On a pedestrian crossing

See HIGHWAY CODE rule 165

728 How will a police officer in a patrol vehicle normally get you to stop?

Mark one answer
- [ ] **A.** Flash the headlights, indicate left and point to the left
- [ ] **B.** Wait until you stop, then approach you
- [ ] **C.** Use the siren, overtake, cut in front and stop
- [ ] **D.** Pull alongside you, use the siren and wave you to stop

See HIGHWAY CODE rule 89

729 There is a police car following you. The police officer flashes the headlights and points to the left. What should you do?

Mark one answer
- [ ] **A.** Turn at the next left
- [ ] **B.** Pull up on the left
- [ ] **C.** Stop immediately
- [ ] **D.** Move over to the left

See HIGHWAY CODE rule 89

730 You approach a junction. The traffic lights are not working. A police officer gives this signal. You should

Mark one answer
- [ ] **A.** turn left only
- [ ] **B.** turn right only
- [ ] **C.** stop level with the officer's arm
- [ ] **D.** stop at the stop line

See HIGHWAY CODE Signals by authorised persons

731 The driver of the car in front is giving this arm signal. What does it mean?

Mark one answer
- [ ] **A.** The driver is slowing down
- [ ] **B.** The driver intends to turn right
- [ ] **C.** The driver wishes to overtake
- [ ] **D.** The driver intends to turn left

See HIGHWAY CODE Signals to other road users

732 Where would you see these road markings?

Mark one answer

- [ ] **A.** At a level crossing
- [ ] **B.** On a motorway slip road
- [ ] **C.** At a pedestrian crossing
- [ ] **D.** On a single-track road

See HIGHWAY CODE rule 109

733 When may you NOT overtake on the left?

Mark one answer

- [ ] **A.** On a free-flowing motorway or dual carriageway
- [ ] **B.** When the traffic is moving slowly in queues
- [ ] **C.** On a one-way street
- [ ] **D.** When the car in front is signalling to turn right

See HIGHWAY CODE rules 116, 117, 242

734 What does this motorway sign mean?

Mark one answer

- [ ] **A.** Change to the lane on your left
- [ ] **B.** Leave the motorway at the next exit
- [ ] **C.** Change to the opposite carriageway
- [ ] **D.** Pull up on the hard shoulder

See HIGHWAY CODE Motorway signals

735 What does this motorway sign mean?

Mark one answer

- [ ] **A.** Temporary minimum speed 50mph
- [ ] **B.** No services for 50 miles
- [ ] **C.** Obstruction 50 metres (164 feet) ahead
- [ ] **D.** Temporary maximum speed 50mph

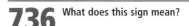

See HIGHWAY CODE Motorway signals

736 What does this sign mean?

Mark one answer

- [ ] **A.** Through traffic to use left lane
- [ ] **B.** Right-hand lane T-junction only
- [ ] **C.** Right-hand lane closed ahead
- [ ] **D.** 11 tonne weight limit

See HIGHWAY CODE Motorway signals

737 On a motorway this sign means

Mark one answer

- [ ] **A.** move over on to the hard shoulder
- [ ] **B.** overtaking on the left only
- [ ] **C.** leave the motorway at the next exit
- [ ] **D.** move to the lane on your left

See HIGHWAY CODE Motorway signals

738 What does '25' mean on this motorway sign?

Mark one answer

- [ ] **A.** The distance to the nearest town
- [ ] **B.** The route number of the road
- [ ] **C.** The number of the next junction
- [ ] **D.** The speed limit on the slip road

See HIGHWAY CODE Direction signs

739 The right-hand lane of a three-lane motorway is

Mark one answer

- [ ] **A.** for lorries only
- [ ] **B.** an overtaking lane
- [ ] **C.** the right-turn lane
- [ ] **D.** an acceleration lane

See HIGHWAY CODE rule 238

740 Where can you find reflective amber studs on a motorway?

Mark one answer

- [ ] **A.** Separating the slip road from the motorway
- [ ] **B.** On the left-hand edge of the road
- [ ] **C.** On the right-hand edge of the road
- [ ] **D.** Separating the lanes

See HIGHWAY CODE rule 111

741 Where on a motorway would you find green reflective studs?

Mark one answer

- [ ] **A.** Separating driving lanes
- [ ] **B.** Between the hard shoulder and the carriageway
- [ ] **C.** At slip road entrances and exits
- [ ] **D.** Between the carriageway and the central reservation

See HIGHWAY CODE rule 111

742 You are travelling along a motorway. You see this sign. You should

Mark one answer

- [ ] **A.** leave the motorway at the next exit
- [ ] **B.** turn left immediately
- [ ] **C.** change lane
- [ ] **D.** move on to the hard shoulder

See HIGHWAY CODE Motorway signals

743 What does this sign mean?

Mark one answer

- [ ] **A.** No motor vehicles
- [ ] **B.** End of motorway
- [ ] **C.** No through road
- [ ] **D.** End of bus lane

See HIGHWAY CODE Information signs

744 Which of these signs means that the national speed limit applies?

Mark one answer

- [ ] **A.**
- [ ] **B.**
- [ ] **C.**
- [ ] **D.**

See HIGHWAY CODE Signs giving orders

745 What is the maximum speed on a single carriageway road?

Mark one answer

- [ ] **A.** 50mph
- [ ] **B.** 60mph
- [ ] **C.** 40mph
- [ ] **D.** 70mph

See HIGHWAY CODE rule 103 table

746 What does this sign mean?

Mark one answer

- [ ] **A.** End of motorway
- [ ] **B.** End of restriction
- [ ] **C.** Lane ends ahead
- [ ] **D.** Free recovery ends

See HIGHWAY CODE Motorway signals

747 This sign is advising you to

Mark one answer

- [ ] **A.** follow the route diversion
- [ ] **B.** follow the signs to the picnic area
- [ ] **C.** give way to pedestrians
- [ ] **D.** give way to cyclists

See HIGHWAY CODE Direction signs

748 Why would this temporary speed limit sign be shown?

Mark one answer

- [ ] **A.** To warn of the end of the motorway
- [ ] **B.** To warn you of a low bridge
- [ ] **C.** To warn you of a junction ahead
- [ ] **D.** To warn of road works ahead

50

³⁄₄ **mile ahead**

See HIGHWAY CODE Traffic signs

749 This traffic sign means there is

Mark one answer

- [ ] **A.** a compulsory maximum speed limit
- [ ] **B.** an advisory maximum speed limit
- [ ] **C.** a compulsory minimum speed limit
- [ ] **D.** an advised separation distance

See HIGHWAY CODE Road works signs

750 You see this sign at a crossroads. You should

Mark one answer
- A. maintain the same speed
- B. carry on with great care
- C. find another route
- D. telephone the police

See HIGHWAY CODE rule 152

751 You are signalling to turn right in busy traffic. How would you confirm your intention safely?

Mark one answer
- A. Sound the horn
- B. Give an arm signal
- C. Flash your headlights
- D. Position over the centre line

See HIGHWAY CODE rule 85

752 What does this sign mean?

Mark one answer
- A. Motorcycles only
- B. No cars
- C. Cars only
- D. No motorcycles

753 You are on a motorway. You see this sign on a lorry that has stopped in the right-hand lane. You should

Mark one answer
- A. move into the right-hand lane
- B. stop behind the flashing lights
- C. pass the lorry on the left
- D. leave the motorway at the next exit

See HIGHWAY CODE Road works signs

754 You are on a motorway. Red flashing lights appear above your lane only. What should you do?

Mark one answer
- A. Continue in that lane and look for further information
- B. Move into another lane in good time
- C. Pull on to the hard shoulder
- D. Stop and wait for an instruction to proceed

See HIGHWAY CODE rule 232

755 A red traffic light means

Mark one answer
- A. you must stop behind the white stop line
- B. you may go straight on if there is no other traffic
- C. you may turn left if it is safe to do so
- D. you must slow down and prepare to stop if traffic has started to cross

See HIGHWAY CODE Traffic light signals

756 The driver of this car is giving an arm signal. What are they about to do?

Mark one answer

- A. Turn to the right
- B. Turn to the left
- C. Go straight ahead
- D. Let pedestrians cross

See HIGHWAY CODE Arm signals

757 Which arm signal tells you that the car you are following is going to turn left?

Mark one answer

A. 　　B.

C. 　　D.

See HIGHWAY CODE Arm signals

758 When may you sound the horn?

Mark one answer

- A. To give you right of way
- B. To attract a friend's attention
- C. To warn others of your presence
- D. To make slower drivers move over

See HIGHWAY CODE rule 92

759 You must not use your horn when you are stationary

Mark one answer

- A. unless a moving vehicle may cause you danger
- B. at any time whatsoever
- C. unless it is used only briefly
- D. except for signalling that you have just arrived

See HIGHWAY CODE rule 92

760 What does this sign mean?

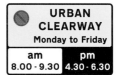

Mark one answer

- A. You can park on the days and times shown
- B. No parking on the days and times shown
- C. No parking at all from Monday to Friday
- D. End of the urban clearway restrictions

See HIGHWAY CODE Signs giving orders

761 What does this sign mean?

Mark one answer

- A. Quayside or river bank
- B. Steep hill downwards
- C. Uneven road surface
- D. Road liable to flooding

See HIGHWAY CODE Warning signs

762 You see this amber traffic light ahead. Which light(s) will come on next?

Mark one answer
- [ ] **A.** Red alone
- [ ] **B.** Red and amber together
- [ ] **C.** Green and amber together
- [ ] **D.** Green alone

See HIGHWAY CODE Traffic light signals

763 The white line painted in the centre of the road means

Mark one answer
- [ ] **A.** oncoming vehicles have priority over you
- [ ] **B.** you should give priority to oncoming vehicles
- [ ] **C.** there is a hazard ahead of you
- [ ] **D.** the area is a national speed limit zone

See HIGHWAY CODE rule 106 & Road markings: Along the carriageway

764 Which sign means you have priority over oncoming vehicles?

Mark one answer

- [ ] **A.**
- [ ] **B.**
- [ ] **C.**
- [ ] **D.**

See HIGHWAY CODE Traffic signs

765 You see this signal overhead on the motorway. What does it mean?

Mark one answer
- [ ] **A.** Leave the motorway at the next exit
- [ ] **B.** All vehicles use the hard shoulder
- [ ] **C.** Sharp bend to the left ahead
- [ ] **D.** Stop, all lanes ahead closed

See HIGHWAY CODE Motorway signals

766 A white line like this along the centre of the road is a

Mark one answer
- [ ] **A.** bus lane marking
- [ ] **B.** hazard warning
- [ ] **C.** give way marking
- [ ] **D.** lane marking

See HIGHWAY CODE rule 106 & Road markings: Along the carriageway

> **TIP** The outside lane of a motorway can't be used by vehicles weighing over 7.5 tonnes, and passenger vehicles over 7.5 tonnes or over 12 metres in length, or adapted to carry more than 8 passengers.

767 What is the purpose of these yellow criss-cross lines on the road?

Mark one answer

- [ ] **A.** To make you more aware of the traffic lights
- [ ] **B.** To guide you into position as you turn
- [ ] **C.** To prevent the junction from becoming blocked
- [ ] **D.** To show you where to stop when the lights change

See HIGHWAY CODE rule 150 & Other road markings

768 What is the reason for the yellow criss-cross lines painted on the road here?

Mark one answer

- [ ] **A.** To mark out an area for trams only
- [ ] **B.** To prevent queuing traffic from blocking the junction on the left
- [ ] **C.** To mark the entrance lane to a car park
- [ ] **D.** To warn you of the tram lines crossing the road

See HIGHWAY CODE rule 150 & Other road markings

769 What is the reason for the area marked in red and white along the centre of this road?

Mark one answer

- [ ] **A.** It is to separate traffic flowing in opposite directions
- [ ] **B.** It marks an area to be used by overtaking motorcyclists
- [ ] **C.** It is a temporary marking to warn of the road works
- [ ] **D.** It is separating the two sides of the dual carriageway

See HIGHWAY CODE rule 109 & Road markings: Along the carriageway

770 Other drivers may sometimes flash their headlights at you. In which situation are they allowed to do this?

Mark one answer

- [ ] **A.** To warn of a radar speed trap ahead
- [ ] **B.** To show that they are giving way to you
- [ ] **C.** To warn you of their presence
- [ ] **D.** To let you know there is a fault with your vehicle

See HIGHWAY CODE rules 90, 91

771 At road works which of the following can control traffic flow?

Mark three answers

- [ ] **A.** A STOP–GO board
- [ ] **B.** Flashing amber lights
- [ ] **C.** A police officer
- [ ] **D.** Flashing red lights
- [ ] **E.** Temporary traffic lights

772
You are approaching a zebra crossing where pedestrians are waiting. Which arm signal might you give?

Mark one answer

A.

B.

C.

D.

See HIGHWAY CODE Arm signals

773
The white line along the side of the road

Mark one answer

A. shows the edge of the carriageway
B. shows the approach to a hazard
C. means no parking
D. means no overtaking

See HIGHWAY CODE Road markings: Along the carriageway

774
You see this white arrow on the road ahead. It means

Mark one answer

A. entrance on the left
B. all vehicles turn left
C. keep left of the hatched markings
D. road bending to the left

See HIGHWAY CODE rule 107

775
How should you give an arm signal to turn left?

Mark one answer

A.

B.

C.

D.

See HIGHWAY CODE Arm signals

776
You are waiting at a T-junction. A vehicle is coming from the right with the left signal flashing. What should you do?

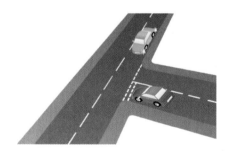

Mark one answer

A. Move out and accelerate hard
B. Wait until the vehicle starts to turn in
C. Pull out before the vehicle reaches the junction
D. Move out slowly

See HIGHWAY CODE rules 86, 146

777 When may you use hazard warning lights when driving?

Mark one answer

- [ ] **A.** Instead of sounding the horn in a built-up area between 11.30pm and 7am
- [ ] **B.** On a motorway or unrestricted dual carriageway, to warn of a hazard ahead
- [ ] **C.** On rural routes, after a warning sign of animals
- [ ] **D.** On the approach to toucan crossings where cyclists are waiting to cross

See HIGHWAY CODE rule 96

778 You are driving on a motorway. There is a slow-moving vehicle ahead. On the back you see this sign. You should

Mark one answer

- [ ] **A.** pass on the right
- [ ] **B.** pass on the left
- [ ] **C.** leave at the next exit
- [ ] **D.** drive no further

See HIGHWAY CODE Road works signs

TIP *The Highway Code* states that the only reason for flashing your lights is **to let others know you are there**. Many people flash their lights to indicate they are **letting another motorist go first**. But in general, you should not assume it is safe to proceed on the basis of such a signal – the lights may not be flashed at you but at someone else.

779 You should NOT normally stop on these markings near schools

~SCHOOL KEEP CLEAR~

Mark one answer

- [ ] **A.** except when picking up children
- [ ] **B.** under any circumstances
- [ ] **C.** unless there is nowhere else available
- [ ] **D.** except to set down children

See HIGHWAY CODE Other road markings

780 Why should you make sure that your indicators are cancelled after turning?

Mark one answer

- [ ] **A.** To avoid flattening the battery
- [ ] **B.** To avoid misleading other road users
- [ ] **C.** To avoid dazzling other road users
- [ ] **D.** To avoid damage to the indicator relay

See HIGHWAY CODE rule 85

781 You are driving in busy traffic. You want to pull up on the left just after a junction on the left. When should you signal?

Mark one answer

- [ ] **A.** As you are passing or just after the junction
- [ ] **B.** Just before you reach the junction
- [ ] **C.** Well before you reach the junction
- [ ] **D.** It would be better not to signal at all

See HIGHWAY CODE rule 85

782 An MOT certificate is normally valid for

Mark one answer
- [ ] A. three years after the date it was issued
- [ ] B. 10,000 miles
- [ ] C. one year after the date it was issued
- [ ] D. 30,000 miles

See HIGHWAY CODE Annexe 3

783 A cover note is a document issued before you receive your

Mark one answer
- [ ] A. driving licence
- [ ] B. insurance certificate
- [ ] C. registration document
- [ ] D. MOT certificate

784 A police officer asks to see your documents. You do not have them with you. You may produce them at a police station within

Mark one answer **NI**
- [ ] A. five days
- [ ] B. seven days
- [ ] C. 14 days
- [ ] D. 21 days

See HIGHWAY CODE Annexe 3

785 You have just passed your practical test. You do not hold a full licence in another category. Within two years you get six penalty points on your licence. What will you have to do?

Mark two answers
- [ ] A. Retake only your theory test
- [ ] B. Retake your theory and practical tests
- [ ] C. Retake only your practical test
- [ ] D. Reapply for your full licence immediately
- [ ] E. Reapply for your provisional licence

See HIGHWAY CODE Annexe 5

786 To drive on the road learners MUST

Mark one answer
- [ ] A. have NO penalty points on their licence
- [ ] B. have taken professional instruction
- [ ] C. have a signed, valid provisional licence
- [ ] D. apply for a driving test within 12 months

See HIGHWAY CODE Annexe 3

787 Before driving anyone else's motor vehicle you should make sure that

Mark one answer
- [ ] A. the vehicle owner has third party insurance cover
- [ ] B. your own vehicle has insurance cover
- [ ] C. the vehicle is insured for your use
- [ ] D. the owner has left the insurance documents in the vehicle

See HIGHWAY CODE Annexe 3

788 Your car needs an MOT certificate. If you drive without one this could invalidate your

Mark one answer
- [ ] A. vehicle service record
- [ ] B. insurance
- [ ] C. road tax disc
- [ ] D. vehicle registration document

See HIGHWAY CODE Annexe 3

TIP Remember, a fine for speeding leads to penalty points on your licence. If you accumulate six penalty points within two years of passing your test, your licence will be revoked.

789 When is it legal to drive a car over three years old without an MOT certificate?

Mark one answer **NI**

☐ A. Up to seven days after the old certificate has run out
☐ B. When driving to an MOT centre to arrange an appointment
☐ C. Just after buying a second-hand car with no MOT
☐ D. When driving to an appointment at an MOT centre

See HIGHWAY CODE Annexe 3

790 To supervise a learner driver you must

Mark two answers

☐ A. have held a full licence for at least 3 years
☐ B. be at least 21
☐ C. be an approved driving instructor
☐ D. hold an advanced driving certificate

See HIGHWAY CODE Annexe 3

791 The cost of your insurance may be reduced if

Mark one answer

☐ A. your car is large and powerful
☐ B. you are using the car for work purposes
☐ C. you have penalty points on your licence
☐ D. you are over 25 years old

792 How old must you be to supervise a learner driver?

Mark one answer

☐ A. 18 years old
☐ B. 19 years old
☐ C. 20 years old
☐ D. 21 years old

See HIGHWAY CODE Annexe 3

793 A newly qualified driver must

Mark one answer

☐ A. display green 'L' plates
☐ B. not exceed 40mph for 12 months
☐ C. be accompanied on a motorway
☐ D. have valid motor insurance

See HIGHWAY CODE Annexe 3

794 What is the legal minimum insurance cover you must have to drive on public roads?

Mark one answer

☐ A. Third party, fire and theft
☐ B. Fully comprehensive
☐ C. Third party only
☐ D. Personal injury cover

See HIGHWAY CODE Annexe 3

795 You have third party insurance. What does this cover?

Mark three answers

☐ A. Damage to your own vehicle
☐ B. Damage to your vehicle by fire
☐ C. Injury to another person
☐ D. Damage to someone's property
☐ E. Damage to other vehicles
☐ F. Injury to yourself

796 For which TWO of these must you show your motor insurance certificate?

Mark two answers

☐ A. When you are taking your driving test
☐ B. When buying or selling a vehicle
☐ C. When a police officer asks you for it
☐ D. When you are taxing your vehicle
☐ E. When having an MOT inspection

See HIGHWAY CODE Annexe 3

797 Vehicle excise duty is often called 'Road Tax' or 'The Tax Disc'. You must

Mark one answer
- [ ] A. keep it with your registration document
- [ ] B. display it clearly on your vehicle
- [ ] C. keep it concealed safely in your vehicle
- [ ] D. carry it on you at all times

See HIGHWAY CODE Annexe 3

798 Motor cars must FIRST have an MOT test certificate when they are

Mark one answer **NI**
- [ ] A. one year old
- [ ] B. three years old
- [ ] C. five years old
- [ ] D. seven years old

See HIGHWAY CODE Annexe 3

799 Your vehicle needs a current MOT certificate. You do not have one. Until you do have one you will not be able to renew your

Mark one answer
- [ ] A. driving licence
- [ ] B. vehicle insurance
- [ ] C. road tax disc
- [ ] D. vehicle registration document

800 Which THREE pieces of information are found on a vehicle registration document?

Mark three answers
- [ ] A. Registered keeper
- [ ] B. Make of the vehicle
- [ ] C. Service history details
- [ ] D. Date of the MOT
- [ ] E. Type of insurance cover
- [ ] F. Engine size

See HIGHWAY CODE Annexe 3

801 You have a duty to contact the licensing authority when

Mark three answers
- [ ] A. you go abroad on holiday
- [ ] B. you change your vehicle
- [ ] C. you change your name
- [ ] D. your job status is changed
- [ ] E. your permanent address changes
- [ ] F. your job involves travelling abroad

See HIGHWAY CODE Annexe 3

802 You must notify the licensing authority when

Mark three answers
- [ ] A. your health affects your driving
- [ ] B. your eyesight does not meet a set standard
- [ ] C. you intend lending your vehicle
- [ ] D. your vehicle requires an MOT certificate
- [ ] E. you change your vehicle

See HIGHWAY CODE rules 79, 81 & Annexe 3

803 Your vehicle is insured third party only. This covers

Mark two answers
- [ ] A. damage to your vehicle
- [ ] B. damage to other vehicles
- [ ] C. injury to yourself
- [ ] D. injury to others
- [ ] E. all damage and injury

804
Your motor insurance policy has an excess of £100. What does this mean?

Mark one answer

A. The insurance company will pay the first £100 of any claim

B. You will be paid £100 if you do not have an accident

C. Your vehicle is insured for a value of £100 if it is stolen

D. You will have to pay the first £100 of any claim

805
When you apply to renew your vehicle excise licence (tax disc) you must produce

Mark one answer

A. a valid insurance certificate

B. the old tax disc

C. the vehicle handbook

D. a valid driving licence

806
What is the legal minimum insurance cover you must have to drive on public roads?

Mark one answer

A. Fire and theft

B. Theft only

C. Third party

D. Fire only

See HIGHWAY CODE Annexe 3

807
Which THREE of the following do you need before you can drive legally?

Mark three answers

A. A valid driving licence with signature

B. A valid tax disc displayed on your vehicle

C. A vehicle service record

D. Proper insurance cover

E. Breakdown cover

F. A vehicle handbook

See HIGHWAY CODE Annexe 3

808
The cost of your insurance may reduce if you

Mark one answer **NI**

A. are under 25 years old

B. do not wear glasses

C. pass the driving test first time

D. take the Pass Plus scheme

809
Which of the following may reduce the cost of your insurance?

Mark one answer **NI**

A. Having a valid MOT certificate

B. Taking a Pass Plus course

C. Driving a powerful car

D. Having penalty points on your licence

810
The Pass Plus scheme has been created for new drivers. What is its main purpose?

Mark one answer **NI**

A. To allow you to drive faster

B. To allow you to carry passengers

C. To improve your basic skills

D. To let you drive on motorways

811 At the scene of an accident you should

Mark one answer

- [ ] A. not put yourself at risk
- [ ] B. go to those casualties who are screaming
- [ ] C. pull everybody out of their vehicles
- [ ] D. leave vehicle engines switched on

See HIGHWAY CODE Annexe 7

812 You are the first to arrive at the scene of an accident. Which FOUR of these should you do?

Mark four answers

- [ ] A. Leave as soon as another motorist arrives
- [ ] B. Switch off the vehicle engine(s)
- [ ] C. Move uninjured people away from the vehicle(s)
- [ ] D. Call the emergency services
- [ ] E. Warn other traffic

See HIGHWAY CODE rule 257

813 An accident has just happened. An injured person is lying in the busy road. What is the FIRST thing you should do to help?

Mark one answer

- [ ] A. Treat the person for shock
- [ ] B. Warn other traffic
- [ ] C. Place them in the recovery position
- [ ] D. Make sure the injured person is kept warm

See HIGHWAY CODE rule 257

TIP At the scene of an accident remain calm and assess the situation. Ensure safety at the scene by controlling the traffic and checking that engines are switched off.

814 You are the first person to arrive at an accident where people are badly injured. Which THREE should you do?

Mark three answers

- [ ] A. Switch on your own hazard warning lights
- [ ] B. Make sure that someone telephones for an ambulance
- [ ] C. Try and get people who are injured to drink something
- [ ] D. Move the people who are injured clear of their vehicles
- [ ] E. Get people who are not injured clear of the scene

See HIGHWAY CODE rule 257

815 You arrive at the scene of a motorcycle accident. The rider is injured. When should the helmet be removed?

Mark one answer

- [ ] A. Only when it is essential
- [ ] B. Always straight away
- [ ] C. Only when the motorcyclist asks
- [ ] D. Always, unless they are in shock

See HIGHWAY CODE rule 257

816 You arrive at a serious motorcycle accident. The motorcyclist is unconscious and bleeding. Your main priorities should be to

Mark three answers

- [ ] A. try to stop the bleeding
- [ ] B. make a list of witnesses
- [ ] C. check the casualty's breathing
- [ ] D. take the numbers of the vehicles involved
- [ ] E. sweep up any loose debris
- [ ] F. check the casualty's airways

See HIGHWAY CODE Annexe 7

817 You arrive at an accident. A motorcyclist is unconscious. Your FIRST priority is the casualty's

Mark one answer

- **A.** breathing
- **B.** bleeding
- **C.** broken bones
- **D.** bruising

See HIGHWAY CODE Annexe 7

818 At an accident a casualty is unconscious. Which THREE of the following should you check urgently?

Mark three answers

- **A.** Circulation
- **B.** Airway
- **C.** Shock
- **D.** Breathing
- **E.** Broken bones

See HIGHWAY CODE Annexe 7

819 You arrive at the scene of an accident. It has just happened and someone is unconscious. Which of the following should be given urgent priority to help them?

Mark three answers

- **A.** Clear the airway and keep it open
- **B.** Try to get them to drink water
- **C.** Check that they are breathing
- **D.** Look for any witnesses
- **E.** Stop any heavy bleeding
- **F.** Take the numbers of vehicles involved

See HIGHWAY CODE Annexe 7

820 At an accident someone is unconscious. Your main priorities should be to

Mark three answers

- **A.** sweep up the broken glass
- **B.** take the names of witnesses
- **C.** count the number of vehicles involved
- **D.** check the airway is clear
- **E.** make sure they are breathing
- **F.** stop any heavy bleeding

See HIGHWAY CODE Annexe 7

821 You have stopped at the scene of an accident to give help. Which THREE things should you do?

Mark three answers

- **A.** Keep injured people warm and comfortable
- **B.** Keep injured people calm by talking to them reassuringly
- **C.** Keep injured people on the move by walking them around
- **D.** Give injured people a warm drink
- **E.** Make sure that injured people are not left alone

See HIGHWAY CODE Annexe 7

822 You arrive at the scene of an accident. It has just happened and someone is injured. Which THREE of the following should be given urgent priority?

Mark three answers

- **A.** Stop any severe bleeding
- **B.** Get them a warm drink
- **C.** Check that their breathing is OK
- **D.** Take numbers of vehicles involved
- **E.** Look for witnesses
- **F.** Clear their airway and keep it open

See HIGHWAY CODE Annexe 7

823 At an accident a casualty has stopped breathing. You should

Mark two answers
- [ ] **A.** remove anything that is blocking the mouth
- [ ] **B.** keep the head tilted forwards as far as possible
- [ ] **C.** raise the legs to help with circulation
- [ ] **D.** try to give the casualty something to drink
- [ ] **E.** keep the head tilted back as far as possible

See HIGHWAY CODE Annexe 7

824 You are at the scene of an accident. Someone is suffering from shock. You should

Mark four answers
- [ ] **A.** reassure them constantly
- [ ] **B.** offer them a cigarette
- [ ] **C.** keep them warm
- [ ] **D.** avoid moving them if possible
- [ ] **E.** loosen any tight clothing
- [ ] **F.** give them a warm drink

See HIGHWAY CODE Annexe 7

825 Which of the following should you NOT do at the scene of an accident?

Mark one answer
- [ ] **A.** Warn other traffic by switching on your hazard warning lights
- [ ] **B.** Call the emergency services immediately
- [ ] **C.** Offer someone a cigarette to calm them down
- [ ] **D.** Ask drivers to switch off their engines

See HIGHWAY CODE Annexe 7

826 There has been an accident. The driver is suffering from shock. You should

Mark two answers
- [ ] **A.** give them a drink
- [ ] **B.** reassure them
- [ ] **C.** not leave them alone
- [ ] **D.** offer them a cigarette
- [ ] **E.** ask who caused the accident

See HIGHWAY CODE Annexe 7

827 You are at the scene of an accident. Someone is suffering from shock. You should

Mark three answers
- [ ] **A.** offer them a cigarette
- [ ] **B.** offer them a warm drink
- [ ] **C.** keep them warm
- [ ] **D.** loosen any tight clothing
- [ ] **E.** reassure them constantly

See HIGHWAY CODE Annexe 7

828 You have to treat someone for shock at the scene of an accident. You should

Mark one answer
- [ ] **A.** reassure them constantly
- [ ] **B.** walk them around to calm them down
- [ ] **C.** give them something cold to drink
- [ ] **D.** cool them down as soon as possible

See HIGHWAY CODE Annexe 7

829 You arrive at the scene of a motorcycle accident. No other vehicle is involved. The rider is unconscious, lying in the middle of the road. The first thing you should do is

Mark one answer
- [ ] **A.** move the rider out of the road
- [ ] **B.** warn other traffic
- [ ] **C.** clear the road of debris
- [ ] **D.** give the rider reassurance

See HIGHWAY CODE rule 257

830 At an accident a small child is not breathing. When giving mouth to mouth you should breathe

Mark one answer
- [ ] **A.** sharply
- [ ] **B.** gently
- [ ] **C.** heavily
- [ ] **D.** rapidly

831 To start mouth to mouth on a casualty you should

Mark three answers
- [ ] **A.** tilt their head forward
- [ ] **B.** clear the airway
- [ ] **C.** turn them on their side
- [ ] **D.** tilt their head back
- [ ] **E.** pinch the nostrils together
- [ ] **F.** put their arms across their chest

See HIGHWAY CODE Annexe 7

832 When you are giving mouth to mouth you should only stop when

Mark one answer
- [ ] **A.** you think the casualty is dead
- [ ] **B.** the casualty can breathe without help
- [ ] **C.** the casualty has turned blue
- [ ] **D.** you think the ambulance is coming

See HIGHWAY CODE Annexe 7

833 You arrive at the scene of an accident. There has been an engine fire and someone's hands and arms have been burnt. You should NOT

Mark one answer
- [ ] **A.** douse the burn thoroughly with cool liquid
- [ ] **B.** lay the casualty down
- [ ] **C.** remove anything sticking to the burn
- [ ] **D.** reassure them constantly

834 You arrive at an accident where someone is suffering from severe burns. You should

Mark one answer
- [ ] **A.** apply lotions to the injury
- [ ] **B.** burst any blisters
- [ ] **C.** remove anything stuck to the burns
- [ ] **D.** douse the burns with cool liquid

835 You arrive at the scene of an accident. A pedestrian has a severe bleeding wound on their leg, although it is not broken. What should you do?

Mark two answers
- [ ] **A.** Dab the wound to stop bleeding
- [ ] **B.** Keep both legs flat on the ground
- [ ] **C.** Apply firm pressure to the wound
- [ ] **D.** Raise the leg to lessen bleeding
- [ ] **E.** Fetch them a warm drink

See HIGHWAY CODE Annexe 7

TIP Remember the **ABC** of First Aid:
A is for Airway
B is for Breathing
C is for Circulation

836

You arrive at the scene of an accident. A passenger is bleeding badly from an arm wound. What should you do?

Mark one answer

- **A.** Apply pressure over the wound and keep the arm down
- **B.** Dab the wound
- **C.** Get them a drink
- **D.** Apply pressure over the wound and raise the arm

See HIGHWAY CODE Annexe 7

837

You arrive at the scene of an accident. A pedestrian is bleeding heavily from a leg wound but the leg is not broken. What should you do?

Mark one answer

- **A.** Dab the wound to stop the bleeding
- **B.** Keep both legs flat on the ground
- **C.** Apply firm pressure to the wound
- **D.** Fetch them a warm drink

See HIGHWAY CODE Annexe 7

838

At an accident a casualty is unconscious but still breathing. You should only move them if

Mark one answer

- **A.** an ambulance is on its way
- **B.** bystanders advise you to
- **C.** there is further danger
- **D.** bystanders will help you to

See HIGHWAY CODE rule 257

839

At an accident you suspect a casualty has back injuries. The area is safe. You should

Mark one answer

- **A.** offer them a drink
- **B.** not move them
- **C.** raise their legs
- **D.** offer them a cigarette

See HIGHWAY CODE rule 257

840

At an accident it is important to look after the casualty. When the area is safe, you should

Mark one answer

- **A.** get them out of the vehicle
- **B.** give them a drink
- **C.** give them something to eat
- **D.** keep them in the vehicle

See HIGHWAY CODE rule 257

841

A tanker is involved in an accident. Which sign would show that the tanker is carrying dangerous goods?

Mark one answer

- **A.** LONG VEHICLE
- **B.** 2YE 1089
- **C.**
- **D.**

See HIGHWAY CODE rule 258 & Vehicle markings

842

The police may ask you to produce which three of these documents following an accident?

Mark three answers

- [ ] **A.** Vehicle registration document
- [ ] **B.** Driving licence
- [ ] **C.** Theory test certificate
- [ ] **D.** Insurance certificate
- [ ] **E.** MOT test certificate
- [ ] **F.** Road tax disc

See HIGHWAY CODE Annexe 3

843

At a railway level crossing the red light signal continues to flash after a train has gone by. What should you do?

Mark one answer

- [ ] **A.** Phone the signal operator
- [ ] **B.** Alert drivers behind you
- [ ] **C.** Wait
- [ ] **D.** Proceed with caution

See HIGHWAY CODE rule 266

844

You see a car on the hard shoulder of a motorway with a HELP pennant displayed. This means the driver is most likely to be

Mark one answer

- [ ] **A.** a disabled person
- [ ] **B.** first aid trained
- [ ] **C.** a foreign visitor
- [ ] **D.** a rescue patrol person

See HIGHWAY CODE rule 252

845

On the motorway the hard shoulder should be used

Mark one answer

- [ ] **A.** to answer a mobile phone
- [ ] **B.** when an emergency arises
- [ ] **C.** for a short rest when tired
- [ ] **D.** to check a road atlas

See HIGHWAY CODE rule 238, 249

846

For which TWO should you use hazard warning lights?

Mark two answers

- [ ] **A.** When you slow down quickly on a motorway because of a hazard ahead
- [ ] **B.** When you have broken down
- [ ] **C.** When you wish to stop on double yellow lines
- [ ] **D.** When you need to park on the pavement

See HIGHWAY CODE rules 96, 248

847

When are you allowed to use hazard warning lights?

Mark one answer

- [ ] **A.** When stopped and temporarily obstructing traffic
- [ ] **B.** When travelling during darkness without headlights
- [ ] **C.** When parked for shopping on double yellow lines
- [ ] **D.** When travelling slowly because you are lost

See HIGHWAY CODE rule 96

848
You are on a motorway. A large box falls on to the road from a lorry. The lorry does not stop. You should

Mark one answer
- [ ] A. go to the next emergency telephone and inform the police
- [ ] B. catch up with the lorry and try to get the driver's attention
- [ ] C. stop close to the box until the police arrive
- [ ] D. pull over to the hard shoulder, then remove the box

See HIGHWAY CODE rule 254

849
There has been an accident. A motorcyclist is lying injured and unconscious. Why should you usually not attempt to remove their helmet?

Mark one answer
- [ ] A. Because they may not want you to
- [ ] B. This could result in more serious injury
- [ ] C. They will get too cold if you do this
- [ ] D. Because you could scratch the helmet

850
After an accident, someone is unconscious in their vehicle. When should you call the emergency services?

Mark one answer
- [ ] A. Only as a last resort
- [ ] B. As soon as possible
- [ ] C. After you have woken them up
- [ ] D. After checking for broken bones

See HIGHWAY CODE rule 257 & Annexe 7

> **TIP** Don't give casualties anything to eat or drink, or offer them a cigarette. Reassure any injured person and keep them warm while waiting for the ambulance to arrive.

851
An accident casualty has an injured arm. They can move it freely, but it is bleeding. Why should you get them to keep it in a raised position?

Mark one answer
- [ ] A. Because it will ease the pain
- [ ] B. It will help them to be seen more easily
- [ ] C. To stop them touching other people
- [ ] D. It will help to reduce the bleeding

852
You are going through a congested tunnel and have to stop. What should you do?

Mark one answer
- [ ] A. Pull up very close to the vehicle in front to save space
- [ ] B. Ignore any message signs as they are never up to date
- [ ] C. Keep a safe distance from the vehicle in front
- [ ] D. Make a U-turn and find another route

853
You are going through a tunnel. What should you look out for that warns of accidents or congestion?

Mark one answer
- [ ] A. Hazard warning lines
- [ ] B. Other drivers flashing their lights
- [ ] C. Variable message signs
- [ ] D. Areas marked with hatch markings

854
You are going through a tunnel. What systems are provided to warn of any accidents or congestion?

Mark one answer
- [ ] A. Double white centre lines
- [ ] B. Variable message signs
- [ ] C. Chevron 'distance markers'
- [ ] D. Rumble strips

855 While driving, a warning light on your vehicle's instrument panel comes on. You should

Mark one answer
- A. continue if the engine sounds alright
- B. hope that it is just a temporary electrical fault
- C. deal with the problem when there is more time
- D. check out the problem quickly and safely

See HIGHWAY CODE Annexe 6

856 You have broken down on a two-way road. You have a warning triangle. You should place the warning triangle at least how far from your vehicle?

Mark one answer
- A. 5 metres (16 feet)
- B. 25 metres (82 feet)
- C. 45 metres (147 feet)
- D. 100 metres (328 feet)

See HIGHWAY CODE rule 248

857 You break down on a level crossing. The lights have not yet begun to flash. Which THREE things should you do?

Mark three answers
- A. Telephone the signal operator
- B. Leave your vehicle and get everyone clear
- C. Walk down the track and signal the next train
- D. Move the vehicle if a signal operator tells you to
- E. Tell drivers behind what has happened

See HIGHWAY CODE rule 272

858 Your vehicle has broken down on an automatic railway level crossing. What should you do FIRST?

Mark one answer
- A. Get everyone out of the vehicle and clear of the crossing
- B. Phone the signal operator so that trains can be stopped
- C. Walk along the track to give warning to any approaching trains
- D. Try to push the vehicle clear of the crossing as soon as possible

See HIGHWAY CODE rule 272

859 Your tyre bursts while you are driving. Which TWO things should you do?

Mark two answers
- A. Pull on the handbrake
- B. Brake as quickly as possible
- C. Pull up slowly at the side of the road
- D. Hold the steering wheel firmly to keep control
- E. Continue on at a normal speed

See HIGHWAY CODE Annexe 6

860 Which TWO things should you do when a front tyre bursts?

Mark two answers
- A. Apply the handbrake to stop the vehicle
- B. Brake firmly and quickly
- C. Let the vehicle roll to a stop
- D. Hold the steering wheel lightly
- E. Grip the steering wheel firmly

See HIGHWAY CODE Annexe 6

861 Your vehicle has a puncture on a motorway. What should you do?

Mark one answer

- A. Drive slowly to the next service area to get assistance
- B. Pull up on the hard shoulder. Change the wheel as quickly as possible
- C. Pull up on the hard shoulder. Use the emergency phone to get assistance
- D. Switch on your hazard lights. Stop in your lane

See HIGHWAY CODE rule 249

862 Which of these items should you carry in your vehicle for use in the event of an accident?

Mark three answers

- A. Road map
- B. Can of petrol
- C. Jump leads
- D. Fire extinguisher
- E. First aid kit
- F. Warning triangle

See HIGHWAY CODE rule 248 & Annexe 7

863 You are in an accident on a two-way road. You have a warning triangle with you. At what distance before the obstruction should you place the warning triangle?

Mark one answer

- A. 25 metres (82 feet)
- B. 45 metres (147 feet)
- C. 100 metres (328 feet)
- D. 150 metres (492 feet)

See HIGHWAY CODE rule 248

864 You have broken down on a two-way road. You have a warning triangle. It should be displayed

Mark one answer

- A. on the roof of your vehicle
- B. at least 150 metres (492 feet) behind your vehicle
- C. at least 45 metres (147 feet) behind your vehicle
- D. just behind your vehicle

See HIGHWAY CODE rule 248

865 You have stalled in the middle of a level crossing and cannot restart the engine. The warning bell starts to ring. You should

Mark one answer

- A. get out and clear of the crossing
- B. run down the track to warn the signal operator
- C. carry on trying to restart the engine
- D. push the vehicle clear of the crossing

See HIGHWAY CODE rule 272

866 You are on the motorway. Luggage falls from your vehicle. What should you do?

Mark one answer

- A. Stop at the next emergency telephone and contact the police
- B. Stop on the motorway and put on hazard lights whilst you pick it up
- C. Walk back up the motorway to pick it up
- D. Pull up on the hard shoulder and wave traffic down

See HIGHWAY CODE rule 254

867 You are on a motorway. When can you use hazard warning lights?

Mark two answers

- A. When a vehicle is following too closely
- B. When you slow down quickly because of danger ahead
- C. When you are towing another vehicle
- D. When driving on the hard shoulder
- E. When you have broken down on the hard shoulder

See HIGHWAY CODE rules 96, 248

868 You are involved in an accident with another vehicle. Someone is injured. Your vehicle is damaged. Which FOUR of the following should you find out?

Mark four answers

- A. Whether the driver owns the other vehicle involved
- B. The other driver's name, address and telephone number
- C. The make and registration number of the other vehicle
- D. The occupation of the other driver
- E. The details of the other driver's vehicle insurance
- F. Whether the other driver is licensed to drive

See HIGHWAY CODE Rules 260, 261

869 You have broken down on a motorway. When you use the emergency telephone you will be asked

Mark three answers

- A. for the number on the telephone that you are using
- B. for your driving licence details
- C. for the name of your vehicle insurance company
- D. for details of yourself and your vehicle
- E. whether you belong to a motoring organisation

870 You lose control of your car and damage a garden wall. No one is around. What must you do?

Mark one answer **NI**

- A. Report the accident to the police within 24 hours
- B. Go back to tell the house owner the next day
- C. Report the accident to your insurance company when you get home
- D. Find someone in the area to tell them about it immediately

See HIGHWAY CODE rule 260

871 Your engine catches fire. What should you do first?

Mark one answer

- A. Lift the bonnet and disconnect the battery
- B. Lift the bonnet and warn other traffic
- C. Call the breakdown service
- D. Call the fire brigade

See HIGHWAY CODE Annexe 6

872 Before driving through a tunnel what should you do?

Mark one answer

- A. Switch your radio off
- B. Remove any sun-glasses
- C. Close your sunroof
- D. Switch on windscreen wipers

See HIGHWAY CODE Rule 82

873 You are driving through a tunnel and the traffic is flowing normally. What should you do?

Mark one answer

- A. Use parking lights
- B. Use front spotlights
- C. Use dipped headlights
- D. Use rear fog lights

874 Before entering a tunnel it is good advice to

Mark one answer

- [ ] A. put on your sun-glasses
- [ ] B. check tyre pressures
- [ ] C. change to a lower gear
- [ ] D. tune your radio to a local channel

875 You are driving through a tunnel. Your vehicle breaks down. What should you do?

Mark one answer

- [ ] A. Switch on hazard warning lights
- [ ] B. Remain in your vehicle
- [ ] C. Wait for the police to find you
- [ ] D. Rely on CCTV cameras seeing you

See HIGHWAY CODE rule 248

876 Your vehicle breaks down in a tunnel. What should you do?

Mark one answer

- [ ] A. Stay in your vehicle and wait for the police
- [ ] B. Stand in the lane behind your vehicle to warn others
- [ ] C. Stand in front of your vehicle to warn oncoming drivers
- [ ] D. Switch on hazard lights then go and call for help immediately

See HIGHWAY CODE rule 248

877 You have an accident while driving through a tunnel. You are not injured but your vehicle cannot be driven. What should you do first?

Mark one answer

- [ ] A. Rely on other drivers phoning for the police
- [ ] B. Switch off the engine and switch on hazard lights
- [ ] C. Take the names of witnesses and other drivers
- [ ] D. Sweep up any debris that is in the road

See HIGHWAY CODE Rule 257

878 When driving through a tunnel you should

Mark one answer

- [ ] A. Look out for variable message signs
- [ ] B. Use your air-conditioning system
- [ ] C. Switch on your rear fog lights
- [ ] D. Always use your windscreen wipers

879 What TWO safeguards could you take against fire risk to your vehicle?

Mark two answers

- [ ] A. Keep water levels above maximum
- [ ] B. Carry a fire extinguisher
- [ ] C. Avoid driving with a full tank of petrol
- [ ] D. Use unleaded petrol
- [ ] E. Check out any strong smell of petrol
- [ ] F. Use low-octane fuel

See HIGHWAY CODE Annexe 6

TIP To be confident that you could be of help in an accident, consider taking a course in First Aid from St John Ambulance or St Andrew's Ambulance Association, or from the British Red Cross. You can find local contact numbers in the phone book.

880

You are towing a small trailer on a busy three-lane motorway. All the lanes are open. You must

Mark two answers

- [ ] **A.** not exceed 60mph
- [ ] **B.** not overtake
- [ ] **C.** have a stabilizer fitted
- [ ] **D.** use only the left and centre lanes

See *HIGHWAY CODE* rules 103 table, 239

881

Any load that is carried on a roof rack MUST be

Mark one answer

- [ ] **A.** securely fastened when driving
- [ ] **B.** carried only when strictly necessary
- [ ] **C.** as light as possible
- [ ] **D.** covered with plastic sheeting

See *HIGHWAY CODE* rule 74

882

You are planning to tow a caravan. Which of these will mostly help to aid the vehicle handling?

Mark one answer

- [ ] **A.** A jockey-wheel fitted to the tow bar
- [ ] **B.** Power steering fitted to the towing vehicle
- [ ] **C.** Anti-lock brakes fitted to the towing vehicle
- [ ] **D.** A stabilizer fitted to the tow bar

883

If a trailer swerves or snakes when you are towing it you should

Mark one answer

- [ ] **A.** ease off the accelerator and reduce your speed
- [ ] **B.** let go of the steering wheel and let it correct itself
- [ ] **C.** brake hard and hold the pedal down
- [ ] **D.** increase your speed as quickly as possible

See *HIGHWAY CODE* rule 74

884

How can you stop a caravan snaking from side to side?

Mark one answer

- [ ] **A.** Turn the steering wheel slowly to each side
- [ ] **B.** Accelerate to increase your speed
- [ ] **C.** Stop as quickly as you can
- [ ] **D.** Slow down very gradually

See *HIGHWAY CODE* rule 74

885

On which TWO occasions might you inflate your tyres to more than the recommended normal pressure?

Mark two answers

- [ ] **A.** When the roads are slippery
- [ ] **B.** When driving fast for a long distance
- [ ] **C.** When the tyre tread is worn below 2mm
- [ ] **D.** When carrying a heavy load
- [ ] **E.** When the weather is cold
- [ ] **F.** When the vehicle is fitted with anti-lock brakes

886

A heavy load on your roof rack will

Mark one answer

- [ ] **A.** improve the road holding
- [ ] **B.** reduce the stopping distance
- [ ] **C.** make the steering lighter
- [ ] **D.** reduce stability

887

Are passengers allowed to ride in a caravan that is being towed?

Mark one answer

- [ ] **A.** Yes if they are over 14
- [ ] **B.** No not at any time
- [ ] **C.** Only if all the seats in the towing vehicle are full
- [ ] **D.** Only if a stabilizer is fitted

888 You are towing a caravan along a motorway. The caravan begins to swerve from side to side. What should you do?

Mark one answer

- [ ] **A.** Ease off the accelerator slowly
- [ ] **B.** Steer sharply from side to side
- [ ] **C.** Do an emergency stop
- [ ] **D.** Speed up very quickly

See HIGHWAY CODE rule 74

889 A trailer must stay securely hitched-up to the towing vehicle. What additional safety device can be fitted to the trailer braking system?

Mark one answer

- [ ] **A.** Stabilizer
- [ ] **B.** Jockey wheel
- [ ] **C.** Corner steadies
- [ ] **D.** Breakaway cable

890 Overloading your vehicle can seriously affect the

Mark two answers

- [ ] **A.** gearbox
- [ ] **B.** steering
- [ ] **C.** handling
- [ ] **D.** battery life
- [ ] **E.** journey time

891 Who is responsible for making sure that a vehicle is not overloaded?

Mark one answer

- [ ] **A.** The driver of the vehicle
- [ ] **B.** The owner of the items being carried
- [ ] **C.** The person who loaded the vehicle
- [ ] **D.** The licensing authority

See HIGHWAY CODE rule 74

892 Which of these is a suitable restraint for a child under three years?

Mark one answer

- [ ] **A.** A child seat
- [ ] **B.** An adult holding a child
- [ ] **C.** An adult seat belt
- [ ] **D.** A lap belt

See HIGHWAY CODE rules 75 chart, 76

893 A child under three years is being carried in your vehicle. They should be secured in a restraint. Which of these is suitable?

Mark one answer

- [ ] **A.** An adult holding a child
- [ ] **B.** A lap belt
- [ ] **C.** A baby carrier
- [ ] **D.** An adult seat belt

See HIGHWAY CODE rules 75 chart, 76

TIP There isn't any room for argument here – passengers can't travel in a vehicle that's being towed.

TIP A stabilizer attached to the tow bar can help in making your tow load or trailer more secure.

Part 4

The Highway Code

Contents

Introduction

The Highway Code is essential reading for everyone. Its rules apply to all road users: pedestrians, horse riders and cyclists, as well as motorcyclists and drivers.

Many of the rules in the Code are legal requirements, and if you disobey these rules you are committing a criminal offence. You may be fined, given penalty points on your licence or be disqualified from driving. In the most serious cases you may be sent to prison. Such rules are identified by the use of the words **MUST/MUST NOT**. In addition, the rule includes an abbreviated reference to the legislation which creates the offence. An explanation of the abbreviations is in Annexe 4: The road user and the law.

Although failure to comply with the other rules of the Code will not, in itself, cause a person to be prosecuted, *The Highway Code* may be used in evidence in any court proceedings under the Traffic Acts to establish liability.

Knowing and applying the rules contained in *The Highway Code* could significantly reduce road accident casualties. Cutting the number of deaths and injuries that occur on our roads every day is a responsibility we all share. *The Highway Code* can help us discharge that responsibility.

Rules for pedestrians

General guidance

1. Pavements or footpaths should be used if provided. Where possible, avoid walking next to the kerb with your back to the traffic. If you have to step into the road, look both ways first.

2. If there is no pavement or footpath, walk on the right-hand side of the road so that you can see oncoming traffic. You should take extra care and
- be prepared to walk in single file, especially on narrow roads or in poor light
- keep close to the side of the road.

It may be safer to cross the road well before a sharp right-hand bend (so that oncoming traffic has a better chance of seeing you). Cross back after the bend.

3. Help other road users to see you. Wear or carry something light coloured, bright or fluorescent in poor daylight conditions. When it is dark, use reflective materials (e.g. armbands, sashes, waistcoats and jackets), which can be seen, by drivers using headlights, up to three times as far away as non-reflective materials.

Be seen in the dark; wear something reflective

4. Young children should not be out alone on the pavement or road (see Rule 7). When taking children out, walk between them and the traffic and hold their hands firmly. Strap very young children into push-chairs or use reins.

5. Organised walks. Groups of people should use a path if available; if one is not, they should keep to the left. Look-outs should be positioned at the front and back of the group, and they should wear fluorescent clothes in daylight and reflective clothes in the dark. At night, the look-out in front should carry a white light and the one at the back a red light. People on the outside of large groups should also carry lights and wear reflective clothing.

6. Motorways. You **MUST NOT** walk on motorways or slip roads except in an emergency (see Rule 249).

Laws RTRA sect 17, MT(E&W)R 1982 as amended & MT(S)R regs 2 &13

Crossing the road

7. The Green Cross Code. The advice given below on crossing the road is for all pedestrians. Children should be taught the Code and should not be allowed out alone until they can understand and use it properly. The age when they can do this is different for each child. Many children cannot judge how fast vehicles are going or how far away they are. Children learn by example, so parents and carers should always use the Code in full when out with their children. They are responsible for deciding at what age children can use it safely by themselves.

a. First find a safe place to cross. It is safer to cross using a subway, a footbridge, an island, a zebra, pelican, toucan or puffin crossing, or where there is a crossing point controlled by a police officer, a school crossing patrol or a traffic warden. Where there is a crossing nearby, use it. Otherwise choose a place where you can see clearly in all directions. Try to avoid crossing between parked cars (see Rule 14) and on blind bends and brows of hills. Move to a space where drivers can see you clearly.

b. Stop just before you get to the kerb, where you can see if anything is coming. Do not get too close to the traffic. If there is no pavement, keep back from the edge of the road but make sure you can still see approaching traffic.

c. Look all around for traffic and listen. Traffic could come from any direction. Listen as well, because you can sometimes hear traffic before you see it.

d. If traffic is coming, let it pass. Look all around again and listen. Do not cross until there is a safe gap in the traffic and you are certain that there is plenty of time. Remember, even if traffic is a long way off, it may be approaching very quickly.

e. When it is safe, go straight across the road – do not run. Keep looking and listening for traffic while you cross, in case there is any traffic you did not see, or in case other traffic appears suddenly.

8. At a junction. When crossing the road, look out for traffic turning into the road, especially from behind you.

9. Pedestrian Safety Barriers. Where there are barriers, cross the road only at the gaps provided for pedestrians. Do not climb over the barriers or walk between them and the road.

10. Tactile paving. Small raised studs which can be felt underfoot may be used to advise blind or partially sighted people that they are approaching a crossing point with a dropped kerb.

11. One-way streets. Check which way the traffic is moving. Do not cross until it is safe to do so without stopping. Bus and cycle lanes may operate in the opposite direction to the rest of the traffic.

12. Bus and cycle lanes. Take care when crossing these lanes as traffic may be moving faster than in the other lanes, or against the flow of traffic.

13. Routes shared with cyclists. Cycle tracks may run alongside footpaths, with a dividing line segregating the two. Keep to the section for pedestrians. Take extra care where cyclists and pedestrians share the same path without separation (see Rule 48).

14. Parked vehicles. If you have to cross between parked vehicles, use the outside edges of the vehicles as if they were the kerb. Stop there and make sure you can see all around and that the traffic can see you. Never cross the road in front of, or behind, any vehicle with its engine running, especially a large vehicle, as the driver may not be able to see you.

15. Reversing vehicles. Never cross behind a vehicle which is reversing, showing white reversing lights or sounding a warning.

16. Moving vehicles. You **MUST NOT** get on to or hold on to a moving vehicle.
Law RTA 1988 sect 26

17. At night. Wear something reflective to make it easier for others to see you (see Rule 3). If there is no pedestrian crossing nearby, cross the road near a street light so that traffic can see you more easily.

Crossings
18. At all crossings. When using any type of crossing you should
- always check that the traffic has stopped before you start to cross or push a pram on to a crossing
- always cross between the studs or over the zebra markings. Do not cross at the side of the crossing or on the zig-zag lines, as it can be dangerous.

You **MUST NOT** loiter on zebra, pelican or puffin crossings.
Laws ZPPPCRGD reg 19 & RTRA sect 25(5)

19. Zebra crossings. Give traffic plenty of time to see you and to stop before you start to cross. Vehicles will need more time when the road is slippery. Remember that traffic does not have to stop until someone has moved on to the crossing. Wait until traffic has stopped from both directions or the road is clear before crossing. Keep looking both ways, and listening, in case a driver or rider has not seen you and attempts to overtake a vehicle that has stopped.

20. Where there is an island in the middle of a zebra crossing, wait on the island and follow Rule 19 before you cross the second half of the road – it is a separate crossing.

21. At traffic lights. There may be special signals for pedestrians. You should only start to cross the road when the green figure shows. If you have started to cross the road and the green figure goes out, you should still have time to reach the other side, but do not delay. If no pedestrian signals have been provided, watch carefully and do not cross until the traffic lights are red and the traffic has stopped. Keep looking and check for traffic that may be turning the corner. Remember that traffic lights may let traffic move in some lanes while traffic in other lanes has stopped.

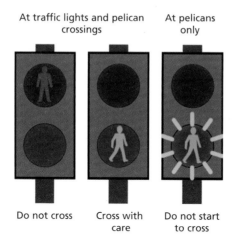

At traffic lights and pelican crossings | At pelicans only

Do not cross | Cross with care | Do not start to cross

Pedestrian signals at traffic lights and pelican crossings

22. Pelican crossings. These are signal-controlled crossings operated by pedestrians. Push the control button to activate the traffic signals. When the red figure shows, do not cross. When a steady green figure shows, check the traffic has stopped then cross with care. When the green figure begins to flash you should not start to cross. If you have already started you should have time to finish crossing safely.

23. At some pelican crossings there is a bleeping sound to indicate to blind or partially-sighted people when the steady green figure is showing, and there may be a tactile signal to help deafblind people.

24. When the road is congested, traffic on your side of the road may be forced to stop even though their lights are green. Traffic may still be moving on the other side of the road, so press the button and wait for the signal to cross.

25. Puffin and toucan crossings. These differ from pelican crossings as there is no flashing green figure phase. On puffin crossings the red and green figures are above the control box on your side of the road. Press the button and wait for the green figure to show. On toucan crossings cyclists are permitted to ride across the road (see Rule 65).

26. 'Staggered' pelican or puffin crossings. When the crossings on each side of the central refuge are not in line they are two separate crossings. On reaching the central island press the button again and wait for a steady green figure.

27. Crossings controlled by an authorised person. Do not cross the road unless you are signalled to do so by a police officer, traffic warden or school crossing patrol. Always cross in front of them.

28. Where there are no controlled crossing points available it is advisable to cross where there is an island in the middle of the road. Use the Green Cross Code to cross to the island and then stop and use it again to cross the second half of the road.

Situations needing extra care

29. Emergency vehicles. If an ambulance, fire engine, police or other emergency vehicle approaches using flashing blue lights, headlights and/or sirens, keep off the road.

30. Buses. Get on or off a bus only when it has stopped to allow you to do so. Watch out for cyclists when you are getting off. Never cross the road directly behind or in front of a bus; wait until it has moved off and you can see clearly in both directions.

31. Tramways. These may run through pedestrian areas. Their path will be marked out by shallow kerbs, changes in the paving or other road surface, white lines or yellow dots. Cross at designated crossings where provided. Flashing amber lights may warn you that a tram is approaching. Elsewhere look both ways along the track before crossing. Do not walk along the track. Trams move quickly and silently and cannot steer to avoid you.

32. Railway level crossings. Do not cross if the red lights show, an alarm is sounding or the barriers are being lowered. The tone of the alarm will change if another train is approaching. If there are no lights, alarms or barriers, stop, look both ways and listen before crossing.

33. Street and pavement repairs. A pavement may be closed temporarily because it is not safe to use. Take extra care if you are directed to walk in or to cross the road.

Rules about animals

Horseriders

34. Safety equipment. Children under the age of 14 **MUST** wear a helmet which complies with the Regulations. It **MUST** be fastened securely. Other riders should also follow this advice.

Law H(PHYR)R

35. Other clothing. You should wear
* boots or shoes with hard soles and heels
* light-coloured or fluorescent clothing in daylight
* reflective clothing if you have to ride at night or in poor visibility.

36. At night. It is safer not to ride on the road at night or in poor visibility, but if you do, make sure your horse has reflective bands above the fetlock joints. Carry a light which shows white to the front and red to the rear.

Riding

37. Before you take a horse on to a road, you should
* ensure all tack fits well and is in good condition
* make sure you can control the horse.

Always ride with other, less nervous horses if you think that your horse will be nervous of traffic. Never ride a horse without a saddle or bridle.

38. Before riding off or turning, look behind you to make sure it is safe, then give a clear arm signal.

39. When riding on the road you should
* keep to the left
* keep both hands on the reins unless you are signalling
* keep both feet in the stirrups
* not carry another person
* not carry anything which might affect your balance or get tangled up with the reins
* keep a horse you are leading to your left
* move in the direction of the traffic flow in a one-way street
* never ride more than two abreast, and ride in single file where the road narrows or on the approach to a bend.

40. You **MUST NOT** take a horse on to a footpath, pavement or cycle track. Use a bridleway where possible.

Laws HA 1835 sect 72 & R(S)A sect 129(5)

41. Avoid roundabouts wherever possible. If you use them you should
- keep to the left and watch out for vehicles crossing your path to leave or join the roundabout
- signal right when riding across exits to show you are not leaving
- signal left just before you leave the roundabout.

Other animals

42. Dogs. Do not let a dog out on the road on its own. Keep it on a short lead when walking on the pavement, road or path shared with cyclists.

43. When in a vehicle make sure dogs or other animals are suitably restrained so they cannot distract you while you are driving or injure you if you stop quickly.

44. Animals being herded. These should be kept under control at all times. You should, if possible, send another person along the road in front to warn other road users, especially at a bend or the brow of a hill. It is safer not to move animals after dark, but if you do, then wear reflective clothing and ensure that lights are carried (white at the front and red at the rear of the herd).

Rules for cyclists

These rules are in addition to those in the following sections, which apply to all vehicles (except the motorway section). See also Annexe 1: Choosing and maintaining your bicycle.

45. Clothing. You should wear
- a cycle helmet which conforms to current regulations
- appropriate clothes for cycling. Avoid clothes which may get tangled in the chain, or in a wheel or may obscure your lights
- light-coloured or fluorescent clothing which helps other road users to see you in daylight and poor light
- reflective clothing and/or accessories (belt, arm or ankle bands) in the dark.

Help yourself to be seen

46. At night your cycle **MUST** have front and rear lights lit. It **MUST** also be fitted with a red rear reflector (and amber pedal reflectors, if manufactured after 1/10/85). White front reflectors and spoke reflectors will also help you be seen.
Law RVLR regs 18 & 24

When cycling
47. Use cycle routes when practicable. They can make your journey safer.

48. Cycle Tracks. These are normally located away from the road, but may occasionally be found alongside footpaths or pavements. Cyclists and pedestrians may be segregated or they may share the same space (unsegregated). When using segregated tracks you **MUST** keep to the

side intended for cyclists. Take care when passing pedestrians, especially children, elderly or disabled people, and allow them plenty of room. Always be prepared to slow down and stop if necessary.
Law HA 1835 sect 72

49. Cycle Lanes. These are marked by a white line (which may be broken) along the carriageway (see Rule 119). Keep within the lane wherever possible.

50. You **MUST** obey all traffic signs and traffic light signals.
Laws RTA 1988 sect 36, TSRGD reg 10

51. You should
- keep both hands on the handlebars except when signalling or changing gear
- keep both feet on the pedals
- not ride more than two abreast
- ride in single file on narrow or busy roads
- not ride close behind another vehicle
- not carry anything which will affect your balance or may get tangled up with your wheels or chain
- be considerate of other road users, particularly blind and partially sighted pedestrians. Let them know you are there when necessary, for example by ringing your bell.

52. You should
- look all around before moving away from the kerb, turning or manoeuvring, to make sure it is safe to do so. Give a clear signal to show other road users what you intend to do (see Signals to other road users)
- look well ahead for obstructions in the road, such as drains, pot-holes and parked vehicles so that you do not have to swerve suddenly to avoid them. Leave plenty of room when passing parked vehicles and watch out for doors being opened into your path
- take extra care near road humps, narrowings and other traffic calming features.

53. You **MUST NOT**
- carry a passenger unless your cycle has been built or adapted to carry one
- hold on to a moving vehicle or trailer
- ride in a dangerous, careless or inconsiderate manner
- ride when under the influence of drink or drugs.
Law RTA 1988 sects 24, 26, 28, 29 & 30 as amended by RTA 1991

54. You **MUST NOT** cycle on a pavement. Do not leave your cycle where it would endanger or obstruct other road users or pedestrians, for example, lying on the pavement. Use cycle parking facilities where provided.
Laws HA 1835 sect 72 & R(S)A sect 129

55. You **MUST NOT** cross the stop line when the traffic lights are red. Some junctions have an advanced stop line to enable you to position yourself ahead of other traffic (see Rule 154).
Laws RTA 1988 sect 36, TSRGD reg 10

56. Bus Lanes. These may be used by cyclists only if the signs include a cycle symbol. Watch out for people getting on or off a bus. Be very careful when overtaking a bus or leaving a bus lane as you will be entering a busier traffic flow.

Road junctions

57. On the left. When approaching a junction on the left, watch out for vehicles turning in front of you, out of or into the side road. Do not ride on the inside of vehicles signalling or slowing down to turn left.

58. Pay particular attention to long vehicles which need a lot of room to manoeuvre at corners. They may have to move over to the right before turning left. Wait until they have completed the manoeuvre because the rear wheels come very close to the kerb while turning. Do not be tempted to ride in the space between them and the kerb.

59. On the right. If you are turning right, check the traffic to ensure it is safe, then signal and move to the centre of the road. Wait until there is a safe gap in the oncoming traffic before completing the turn. It may be safer to wait on the left until there is a safe gap or to dismount and push your cycle across the road.

60. Dual carriageways. Remember that traffic on most dual carriageways moves quickly. When crossing wait for a safe gap and cross each carriageway in turn. Take extra care when crossing slip roads.

Roundabouts

61. Full details about the correct procedure at roundabouts are contained in Rules 160–166. Roundabouts can be hazardous and should be approached with care.

62. You may feel safer either keeping to the left on the roundabout or dismounting and walking your cycle round on the pavement or verge. If you decide to keep to the left you should

- be aware that drivers may not easily see you
- take extra care when cycling across exits and you may need to signal right to show you are not leaving the roundabout
- watch out for vehicles crossing your path to leave or join the roundabout.

63. Give plenty of room to long vehicles on the roundabout as they need more space to manoeuvre. Do not ride in the space they need to get round the roundabout. It may be safer to wait until they have cleared the roundabout.

Crossing the road

64. Do not ride across a pelican, puffin or zebra crossing. Dismount and wheel your cycle across.

65. Toucan crossings. These are light-controlled crossings which allow cyclists and pedestrians to cross at the same time. They are push button operated. Pedestrians and cyclists will see the green signal together. Cyclists are permitted to ride across.

66. Cycle-only crossings. Cycle tracks on opposite sides of the road may be linked by signalled crossings. You may ride across but you **MUST NOT** cross until the green cycle symbol is showing.

Law TSRGD reg 33(1)

Rules for motorcyclists

These Rules are in addition to those in the following sections which apply to all vehicles. For motorcycle licence requirements see Annexe 2: Motorcycle licence requirements.

General

67. On all journeys, the rider and pillion passenger on a motorcycle, scooter or moped **MUST** wear a protective helmet. Helmets **MUST** comply with the Regulations and they **MUST** be fastened securely. It is also advisable to wear eye protectors, which **MUST** comply with the Regulations. Consider wearing ear protection. Strong boots, gloves and suitable clothing may help to protect you if you fall off.

Laws RTA 1988 sects 16 &17 & MC(PH)R as amended reg 4, & RTA sect 18 & MC(EP)R as amended reg 4

68. You **MUST NOT** carry more than one pillion passenger and he/she **MUST** sit astride the machine on a proper seat and should keep both feet on the footrests.

Law RTA 1988 sect 23

69. Daylight riding. Make yourself as visible as possible from the side as well as the front and rear. You could wear a white or brightly coloured helmet. Wear fluorescent clothing or strips. Dipped headlights, even in good daylight, may also make you more conspicuous.

Make sure you can be seen

70. Riding in the dark. Wear reflective clothing or strips to improve your chances of being seen in the dark. These reflect light from the headlamps of other vehicles making you more visible from a long distance. See Rules 93–96 for lighting requirements.

71. Manoeuvring. You should be aware of what is behind and to the sides before manoeuvring. Look behind you; use mirrors if they are fitted. When overtaking traffic queues look out for pedestrians crossing between vehicles and vehicles emerging from junctions.
Remember: Observation – Signal – Manoeuvre.

Rules for drivers and motorcyclists

72. Vehicle condition. You **MUST** ensure your vehicle and trailer complies with the full requirements of the Road Vehicles (Construction and Use) Regulations and Road Vehicles Lighting Regulations. (See Annexe 6: Vehicle maintenance safety and security).

73. Before setting off. You should ensure that
- you have planned your route and allowed sufficient time
- clothing and footwear do not prevent you using the controls in the correct manner
- you know where all the controls are and how to use them before you need them. All vehicles are different; do not wait until it is too late to find out
- your mirrors and seat are adjusted correctly to ensure comfort, full control and maximum vision
- head restraints are properly adjusted to reduce the risk of neck injuries in the event of an accident
- you have sufficient fuel before commencing your journey, especially if it includes motorway driving. It can be dangerous to lose power when driving in traffic.

74. Vehicle towing and loading. As a driver
- you **MUST NOT** tow more than your licence permits you to
- you **MUST NOT** overload your vehicle or trailer. You should not

tow a weight greater than that recommended by the manufacturer of your vehicle

- you **MUST** secure your load and it **MUST NOT** stick out dangerously
- you should properly distribute the weight in your caravan or trailer with heavy items mainly over the axle(s) and ensure a downward load on the tow ball. Manufacturer's recommended weight and tow ball load should not be exceeded. This should avoid the possibility of swerving or snaking and going out of control. If this does happen, ease off the accelerator and reduce speed gently to regain control.

Law CUR reg 100, MVDL reg 43

Seat Belts

75. You **MUST** wear a seat belt if one is available, unless you are exempt. Those exempt from the requirement include the holders of medical exemption certificates and people making local deliveries in a vehicle designed for the purpose.

Laws RTA 1988 sects 14 & 15, MV(WSB)R & MV(WSBCFS)R

Seat belt requirements

This table summarises the main legal requirements for wearing seat belts

	FRONT SEAT (all vehicles)	REAR SEAT (cars and small minibuses*)	WHOSE RESPONSIBILITY
DRIVER	**MUST** be worn if fitted		**DRIVER**
CHILD under 3 years of age	Appropriate child restraint **MUST** be worn	Appropriate child restraint **MUST** be worn *if available*	**DRIVER**
CHILD aged 3 to 11 and under 1.5 metres (about 5 feet) in height	Appropriate child restraint **MUST** be worn *if available.* If not, an adult seat belt **MUST** be worn	Appropriate child restraint **MUST** be worn *if available.* If not, an adult seat belt **MUST** be worn *if available*	**DRIVER**
CHILD aged 12 or 13 or younger child 1.5 metres or more in height	Adult seat belt **MUST** be worn *if available*	Adult seat belt **MUST** be worn *if available*	**DRIVER**
PASSENGER over the age of 14	**MUST** be worn *if available*	**MUST** be worn *if available*	**PASSENGER**

*Minibuses with an unladen weight of 2540kg or less

76. The driver **MUST** ensure that all children under 14 years of age wear seat belts or sit in an approved child restraint. This should be a baby seat, child seat, booster seat or booster cushion appropriate to the child's weight and size, fitted to the manufacturer's instructions.
Laws RTA 1988 sects 14 & 15, MV(WSB)R & MV(WSBCFS)R

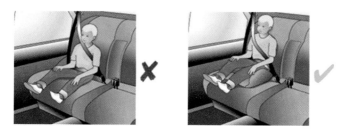

Make sure children wear the correct restraint

77. You **MUST** wear seatbelts in minibuses with an unladen weight of 2540 kg or less. You should wear them in large minibuses and coaches where available.
Laws RTA 1988 sects 14 & 15, MV(WSB)R & MV(WSBCFS)R

78. Children in cars. Drivers who are carrying children in cars should ensure that
- children do not sit behind the rear seats in an estate car or hatchback, unless a special child seat has been fitted
- the child safety door locks, where fitted, are used when children are in the car
- children are kept under control
- a rear-facing baby seat is **NEVER** fitted into a seat protected by an airbag.

Fitness to drive
79. Make sure that you are fit to drive. You **MUST** report to the Driver and Vehicle Licensing Agency (DVLA) any health condition likely to affect your driving.
Law RTA 1988 sect 94

80. Driving when you are tired greatly increases your accident risk. To minimise this risk
- make sure you are fit to drive. Do not undertake a long journey (longer than an hour) if you feel tired
- avoid undertaking long journeys between midnight and 6am, when natural alertness is at a minimum

- plan your journey to take sufficient breaks. A minimum break of at least 15 minutes after every two hours of driving is recommended
- if you feel at all sleepy, stop in a safe place. Do not stop on the hard shoulder of a motorway
- the most effective ways to counter sleepiness are to take a short nap (up to 15 minutes) or drink, for example, two cups of strong coffee. Fresh air, exercise or turning up the radio may help for a short time, but are not as effective.

81. Vision. You **MUST** be able to read a vehicle number plate from a distance of 20.5 metres (67 feet – about five car lengths) in good daylight. From September 2001, you **MUST** be able to read a new style number plate from a distance of 20 metres (66 feet). If you need to wear glasses (or contact lenses) to do this, you **MUST** wear them at all times whilst driving. The police have the power to require a driver, at any time, to undertake an eyesight test in good daylight.
Laws RTA 1988 sect 96 & MV(DL)R reg 40 & sch 8

82. At night or in poor visibility, do not use tinted glasses, lenses or visors or anything that restricts vision.

Alcohol and drugs
83. Do not drink and drive as it will seriously affect your judgement and abilities. You **MUST NOT** drive with a breath alcohol level higher than 35 µg /100 ml or a blood alcohol level of more than 80 mg/100 ml. Alcohol will
- give a false sense of confidence
- reduce co-ordination and slow down reactions
- affect judgement of speed, distance and risk
- reduce your driving ability, even if you are below the legal limit
- take time to leave your body; you may be unfit to drive in the evening after drinking at lunchtime, or in the morning after drinking the previous evening. If you are going to drink, arrange another means of transport.
Law RTA 1988 sects 4, 5 & 11(2)

84. You **MUST NOT** drive under the influence of drugs or medicine. Check the instructions or ask your doctor or pharmacist. Using illegal drugs is highly dangerous. Never take them before driving; the effects are unpredictable, but can be even more severe than alcohol and may result in fatal or serious road accidents.
Law RTA 1988 sect 4

General rules, techniques and advice for all drivers and riders

This section should be read by all drivers, motorcyclists and cyclists. The rules in *The Highway Code* do not give you the right of way in any circumstance, but they advise you when you should give way to others. Always give way if it can help to avoid an accident.

Signals

85. Signals warn and inform other road users, including pedestrians (see Signals to other road users), of your intended actions.

You should
- give clear signals in plenty of time, having checked it is not misleading to signal at that time
- use them, if necessary, before changing course or direction, stopping or moving off
- cancel them after use
- make sure your signals will not confuse others. If, for instance you want to stop after a side road, do not signal until you are passing the road. If you signal earlier it may give the impression that you intend to turn into the road. Your brake lights will warn traffic behind you that you are slowing down
- use an arm signal to emphasise or reinforce your signal if necessary. Remember that signalling does not give you priority.

86. You should also
- watch out for signals given by other road users and proceed only when you are satisfied that it is safe
- be aware that an indicator on another vehicle may not have been cancelled.

87. You **MUST** obey signals given by police officers and traffic wardens (see Signals by authorised persons) and signs used by school crossing patrols.
Laws RTRA sect 28, RTA 1988 sect 35 and FTWO art 3

Traffic light signals and traffic signs
88. You **MUST** obey all traffic light signals (see Light signals controlling traffic) and traffic signs giving orders, including temporary signals & signs (see Traffic Signs and Road works signs). Make sure you know, understand and act on all other traffic and information signs and road

markings.
Laws RTA 1988 sect 36, TSRGD regs 10,15,16,25,26 & 33

89. Police stopping procedures. If the police want to stop your
vehicle they will, where possible, attract your attention by
* flashing blue lights or headlights or sounding their siren or horn
* directing you to pull over to the side by pointing and/or using the
  left indicator.

You **MUST** then pull over and stop as soon as it is safe to do so. Then
switch off your engine.
Law RTA 1988 sect 163

90. Flashing headlights. Only flash your headlights to let other road
users know that you are there. Do not flash your headlights in an
attempt to intimidate other road users.

91. If another driver flashes his headlights never assume that it is a
signal to go. Use your own judgement and proceed carefully.

92. The horn. Use only while your vehicle is moving and you need to
warn other road users of your presence. Never sound your horn
aggressively. You **MUST NOT** use your horn
* while stationary on the road
* when driving in a built up area between the hours of 11.30 pm
  and 7.00 am

except when another vehicle poses a danger.
Law CUR reg 99

Lighting requirements

93. You **MUST**
* use headlights at night, except on restricted roads (those with
  street lights not more than 185 metres (600 feet) apart and which
  are generally subject to a speed limit of 30 mph)
* use headlights when visibility is seriously reduced (see Rule 201).
* ensure all sidelights and rear registration plate lights are lit at night.

Laws RVLR regs 24 & 25 & RV(R&L)R reg 19

94. You **MUST NOT**
* use any lights in a way which would dazzle or cause discomfort to
  other road users
* use front or rear fog lights unless visibility is seriously reduced. You
  MUST switch them off when visibility improves to avoid dazzling
  other road users.

Law RVLR reg 27

95. You should also

- use dipped headlights, or dim-dip if fitted, at night in built-up areas and in dull daytime weather, to ensure that you can be seen
- keep your headlights dipped when overtaking until you are level with the other vehicle and then change to main beam if necessary, unless this would dazzle oncoming traffic
- slow down, and if necessary stop, if you are dazzled by oncoming headlights.

96. Hazard warning lights. These may be used when your vehicle is stationary, to warn that it is temporarily obstructing traffic. Never use them as an excuse for dangerous or illegal parking. You **MUST NOT** use hazard warning lights whilst driving unless you are on a motorway or unrestricted dual carriageway and you need to warn drivers behind you of a hazard or obstruction ahead. Only use them for long enough to ensure that your warning has been observed.

Law RVLR reg 27

Control of the vehicle

Braking

97. In normal circumstances. The safest way to brake is to do so early and lightly. Brake more firmly as you begin to stop. Ease the pressure off just before the vehicle comes to rest to avoid a jerky stop.

98. In an emergency. Brake immediately. Try to avoid braking so harshly that you lock your wheels. Locked wheels can lead to skidding.

99. Skids. Skidding is caused by the driver braking, accelerating or steering too harshly or driving too fast for the road conditions. If skidding occurs, ease off the brake or accelerator and try to steer smoothly in the direction of the skid. For example, if the rear of the vehicle skids to the right, steer quickly and smoothly to the right to recover.

Rear of car skids to the right   Driver steers to the right

100. ABS. The presence of an anti-lock braking system should not cause you to alter the way you brake from that indicated in Rule 97. However in the case of an emergency, apply the footbrake rapidly and firmly; do not release the pressure until the vehicle has slowed to the desired speed. The ABS should ensure that steering control will be retained.

101. Brakes affected by water. If you have driven through deep water your brakes may be less effective. Test them at the first safe opportunity by pushing gently on the brake pedal to make sure that they work. If they are not fully effective, gently apply light pressure while driving slowly. This will help to dry them out.

102. Coasting. This term describes a vehicle travelling in neutral or with the clutch pressed down. Do not coast, whatever the driving conditions. It reduces driver control because
- engine braking is eliminated
- vehicle speed downhill will increase quickly
- increased use of the footbrake can reduce its effectiveness
- steering response will be affected particularly on bends and corners
- it may be more difficult to select the appropriate gear when needed.

Speed limits
103. You **MUST NOT** exceed the maximum speed limits for the road and for your vehicle (see the table on the next page). Street lights usually mean that there is a 30 mph speed limit unless there are signs showing another limit.

Law RTRA sects 81,86,89 & sch 6

Speed Limits

Type of vehicle	Built-up areas* MPH	Elsewhere Single carriageways MPH	Elsewhere Dual carriageways MPH	Motorways MPH
Cars & motorcycles (including car derived vans up to 2 tonnes maximum laden weight)	30	60	70	70
Cars towing caravans or trailers (including car derived vans and motorcycles)	30	50	60	60
Buses & coaches (not exceeding 12 metres in overall length)	30	50	60	70
Goods vehicles (not exceeding 7.5 tonnes maximum laden wieght)	30	50	60	70†
Goods vehicles (exceeding 7.5 tonnes maximum laden wieght)	30	40	50	60

These are the national speed limits and apply to all roads unless signs show otherwise.
*The 30mph limit applies to all traffic on all roads in England and Wales (only class C and unclassified roads in Scotland) with street lighting unless signs show otherwise.
†60 if articulated or towing a trailer

104. The speed limit is the absolute maximum and does not mean it is safe to drive at that speed irrespective of conditions. Driving at speeds too fast for the road and traffic conditions can be dangerous. You should always reduce your speed when
- the road layout or condition presents hazards, such as bends
- sharing the road with pedestrians and cyclists, particularly children, and motorcyclists
- weather conditions make it safer to do so
- driving at night as it is harder to see other road users.

Stopping distances

105. Drive at a speed that will allow you to stop well within the distance you can see to be clear. You should
- leave enough space between you and the vehicle in front so that you can pull up safely if it suddenly slows down or stops. The safe rule is never to get closer than the overall stopping distance (see Typical Stopping Distances diagram, on the next page)
- allow at least a two-second gap between you and the vehicle in front on roads carrying fast traffic. The gap should be at least doubled on wet roads and increased still further on icy roads
- remember, large vehicles and motorcycles need a greater distance to stop.

Use a fixed point to help measure a two second gap

Typical stopping Distances

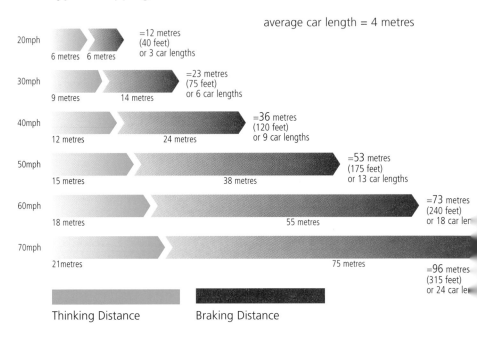

average car length = 4 metres

20mph	6 metres 6 metres	=12 metres (40 feet) or 3 car lengths
30mph	9 metres 14 metres	=23 metres (75 feet) or 6 car lengths
40mph	12 metres 24 metres	=36 metres (120 feet) or 9 car lengths
50mph	15 metres 38 metres	=53 metres (175 feet) or 13 car lengths
60mph	18 metres 55 metres	=73 metres (240 feet) or 18 car len
70mph	21metres 75 metres	=96 metres (315 feet) or 24 car le

Thinking Distance   Braking Distance

Lines and lane markings on the road

Diagrams of all lines shown in Road markings

106. A broken white line. This marks the centre of the road. When this line lengthens and the gaps shorten, it means that there is a hazard ahead. Do not cross it unless you can see the road is clear well ahead and wish to overtake or turn off.

107. Double white lines where the line nearest to you is broken. This means you may cross the lines to overtake if it is safe, provided you can complete the manoeuvre before reaching a solid white line on your side. White arrows on the road indicate when you need to get back onto your side of the road.

108. Double white lines where the line nearest you is solid. This means you **MUST NOT** cross or straddle it unless it is safe and you need to enter adjoining premises or a side road. You may cross the line if necessary to pass a stationary vehicle, or overtake a pedal cycle, horse or road maintenance vehicle, if they are travelling at 10 mph or less.

Laws RTA sect 36 & TSRGD regs 10 & 26

109. Areas of white diagonal stripes or chevrons painted on the road. These are to separate traffic lanes or to protect traffic turning right.

- If the area is bordered by a solid white line, you should not enter it except in an emergency.
- If the area is bordered by a broken white line, you should not enter the area unless it is necessary and you can see that it is safe to do so.
- If the area is on a motorway and consists of a triangle bounded by continuous white lines marked by chevrons, you **MUST NOT** enter it except in an emergency.

Laws MT(E&W)R regs 5, 9,& 10 & MT(S)R regs 4, 8 & 9

110. Lane dividers. These are short broken white lines which are used on wide carriageways to divide them into lanes. You should keep between them.

111. Reflective road studs may be used with white lines.

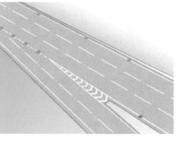

- White studs mark the lanes or the middle of the road.
- Red studs mark the left edge of the road.
- Amber studs mark the central reservation of a dual carriageway or motorway.
- Green studs mark the edge of the main carriageway at lay-bys, side roads and slip roads.

Multi-lane carriageways

Lane discipline

112. If you need to change lane, first use your mirrors and check your blind spots (the areas you are unable to see in the mirrors) to make sure you will not force another driver or rider to swerve or slow down. When it is safe to do so, signal to indicate your intentions to other road users and when clear move over.

113. You should follow the signs and road markings and get into lane as directed. In congested road conditions do not change lanes unnecessarily.

Single carriageway

114. Where a single carriageway has three lanes and the road markings or signs do not give priority to traffic in either direction

- use the middle lane only for overtaking or turning right. Remember, you have no more right to use the middle lane than a driver coming from the opposite direction
- do not use the right-hand lane.

115. Where a single carriageway has four or more lanes, use only the lanes that signs or markings indicate.

Dual carriageways

116. On a two-lane dual carriageway you should stay in the left-hand lane. Use the right-hand lane for overtaking or turning right. If you use it for overtaking move back to the left-hand lane when it is safe to do so.

117. On a three-lane dual carriageway, you may use the middle lane or the right-hand lane to overtake but return to the middle and then the left-hand lane when it is safe.

118. Climbing and crawler lanes. These are provided on some hills. Use this lane if you are driving a slow moving vehicle or if there are vehicles behind you wishing to overtake.

119. Cycle lanes. These are shown by road markings and signs. You **MUST NOT** drive or park in a cycle lane marked by a solid white line during its times of operation. Do not drive or park in a cycle lane marked by a broken white line unless it is unavoidable. You **MUST NOT** park in any cycle lane whilst waiting restrictions apply.

Law RTRA sects 5 & 8

120. Bus and tram lanes. These are shown by road markings and signs. You **MUST NOT** drive or stop in a tram lane or in a bus lane during its period of operation unless the signs indicate you may do so.
Law RTRA sects 5 & 8

121. One-way streets. Traffic **MUST** travel in the direction indicated by signs. Buses and/or cycles may have a contraflow lane. Choose the correct lane for your exit as soon as you can. Do not change lanes suddenly. Unless road signs or markings indicate otherwise, you should use
- the left-hand lane when going left
- the right-hand lane when going right
- the most appropriate lane when going straight ahead.

Remember – traffic could be passing on both sides.
Laws RTA 1988 sect 36 & RTRA sects 5 & 8

General advice

122. You MUST NOT
- drive dangerously
- drive without due care and attention
- drive without reasonable consideration for other road users.

Law RTA 1988 sects 2 & 3 as amended by RTA 1991

123. You **MUST NOT** drive on or over a pavement, footpath or bridleway except to gain lawful access to property.
Laws HA 1835 sect 72 & RTA sect 34

124. Adapt your driving to the appropriate type and condition of road you are on. In particular
- do not treat speed limits as a target. It is often not appropriate or safe to drive at the maximum speed limit
- take the road and traffic conditions into account. Be prepared for unexpected or difficult situations, for example, the road being blocked beyond a blind bend. Be prepared to adjust your speed as a precaution
- where there are junctions, be prepared for vehicles emerging
- in side roads and country lanes look out for unmarked junctions where nobody has priority
- try to anticipate what pedestrians and cyclists might do.
  If pedestrians, particularly children, are looking the other way, they may step out into the road without seeing you.

125. Be considerate. Be careful of and considerate towards other road users. You should

- try to be understanding if other drivers cause problems; they may be inexperienced or not know the area well
- be patient; remember that anyone can make a mistake
- not allow yourself to become agitated or involved if someone is behaving badly on the road. This will only make the situation worse. Pull over, calm down and, when you feel relaxed, continue your journey
- slow down and hold back if a vehicle pulls out into your path at a junction. Allow it to get clear. Do not over-react by driving too close behind it.

126. Safe driving needs concentration. Avoid distractions when driving such as

- loud music (this may mask other sounds)
- trying to read maps
- inserting a cassette or CD or tuning a radio
- arguing with your passengers or other road users
- eating and drinking.

Mobile phones and in-car technology

127. You **MUST** exercise proper control of your vehicle at all times. Never use a hand held mobile phone or microphone when driving. Using hands free equipment is also likely to distract your attention from the road. It is far safer not to use any telephone while you are driving – find a safe place to stop first.

Law RTA 1988 sects 2 & 3 & CUR reg 104

128. There is a danger of driver distraction being caused by in-vehicle systems such as route guidance and navigation systems, congestion warning systems, PCs, multi-media, etc. Do not operate, adjust or view any such system if it will distract your attention while you are driving; you **MUST** exercise proper control of your vehicle at all times. If necessary find a safe place to stop first.

Law RTA 1988 sects 2 & 3 & CUR reg 104

In slow moving traffic

129. You should

- reduce the distance between you and the vehicle ahead to maintain traffic flow
- never get so close to the vehicle in front that you cannot stop safely
- leave enough space to be able to manoeuvre if the vehicle in front breaks down or an emergency vehicle needs to get past

- not change lanes to the left to overtake
- allow access into and from side roads, as blocking these will add to congestion.

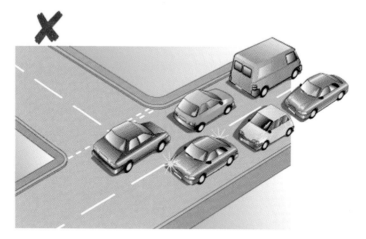

Do not block access to a side road

Driving in built up areas

130. Narrow residential streets. You should drive slowly and carefully on streets where there are likely to be pedestrians, cyclists and parked cars. In some areas a 20 mph maximum speed limit may be in force. Look out for

- vehicles emerging from junctions
- vehicles moving off
- car doors opening
- pedestrians
- children running out from between parked cars
- cyclists and motorcyclists.

131. Traffic calming measures. On some roads there are features such as road humps, chicanes and narrowings which are intended to slow you down. When you approach these features reduce your speed. Allow cyclists and motorcyclists room to pass through them. Maintain a reduced speed along the whole of the stretch of road within the calming measures. Give way to oncoming traffic if directed to do so by signs. You should not overtake other moving vehicles whilst in these areas.

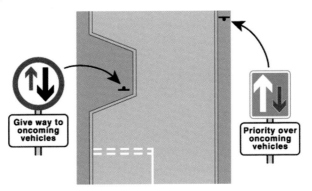

Chicanes may be used to slow traffic down

Country roads

132. Take extra care on country roads and reduce your speed at approaches to bends, which can be sharper than they appear, and at minor junctions and turnings, which may be partially hidden. Be prepared for pedestrians, horse riders and cyclists walking or riding in the road. You should also reduce your speed where country roads enter villages.

133. Single-track roads. These are only wide enough for one vehicle. They may have special passing places. If you see a vehicle coming towards you, or the driver behind wants to overtake, pull into a passing place on your left, or wait opposite a passing place on your right. Give way to vehicles coming uphill whenever you can. If necessary, reverse until you reach a passing place to let the other vehicle pass.

134. Do not park in passing places.

Using the road

General rules

135. Before moving off you should
- use all mirrors to check the road is clear
- look round to check the blind spots (the areas you are unable to see in the mirrors)
- signal if necessary before moving out
- look round for a final check.

Move off only when it is safe to do so.

Check the blind spot before moving off

136. Once moving you should
- keep to the left, unless road signs or markings indicate otherwise. The exceptions are when you want to overtake, turn right or pass parked vehicles or pedestrians in the road
- keep well to the left on right-hand bends. This will improve your view of the road and help avoid the risk of colliding with traffic approaching from the opposite direction
- keep both hands on the wheel, where possible. This will help you to remain in full control of the vehicle at all times
- be aware of other vehicles especially cycles and motorcycles. These are more difficult to see than larger vehicles and their riders are particularly vulnerable. Give them plenty of room, especially if you are driving a long vehicle or towing a trailer
- select a lower gear before you reach a long downhill slope. This will help to control your speed
- when towing, remember the extra length will affect overtaking and manoeuvring. The extra weight will also affect the braking and acceleration.

Mirrors

137. All mirrors should be used effectively throughout your journey. You should

- use your mirrors frequently so that you always know what is behind and to each side of you
- use them in good time before you signal or change direction or speed
- be aware that mirrors do not cover all areas and there will be blind spots. You will need to look round and check.

Remember: Mirrors – Signal – Manoeuvre

Overtaking

138. Before overtaking you should make sure

- the road is sufficiently clear ahead
- the vehicle behind is not beginning to overtake you
- there is a suitable gap in front of the vehicle you plan to overtake.

139. Overtake only when it is safe to do so. You should

- not get too close to the vehicle you intend to overtake
- use your mirrors, signal when it is safe to do so, take a quick sideways glance into the blind spot area and then start to move out
- not assume that you can simply follow a vehicle ahead which is overtaking; there may only be enough room for one vehicle
- move quickly past the vehicle you are overtaking, once you have started to overtake. Allow plenty of room. Move back to the left as soon as you can but do not cut in
- take extra care at night and in poor visibility when it is harder to judge speed and distance
- give way to oncoming vehicles before passing parked vehicles or other obstructions on your side of the road
- only overtake on the left if the vehicle in front is signalling to turn right, and there is room to do so
- stay in your lane if traffic is moving slowly in queues. If the queue on your right is moving more slowly than you are, you may pass on the left
- give motorcyclists, cyclists and horse riders at least as much room as you would a car when overtaking (see Rules 188, 189 and 191).

Remember: Mirrors – Signal – Manoeuvre

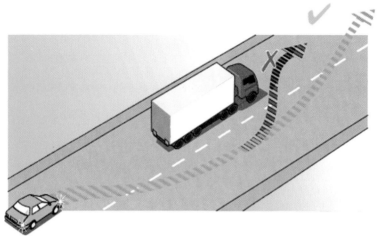

Do not cut in too quickly

140. Large vehicles. Overtaking these is more difficult.
You should
- drop back to increase your ability to see ahead. Getting too close to large vehicles will obscure your view of the road ahead and there may be another slow moving vehicle in front
- make sure that you have enough room to complete your overtaking manoeuvre before committing yourself. It takes longer to pass a large vehicle. If in doubt do not overtake
- not assume you can follow a vehicle ahead which is overtaking a long vehicle. If a problem develops, they may abort overtaking and pull back in.

141. You **MUST NOT** overtake
- if you would have to cross or straddle double white lines with a solid line nearest to you (but see Rule 108)
- if you would have to enter an area designed to divide traffic, if it is surrounded by a solid white line
- the nearest vehicle to a pedestrian crossing, especially when it has stopped to let pedestrians cross
- if you would have to enter a lane reserved for buses, trams or cycles during its hours of operation
- after a 'No Overtaking' sign and until you pass a sign cancelling the restriction.

Laws RTA 1988 sect 36, TSRGD reg 10, ZPPPCR reg 24

142. DO NOT overtake if there is any doubt, or where you cannot see far enough ahead to be sure it is safe. For example, when you are approaching
- a corner or bend
- a hump bridge
- the brow of a hill.

143. DO NOT overtake where you might come into conflict with other road users. For example
- approaching or at a road junction on either side of the road
- where the road narrows
- when approaching a school crossing patrol
- between the kerb and a bus or tram when it is at a stop
- where traffic is queuing at junctions or road works
- when you would force another vehicle to swerve or slow down
- at a level crossing
- when a vehicle is indicating right, even if you believe the signal should have been cancelled. Do not take a risk; wait for the signal to be cancelled.

144. Being overtaken. If a driver is trying to overtake you, maintain a steady course and speed, slowing down if necessary to let the vehicle pass. Never obstruct drivers who wish to pass. Speeding up or driving unpredictably while someone is overtaking you is dangerous. Drop back to maintain a two-second gap if someone overtakes and pulls into the gap in front of you.

145. Do not hold up a long queue of traffic, especially if you are driving a large or slow moving vehicle. Check your mirrors frequently, and if necessary, pull in where it is safe and let traffic pass.

Road junctions
146. Take extra care at junctions. You should
- watch out for cyclists, motorcyclists and pedestrians as they are not always easy to see
- watch out for pedestrians crossing a road into which you are turning. If they have started to cross they have priority, so give way
- watch out for long vehicles which may be turning at a junction ahead; they may have to use the whole width of the road to make the turn (see Rule 196)
- not assume, when waiting at a junction, that a vehicle coming from the right and signalling left will actually turn. Wait and make sure
- not cross or join a road until there is a gap large enough for you to do so safely.

147. You **MUST** stop behind the line at a junction with a 'Stop' sign and a solid white line across the road. Wait for a safe gap in the traffic before you move off.
Laws RTA 1988 sect 36 & TSRGD regs 10 & 16

148. The approach to a junction may have a 'Give Way' sign or a triangle marked on the road. You **MUST** give way to traffic on the main road when emerging from a junction with broken white lines across the road.
Laws RTA 1988 sect 36 & TSRGD regs 10 & 25

149. Dual carriageways. When crossing or turning right, first assess whether the central reservation is deep enough to protect the full length of your vehicle.
- If it is, then you should treat each half of the carriageway as a separate road. Wait in the central reservation until there is a safe gap in the traffic on the second half of the road.
- If the central reservation is too shallow for the length of your vehicle, wait until you can cross both carriageways in one go.

Assess your vehicle's length and do not obstruct traffic

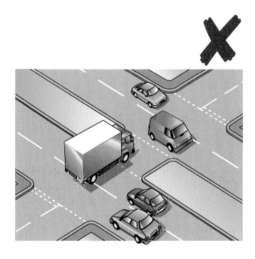

150. Box junctions. These have criss-cross yellow lines painted on the road (see Road markings). You **MUST NOT** enter the box until your exit road or lane is clear. However, you may enter the box and wait when you want to turn right, and are only stopped from doing so by oncoming traffic, or by other vehicles waiting to turn right.
Law TSRGD reg 10(1)

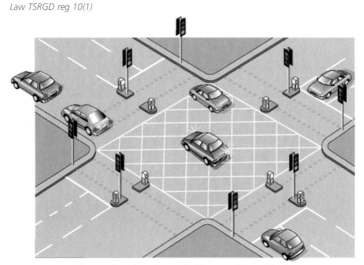

Enter a box junction only if your exit road is clear

Junctions controlled by traffic lights

151. You **MUST** stop behind the white 'Stop' line across your side of the road unless the light is green. If the amber light appears you may go on only if you have already crossed the stop line or are so close to it that to stop might cause an accident.
Laws RTA 1988 sect 36 & TSRGD regs 10 & 33

152. You **MUST NOT** move forward over the white line when the red light is showing. Only go forward when the traffic lights are green if there is room for you to clear the junction safely or you are taking up a position to turn right. If the traffic lights are not working, proceed with caution.
Laws RTA 1988 sect 36 & TSRGD regs 10 & 33

153. Green filter arrow. This indicates a filter lane only. Do not enter that lane unless you want to go in the direction of the arrow. You may proceed in the direction of the green arrow when it, or the full green light shows. Give other traffic, especially cyclists, time and room to move into the correct lane.

154. Advanced stop lines. Some junctions have advanced stop lines or bus advance areas to allow cycles and buses to be positioned ahead of other traffic. Motorists **MUST** wait behind the first white line reached, and not encroach on the marked area. Allow cyclists and buses time and space to move off when the green signal shows.

Laws RTA 1988 sect 36 & TSRGD regs 10 & 33

Do not encroach on the area marked for cyclists

Turning right
155. Well before you turn right you should
- use your mirrors to make sure you know the position and movement of traffic behind you
- give a right-turn signal
- take up a position just left of the middle of the road or in the space marked for traffic turning right
- leave room for other vehicles to pass on the left, if possible.

Position your vehicle correctly to avoid obstructing traffic

156. Wait until there is a safe gap between you and any oncoming vehicle. Watch out for cyclists, motorcyclists and pedestrians. Check your mirrors and blind spot again to make sure you are not being overtaken, then make the turn. Do not cut the corner. Take great care when turning into a main road; you will need to watch for traffic in both directions and wait for a safe gap.
Remember: Mirrors – Signal – Manoeuvre

157. When turning at a cross roads where an oncoming vehicle is also turning right, there is a choice of two methods
* turn right side to right side; keep the other vehicle on your right and turn behind it. This is generally the safest method as you have a clear view of any approaching traffic when completing your turn
* left side to left side, turning in front of each other. This can block your view of oncoming vehicles, so take extra care.

Road layout, markings or how the other vehicle is positioned can determine which course should be taken.

Turning right side to right side

Turning left side to left side

Turning left
158. Use your mirrors and give a left-turn signal well before you turn left. Do not overtake just before you turn left and watch out for traffic coming up on your left before you make the turn, especially if driving a large vehicle. Cyclists and motorcyclists in particular may be hidden from your view.

Do not cut in on cyclists

159. When turning
- keep as close to the left as is safe and practical
- give way to any vehicles using a bus lane, cycle lane or tramway from either direction.

Roundabouts

160. On approaching a roundabout take notice and act on all the information available to you, including traffic signs, traffic lights and lane markings which direct you into the correct lane. You should
- use **Mirrors – Signal – Manoeuvre** at all stages
- decide as early as possible which exit you need to take
- give an appropriate signal (see Rule 162). Time your signals so as not to confuse other road users
- get into the correct lane
- adjust your speed and position to fit in with traffic conditions
- be aware of the speed and position of all the traffic around you.

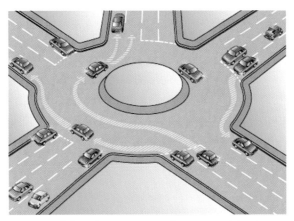

Follow the correct procedure at roundabouts

161. When reaching the roundabout you should
- give priority to traffic approaching from your right, unless directed otherwise by signs, road markings or traffic lights
- check whether road markings allow you to enter the roundabout without giving way. If so, proceed, but still look to the right before joining
- watch out for vehicles already on the roundabout; be aware they may not be signalling correctly or at all
- look forward before moving off to make sure traffic in front has moved off.

162. Signals and position, unless signs or markings indicate otherwise.

When taking the first exit
- signal left and approach in the left-hand lane
- keep to the left on the roundabout and continue signalling left to leave.

When taking any intermediate exit
- select the appropriate lane on approach to and on the roundabout, signaling where necessary
- stay in this lane until you need to alter course to exit the roundabout
- signal left after you have passed the exit before the one you want.

When taking the last exit or going full circle
- signal right and approach in the right-hand lane
- keep to the right on the roundabout until you need to change lanes to exit the roundabout
- signal left after you have passed the exit before the one you want.

When there are more than three lanes at the entrance to a roundabout, use the most appropriate lane on approach and through it.

163. In all cases watch out for and give plenty of room to
- pedestrians who may be crossing the approach and exit roads
- traffic crossing in front of you on the roundabout, especially vehicles intending to leave by the next exit
- traffic which may be straddling lanes or positioned incorrectly
- motorcyclists
- cyclists and horse riders who may stay in the left-hand lane and signal right if they intend to continue round the roundabout
- long vehicles (including those towing trailers) which might have to take a different course approaching or on the roundabout because of their length. Watch out for their signals.

164. Mini-roundabouts. Approach these in the same way as normal roundabouts. All vehicles **MUST** pass round the central markings except large vehicles which are physically incapable of doing so. Remember, there is less space to manoeuvre and less time to signal. Beware of vehicles making U-turns.

Laws RTA 1988 sect 36 & TSRGD 10(1)

165. At double mini-roundabouts treat each roundabout separately and give way to traffic from the right.

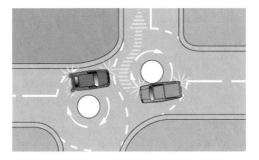

Treat each roundabout separately

166. Multiple roundabouts. At some complex junctions, there may be a series of mini-roundabouts at the intersections. Treat each mini-roundabout separately and follow the normal rules.

Pedestrian crossings

167. You **MUST NOT** park on a crossing or in the area covered by the zig-zag lines. You **MUST NOT** overtake the moving vehicle nearest the crossing or the vehicle nearest the crossing which has stopped to give way to pedestrians.

Laws ZPPPCRGD regs 18, 20 & 24 & RTRA sect 25(5)

168. In queuing traffic, you should keep the crossing clear.

Keep the crossing clear

169. You should take extra care where the view of either side of the crossing is blocked by queuing traffic or incorrectly parked vehicles. Pedestrians may be crossing between stationary vehicles.

170. Allow pedestrians plenty of time to cross and do not harass them by revving your engine or edging forward.

171. Zebra crossings. As you approach a zebra crossing
- look out for people waiting to cross and be ready to slow down or stop to let them cross
- you **MUST** give way when someone has moved onto a crossing
- allow more time for stopping on wet or icy roads
- do not wave people across; this could be dangerous if another vehicle is approaching
- be aware of pedestrians approaching from the side of the crossing.

Law ZPPPCR reg 25

Signal-controlled crossings

172. Pelican crossings. These are signal-controlled crossings where flashing amber follows the red 'Stop' light. You **MUST** stop when the red light shows. When the amber light is flashing, you **MUST** give way to any pedestrians on the crossing. If the amber light is flashing and there are no pedestrians on the crossing, you may proceed with caution.

Laws ZPPPCRGD regs 23 & 26 & RTRA sect 25(5)

Allow pedestrians to cross when the amber light is flashing

173. Pelican crossings which go straight across the road are one crossing, even when there is a central island. You **MUST** wait for pedestrians who are crossing from the other side of the island.

Law ZPPPCRGD reg 26 & RTRA sect 25(5)

174. Give way to pedestrians who are still crossing after the signal for vehicles has changed to green.

175. Toucan and puffin crossings. These are similar to pelican crossings, but there is no flashing amber phase.

Reversing

176. Choose an appropriate place to manoeuvre. If you need to turn your car around, wait until you find a safe place. Try not to reverse or turn round in a busy road; find a quiet side road or drive round a block of side streets.

177. Do not reverse from a side road into a main road. When using a driveway, reverse in and drive out if you can.

178. Look carefully before you start reversing. You should
- use all your mirrors
- check the 'blind spot' behind you (the part of the road you cannot see easily in the mirrors)
- check there are no pedestrians, particularly children, cyclists, or obstructions in the road behind you
- look mainly through the rear window
- check all around just before you start to turn and be aware that the front of your vehicle will swing out as you turn
- get someone to guide you if you cannot see clearly.

Check all round when reversing

179. You **MUST NOT** reverse your vehicle further than necessary.
Law CUR reg 106

Road users requiring extra care

180. The most vulnerable road users are pedestrians, cyclists, motorcyclists and horse riders. It is particularly important to be aware of children, elderly and disabled people, and learner and inexperienced drivers and riders.

Pedestrians
181. In urban areas there is a risk of pedestrians, especially children, stepping unexpectedly into the road. You should drive with the safety of children in mind at a speed suitable for the conditions.

182. Drive carefully and slowly when
- in crowded shopping streets or residential areas
- driving past bus and tram stops; pedestrians may emerge suddenly into the road
- passing parked vehicles, especially ice cream vans; children are more interested in ice cream than traffic and may run into the road unexpectedly
- needing to cross a pavement; for example, to reach a driveway. Give way to pedestrians on the pavement.
- reversing into a side road; look all around the vehicle and give way to any pedestrians who may be crossing the road
- turning at road junctions; give way to pedestrians who are already crossing the road into which you are turning
- the pavement is closed due to street repairs and pedestrians are directed to use the road.

Watch out for children in busy areas

183. Particularly vulnerable pedestrians. These include
- children and elderly pedestrians who may not be able to judge your speed and could step into the road in front of you. At 40 mph your vehicle will probably kill any pedestrians it hits. At 20 mph there is only a 1 in 20 chance of the pedestrian being killed. So kill your speed

- elderly pedestrians who may need more time to cross the road. Be patient and allow them to cross in their own time. Do not hurry them by revving your engine or edging forward
- blind and partially sighted people who may be carrying a white cane (white with a red band for deaf and blind people) or using a guide dog
- people with disabilities. Those with hearing problems may not be aware of your vehicle approaching. Those with walking difficulties require more time.

184. Near schools. Drive slowly and be particularly aware of young cyclists and pedestrians. In some places, there may be a flashing amber signal below the 'School' warning sign which tells you that there may be children crossing the road ahead. Drive very slowly until you are clear of the area.

185. Drive carefully when passing a stationary bus showing a 'School Bus' sign (see Vehicle markings) as children may be getting on or off.

186. You **MUST** stop when a school crossing patrol shows a 'Stop' for children sign (see Traffic signs).
Law RTRA sect 28

Motorcyclists and cyclists

187. It is often difficult to see motorcyclists and cyclists especially when they are coming up from behind, coming out of junctions and at roundabouts. Always look out for them when you are emerging from a junction.

Look out for motorcyclists at junctions

188. When passing motorcyclists and cyclists, give them plenty of room (see Rule 139). If they look over their shoulder whilst you are following them it could mean that they may soon attempt to turn right. Give them time and space to do so.

189. Motorcyclists and cyclists may suddenly need to avoid uneven road surfaces and obstacles such as draincovers or oily, wet or icy patches on the road. Give them plenty of room.

Other road users

190. Animals. When passing animals, drive slowly. Give them plenty of room and be ready to stop. Do not scare animals by sounding your horn or revving your engine. Look out for animals being led or ridden on the road and take extra care and keep your speed down at left-hand bends and on narrow country roads. If a road is blocked by a herd of animals, stop and switch off your engine until they have left the road. Watch out for animals on unfenced roads.

191. Horse riders. Be particularly careful of horses and riders, especially when overtaking. Always pass wide and slow. Horse riders are often children, so take extra care and remember riders may ride in double file when escorting a young or inexperienced horse rider. Look out for horse riders' signals and heed a request to slow down or stop. Treat all horses as a potential hazard and take great care.

192. Elderly drivers. Their reactions may be slower than other drivers. Make allowance for this.

193. Learners and inexperienced drivers. They may not be so skilful at reacting to events. Be particularly patient with learner drivers and young drivers. Drivers who have recently passed their test may display a 'new driver' plate or sticker.

Other vehicles

194. Emergency vehicles. You should look and listen for ambulances, fire engines, police or other emergency vehicles using flashing blue, red or green lights, headlights or sirens. When one approaches do not panic. Consider the route of the emergency vehicle and take appropriate action to let it pass. If necessary, pull to the side of the road and stop, but do not endanger other road users.

195. Powered vehicles used by disabled people. These small vehicles travel at a maximum speed of 8 mph. On a dual carriageway they **MUST** have a flashing amber light, but on other roads you may not have that advance warning.

Law RVLR reg 17(1)

196. Large vehicles. These may need extra road space to turn or to deal with a hazard that you are not able to see. If you are following a large vehicle, such as a bus or articulated lorry, be prepared to stop and wait if it needs room or time to turn.

Long vehicles need extra room

197. Large vehicles can block your view. Your ability to see and to plan ahead will be improved if you pull back to increase your separation distance.

198. Buses, coaches and trams. Give priority to these vehicles when you can do so safely, especially when they signal to pull away from stops. Look out for people getting off a bus or tram and crossing the road.

199. Electric vehicles. Be careful of electric vehicles such as milk floats and trams. Trams move quickly but silently and cannot steer to avoid you.

200. Vehicles with flashing amber lights. These warn of a slow-moving vehicle (such as a road gritter or recovery vehicle) or a vehicle which has broken down, so approach with caution.

Driving in adverse weather conditions

201. You **MUST** use headlights when visibility is seriously reduced, generally when you cannot see for more than 100 metres (328 feet). You may also use front or rear fog lights but you **MUST** switch them off when visibility improves (see Rule 211).

Law RVLR regs 25 & 27

Wet weather

202. In wet weather, stopping distances will be at least double those required for stopping on dry roads (see Rule 105 and Typical Stopping Distances diagram). This is because your tyres have less grip on the road. In wet weather

- you should keep well back from the vehicle in front. This will increase your ability to see and plan ahead
- if the steering becomes unresponsive, it probably means that water is preventing the tyres from gripping the road.
  Ease off the accelerator and slow down gradually
- the rain and spray from vehicles may make it difficult to see and be seen.

Icy and snowy weather

203. In winter check the local weather forecast for warnings of icy or snowy weather. **DO NOT** drive in these conditions unless your journey is essential. If it is, take great care. Carry a spade, warm clothing, a warm drink and emergency food in case your vehicle breaks down.

204. Before you set off

- you **MUST** be able to see, so clear all snow and ice from all your windows
- you **MUST** ensure that lights and number plates are clean
- make sure the mirrors are clear and the windows are de-misted thoroughly.

Laws CUR reg 30 & RVLR reg 23

Make sure your windscreen is completely clear

205. When driving in icy or snowy weather

- drive with care, even if the roads have been gritted
- keep well back from the vehicle in front as stopping distances can be ten times greater than on dry roads
- take care when overtaking gritting vehicles, particularly if you are riding a motorcycle
- watch out for snowploughs which may throw out snow on either side. Do not overtake them unless the lane you intend to use has been cleared
- be prepared for the road conditions changing over relatively short distances.

206. Drive extremely carefully when the roads are icy. Avoid sudden actions as these could cause a skid. You should

- drive at a slow speed in as high a gear as possible; accelerate and brake very gently
- drive particularly slowly on bends where skids are more likely. Brake progressively on the straight before you reach a bend. Having slowed down, steer smoothly round the bend, avoiding sudden actions
- check your grip on the road surface when there is snow or ice by choosing a safe place to brake gently. If the steering feels unresponsive this may indicate ice and your vehicle losing its grip on the road. When travelling on ice, tyres make virtually no noise.

Windy weather

207. High sided vehicles are most affected by windy weather, but strong gusts can also blow a car, cyclist or motorcyclist off course. This can happen at open stretches of road exposed to strong cross winds, or when passing bridges or gaps in hedges.

208. In very windy weather your vehicle may be affected by turbulence created by large vehicles. Motorcyclists are particularly affected, so keep well back from them when they are overtaking a high-sided vehicle.

Fog

209. Before entering fog check your mirrors then slow down. If the word 'Fog' is shown on a roadside signal but the road is clear, be prepared for a bank of fog or drifting patchy fog ahead. Even if it seems to be clearing, you can suddenly find yourself in thick fog.

210. When driving in fog you should

- use your lights as required in Rule 201
- keep a safe distance behind the vehicle in front. Rear lights can give a false sense of security

- be able to pull up within the distance you can see clearly. This is particularly important on motorways and dual carriageways, as vehicles are travelling faster
- use your windscreen wipers and demisters
- beware of other drivers not using headlights
- not accelerate to get away from a vehicle which is too close behind you
- check your mirrors before you slow down. Then use your brakes so that your brake lights warn drivers behind you that you are slowing down
- stop in the correct position at a junction with limited visibility and listen for traffic. When you are sure it is safe to emerge, do so positively and do not hesitate in a position that puts you directly in the path of approaching vehicles.

211. You **MUST NOT** use front or rear fog lights unless visibility is seriously reduced (see Rule 201) as they dazzle other road users and can obscure your brake lights. You **MUST** switch them off when visibility improves.
Law RVLR regs 25 & 27

Hot weather
212. Keep your vehicle well ventilated to avoid drowsiness. Be aware that the road surface may become soft or if it rains after a dry spell it may become slippery. These conditions could affect your steering and braking.

Waiting and parking

213. You **MUST NOT** wait or park where there are restrictions shown by
- yellow lines along the edge of the carriageway (see Road markings)
- school entrance markings on the carriageway.

The periods when restrictions apply are shown on upright signs, usually at intervals along the road, parallel to the kerb.
Law RTRA sects 5&8

Parking
214. Use off-street parking areas, or bays marked out with white lines on the road as parking places, wherever possible. If you have to stop on the road side

- stop as close as you can to the side
- do not stop too close to a vehicle displaying an Orange Badge, remember, they may need more room to get in or out
- you **MUST** switch off the engine, headlights and fog lights
- you **MUST** apply the handbrake before leaving the vehicle
- you **MUST** ensure you do not hit anyone when you open your door
- it is safer for your passengers (especially children) to get out of the vehicle on the side next to the kerb
- lock your vehicle.

Laws CUR reg 98,105 & 107, RVLR reg 27 & RTA 1988 sect 42

Check before opening your door

215. You **MUST NOT** stop or park on
- the carriageway or the hard shoulder of a motorway except in an emergency (see Rule 244)
- a pedestrian crossing, including the area marked by the zig-zag lines (see Rule 167)
- a Clearway (see Traffic Signs)
- a Bus Stop Clearway within its hours of operation
- an Urban Clearway within its hours of operation, except to pick up or set down passengers (see Traffic Signs)
- a road marked with double white lines, except to pick up or set down passengers
- a bus, tram or cycle lane during its period of operation
- a cycle track
- red lines, in the case of specially designated 'red routes', unless otherwise indicated by signs.

Laws MT(E&W)R regs 7 & 9, MT(S)R regs 6 & 8, ZPPPCRGD regs 18 & 20, RTRA sects 5 & 8, TSRGD regs 10 & 26, RTA 1988 sects 36 & 21(1)

216. You **MUST NOT** park in parking spaces reserved for specific users, such as Orange Badge holders or residents, unless entitled to do so.
Law RTRA sects 5 & 8

217. DO NOT park your vehicle or trailer on the road where it would endanger, inconvenience or obstruct pedestrians or other road users. For example, do not stop
- near a school entrance
- anywhere you would prevent access for Emergency Services
- at or near a bus stop or taxi rank
- on the approach to a level crossing
- opposite or within 10 metres (32 feet) of a junction, except in an authorised parking space
- near the brow of a hill or hump bridge
- opposite a traffic island or (if this would cause an obstruction) another parked vehicle
- where you would force other traffic to enter a tram lane
- where the kerb has been lowered to help wheelchair users
- in front of an entrance to a property
- on a bend.

218. DO NOT park partially or wholly on the pavement unless signs permit it. Parking on the pavement can obstruct and seriously inconvenience pedestrians, people in wheelchairs, the visually impaired and people with prams or pushchairs.

219. Controlled Parking Zones. The zone entry signs indicate the times when the waiting restrictions within the zone are in force. Parking may be allowed in some places at other times. Otherwise parking will be within separately signed and marked bays.

220. Goods vehicles. Vehicles with a maximum laden weight of over 7.5 tonnes (including any trailer) **MUST NOT** be parked on a verge, pavement or any land situated between carriageways, without police permission. The only exception is when parking is essential for loading and unloading, in which case the vehicle **MUST NOT** be left unattended.
Law RTA 1988 sect 19

221. Loading and unloading. Do not load or unload where there are yellow markings on the kerb and upright signs advise restrictions are in place (see Road markings). This may be permitted where parking is otherwise restricted. On red routes, specially marked and signed bays indicate where and when loading and unloading is permitted.
Law RTRA sects 5 & 8

Parking at night

222. You **MUST NOT** park on a road at night facing against the direction of the traffic flow unless in a recognised parking space.
Laws CUR reg 101 & RVLR reg 24

223. All vehicles **MUST** display parking lights when parked on a road or a lay-by on a road with a speed limit greater than 30 mph.
Law RVLR reg 24

224. Cars, goods vehicles not exceeding 1525kg unladen, invalid carriages and motorcycles may be parked without lights on a road (or lay-by) with a speed limit of 30 mph or less if they are
- at least 10 metres (32 feet) away from any junction, close to the kerb and facing in the direction of the traffic flow
- in a recognised parking place or lay-by.

Other vehicles and trailers, and all vehicles with projecting loads, **MUST NOT** be left on a road at night without lights.
Law RVLR reg 24

225. Parking in fog. It is especially dangerous to park on the road in fog. If it is unavoidable, leave your parking lights or sidelights on.

226. Parking on hills. If you park on a hill you should
- park close to the kerb and apply the handbrake firmly
- select a forward gear and turn your steering wheel away from the kerb when facing uphill
- select reverse gear and turn your steering wheel towards the kerb when facing downhill
- use 'park' if your car has an automatic gearbox.

Motorways

Many other Rules apply to motorway driving, either wholly or in part: Rules 43, 67–105, 109–113, 118, 122, 126–128, 135, 137, 194, 196, 200, 201–212, 248–252, 254–264.

General

227. Prohibited vehicles. Motorways **MUST NOT** be used by pedestrians, holders of provisional car or motorcycle driving licences unless exempt, riders of motorcycles under 50cc, cyclists and horse riders. Certain slow-moving vehicles and those carrying oversized loads (except by special permission), agricultural vehicles and most invalid carriages are also prohibited.

Laws HA 1980 sects 16, 17 & sch 4, MT(E&W)R reg 4, MT(E&W)(A)R, R(S)A sects 7 ,8 & sch 3 & MT(S)R reg 10

228. Traffic on motorways usually travels faster than on other roads, so you have less time to react. It is especially important to use your mirrors earlier and look much further ahead than you would on other roads.

Motorway signals

229. Motorway signals (see Light signals controlling traffic) are used to warn you of a danger ahead. For example, there may be an accident, fog, or a spillage, which you may not immediately be able to see.

230. Signals situated on the central reservation apply to all lanes. On very busy stretches, signals may be overhead with a separate signal for each lane.

231. Amber flashing lights. These warn of a hazard ahead. The signal may show a temporary maximum speed limit, lanes that are closed or a message such as 'Fog'. Adjust your speed and look out for the danger until you pass a signal which is not flashing or one that gives the 'All clear' sign and you are sure it is safe to increase your speed.

232. Red flashing lights. If red lights on the overhead signals flash above your lane (there may also be a red 'X') you **MUST NOT** go beyond the signal in that lane. If red lights flash on a signal in the central reservation or at the side of the road, you **MUST NOT** go beyond the signal in any lane.

Laws RTA 1988 sect 36 & TSRGD reg 10

Driving on the motorway

Joining the motorway

233. When you join the motorway you will normally approach it from a road on the left (a slip road) or from an adjoining motorway. You should

- give priority to traffic already on the motorway
- check the traffic on the motorway and adjust your speed to fit safely into the traffic flow in the left-hand lane
- not cross solid white lines that separate lanes
- stay on the slip road if it continues as an extra lane on the motorway
- remain in the left-hand lane long enough to adjust to the speed of traffic before considering overtaking.

On the motorway

234. When you can see well ahead and the road conditions are good, you should

- drive at a steady cruising speed which you and your vehicle can handle safely and is within the speed limit (see Rule 103 and Speed limits diagram)
- keep a safe distance from the vehicle in front and increase the gap on wet or icy roads, or in fog (see Rules 105 & 210).

235. You **MUST NOT** exceed 70 mph, or the maximum speed limit permitted for your vehicle (see Rule 103 and Speed limits diagram). If a lower speed limit is in force, either permanently or temporarily, at roadworks for example, you **MUST NOT** exceed the lower limit. On some motorways, mandatory motorway signals (which display the speed within a red ring) are used to vary the maximum speed limit to improve traffic flow. You **MUST NOT** exceed this speed limit.
Law RTRA sects 17, 86, 89 & sch 6

236. The monotony of driving on a motorway can make you feel sleepy. To minimise the risk, follow the advice in Rule 80.

237. You **MUST NOT** reverse, cross the central reservation, or drive against the traffic flow. If you have missed your exit, or have taken the wrong route, carry on to the next exit.
Laws MT(E&W)R regs 6 & 7 & MT(S)R regs 4 & 7

Lane discipline

238. You should drive in the left-hand lane if the road ahead is clear. If you are overtaking a number of slower moving vehicles it may be safer to remain in the centre or outer lanes until the manoeuvre is completed rather than continually changing lanes. Return to the left-hand lane once you have overtaken all the vehicles or if you are delaying traffic

behind you. Slow moving or speed restricted vehicles should always remain in the left-hand lane of the carriageway unless overtaking. You **MUST NOT** drive on the hard shoulder except in an emergency or if directed to do so by signs.
Laws MT(E&W)R reg 5 & MT(S)R reg 4

239. The right-hand lane of a motorway with three or more lanes **MUST NOT** be used (except in prescribed circumstances) if you are driving
- any vehicle drawing a trailer
- a goods vehicle with a maximum laden weight over 7.5 tonnes
- a passenger vehicle with a maximum laden weight exceeding 7.5 tonnes constructed or adapted to carry more than eight seated passengers in addition to the driver.

Laws MT(E&W)R reg 12 & MT(S)R reg 11A

240. Approaching a junction. Look well ahead for signals or signs. Direction signs may be placed over the road. If you need to change lanes, do so in good time. At some junctions a lane may lead directly off the motorway. Only get in that lane if you wish to go in the direction indicated on the overhead signs.

Overtaking

241. Do not overtake unless you are sure it is safe to do so. Overtake only on the right. You should
- check your mirrors
- take time to judge the speeds correctly
- make sure that the lane you will be joining is sufficiently clear ahead and behind
- take a quick sideways glance into the blind spot area to verify the position of a vehicle that may have disappeared from your view in the mirror
- remember that traffic may be coming up behind you very quickly. Check your mirrors carefully. When it is safe to do so, signal in plenty of time, then move out
- ensure you do not cut in on the vehicle you have overtaken
- be especially careful at night and in poor visibility when it is harder to judge speed and distance.

242. Do not overtake on the left or move to a lane on your left to overtake. In congested conditions, where adjacent lanes of traffic are moving at similar speeds, traffic in left-hand lanes may sometimes be moving faster than traffic to the right. In these conditions you may keep up with the traffic in your lane even if this means passing traffic in the lane to your right. Do not weave in and out of lanes to overtake.

243. You **MUST NOT** use the hard shoulder for overtaking.
Laws MT(E&W)R regs 5 & 9 & MT(S)R reg 4

Stopping

244. You **MUST NOT** stop on the carriageway, hard shoulder, slip road, central reservation or verge except in an emergency, or when told to do so by the police, an emergency sign or by flashing red light signals.
Laws MT(E&W)R regs 7(1), 9 & 10 & MT(S)R regs 6(1), 8 & 9

245. You **MUST NOT** pick up or set down anyone, or walk on a motorway, except in an emergency.
Laws RTRA sect 17 & MT(E&W)R reg 15

Leaving the motorway

246. Unless signs indicate that a lane leads directly off the motorway, you will normally leave the motorway by a slip road on your left. You should

- watch for the signs letting you know you are getting near your exit
- move into the left-hand lane well before reaching your exit
- signal left in good time and reduce your speed on the slip road as necessary.

247. On leaving the motorway or using a link road between motorways, your speed may be higher than you realise – 50 mph may feel like 30 mph. Check your speedometer and adjust your speed accordingly. Some slip roads and link roads have sharp bends, so you will need to slow down.

Breakdowns and accidents

Breakdowns

248. If your vehicle breaks down, think first of other road users and
- get your vehicle off the road if possible
- warn other traffic by using your hazard warning lights if your vehicle is causing an obstruction
- put a warning triangle on the road at least 45 metres (147 feet) behind your broken down vehicle on the same side of the road, or use other permitted warning devices if you have them. Always take great care when placing them, but never use them on motorways
- keep your sidelights on if it is dark or visibility is poor
- do not stand (or let anybody else stand), between your vehicle and oncoming traffic
- at night or in poor visibility do not stand where you will prevent other road users seeing your lights.

Additional rules for the motorway

249. If your vehicle develops a problem, leave the motorway at the next exit or pull into a service area. If you cannot do so, you should
- pull on to the hard shoulder and stop as far to the left as possible, with your wheels turned to the left
- try to stop near an emergency telephone (situated at approximately one mile intervals along the hard shoulder)
- leave the vehicle by the left-hand door and ensure your passengers do the same. You **MUST** leave any animals in the vehicle or, in an emergency, keep them under proper control on the verge
- do not attempt even simple repairs
- ensure that passengers keep away from the carriageway and hard shoulder, and that children are kept under control
- walk to an emergency telephone on your side of the carriageway (follow the arrows on the posts at the back of the hard shoulder) - the telephone is free of charge and connects directly to the police. Use these in preference to a mobile phone (see Rule 257)
- give full details to the police; also inform them if you are a vulnerable motorist such as a woman travelling alone
- return and wait near your vehicle (well away from the carriageway and hard shoulder)
- if you feel at risk from another person, return to your vehicle by a left-hand door and lock all doors. Leave your vehicle again as soon as you feel this danger has passed.

Laws MT(E&W)R reg 14 & MT(S)R reg 12

Keep well back from the hard shoulder

250. Before you rejoin the carriageway after a breakdown, build up speed on the hard shoulder and watch for a safe gap in the traffic. Be aware that other vehicles may be stationary on the hard shoulder.

251. If you cannot get your vehicle on to the hard shoulder
- do not attempt to place any warning device on the carriageway
- switch on your hazard warning lights
- leave your vehicle only when you can safely get clear of the carriageway.

Disabled drivers
252. If you have a disability which prevents you from following the above advice you should
- stay in your vehicle
- switch on your hazard warning lights
- display a 'Help' pennant or, if you have a car or mobile telephone, contact the emergency services and be prepared to advise them of your location.

Obstructions
253. If anything falls from your vehicle (or any other vehicle) on to the road, stop and retrieve it only if it is safe to do so.

254. Motorways. On a motorway do not try to remove the obstruction yourself. Stop at the next emergency telephone and call the police.

Accidents

255. Warning signs or flashing lights. If you see or hear emergency vehicles in the distance be aware there may be an accident ahead.

256. When passing the scene of an accident do not be distracted or slow down unnecessarily (for example if an accident is on the other side of a dual carriageway). This may cause another accident or traffic congestion, but see Rule 257.

257. If you are involved in an accident or stop to give assistance
- use your hazard warning lights to warn other traffic
- ask drivers to switch off their engines and stop smoking
- arrange for the emergency services to be called immediately with full details of the accident location and any casualties (on a motorway, use the emergency telephone which allows easy location by the emergency services. If you use a mobile phone, first make sure you have identified your location from the marker posts on the side of the hard shoulder)
- move uninjured people away from the vehicles to safety; on a motorway this should, if possible, be well away from the traffic, the hard shoulder and the central reservation
- do not move injured people from their vehicles unless they are in immediate danger from fire or explosion
- do not remove a motorcyclist's helmet unless it is essential to do so
- be prepared to give first aid as shown in Annexe 7: First Aid on the road
- stay at the scene until emergency services arrive.
If you are involved in any other medical emergency on the motorway you should contact the emergency services in the same way.

Accidents involving dangerous goods

258. Vehicles carrying dangerous goods in packages will be marked with plain orange reflective plates. Road tankers and vehicles carrying tank containers of dangerous goods will have hazard warning plates (see Vehicle markings).

259. If an accident involves a vehicle containing dangerous goods, follow the advice in Rule 257 and, in particular
- switch off engines and **DO NOT SMOKE**
- keep well away from the vehicle and do not be tempted to try to rescue casualties as you yourself could become one
- call the emergency services and give as much information as possible about the labels and markings on the vehicle.
  DO NOT use a mobile phone close to a vehicle carrying flammable loads.

Documentation

260. If you are involved in an accident which causes damage or injury to any other person, vehicle, animal or property, you **MUST**
- stop
- give your own and the vehicle owner's name and address, and the registration number of the vehicle, to anyone having reasonable grounds for requiring them
- if you do not give your name and address at the time of the accident, report the accident to the police as soon as reasonably practicable, and in any case within 24 hours.

Law RTA 1988 sect 170

261. If another person is injured and you do not produce your insurance certificate at the time of the accident to a police officer or to anyone having reasonable grounds to request it, you **MUST**
- report the accident to the police as soon as possible and in any case within 24 hours
- produce your insurance certificate for the police within seven days.

Law RTA 1988 sect 170

Road works

262. When the 'Road Works Ahead' sign is displayed, you will need to be more watchful and look for additional signs providing more specific instructions.
- You **MUST NOT** exceed any temporary maximum speed limit.
- Use your mirrors and get into the correct lane for your vehicle in good time and as signs direct.
- Do not switch lanes to overtake queuing traffic.
- Do not drive through an area marked off by traffic cones.
- Watch out for traffic entering or leaving the works area, but do not be distracted by what is going on there.
- Bear in mind that the road ahead may be obstructed by the works or by slow moving or stationary traffic.

Law RTRA sect 16

Additional rules for high speed roads
263. Take special care on motorways and other high speed dual carriageways.
- One or more lanes may be closed to traffic and a lower speed limit may apply.
- Works vehicles that are slow moving or stationary with a large 'Keep Left' or 'Keep Right' sign on the back are sometimes used to close lanes for repairs.
- Check mirrors, slow down and change lanes if necessary.
- Keep a safe distance from the vehicle in front (see Rule 105).

264. Contraflow systems mean that you may be travelling in a narrower lane than normal and with no permanent barrier between you and oncoming traffic. The hard shoulder may be used for traffic, but be aware that there may be broken down vehicles ahead of you. Keep a good distance from the vehicle ahead and observe any temporary speed limits.

Railway level crossings

265. A level crossing is where a road crosses a railway line. Approach and cross it with care. Never drive on to a crossing until the road is clear on the other side and do not get too close to the car in front. Never stop or park on, or near, a crossing.

Controlled crossings

266. Most crossings have traffic light signals with a steady amber light, twin flashing red stop lights (see Light signals controlling traffic and Traffic signs) and an audible alarm for pedestrians. They may have full, half or no barriers.

- You **MUST** always obey the flashing red stop lights.
- You **MUST** stop behind the white line across the road.
- Keep going if you have already crossed the white line when the amber light comes on.
- You **MUST** wait if a train goes by and the red lights continue to flash. This means another train will be passing soon.
- Only cross when the lights go off and barriers open.
- Never zig-zag around half-barriers, they lower automatically because a train is approaching.
- At crossings where there are no barriers, a train is approaching when the lights show.

Laws RTA 1988 sect 36 & TSRGD reg 10

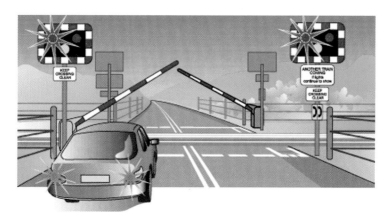

Stop when the traffic lights show

267. Railway telephones. If you are driving a large or slow-moving vehicle, or herding animals, a train could arrive before you are clear of the crossing. You **MUST** obey any sign instructing you to use the railway telephone to obtain permission to cross. You **MUST** also telephone when clear of the crossing.
Laws RTA 1988 sect 36 & TSRGD reg 10

268. Crossings without traffic lights. Vehicles should stop and wait at the barrier or gate when it begins to close and not cross until the barrier or gate opens.

User-operated gates or barriers
269. Some crossings have 'Stop' signs and small red and green lights. You **MUST NOT** cross when the red light is showing, only cross if the green light is on. If crossing with a vehicle, you should
- open the gates or barriers on both sides of the crossing
- check that the green light is still on and cross quickly
- close the gates or barriers when you are clear of the crossing.

Laws RTA 1988 sect 36 & TSRGD reg 10

270. If there are no lights, follow the procedure in Rule 269. Stop, look both ways and listen before you cross. If there is a railway telephone, always use it to contact the signal operator to make sure it is safe to cross. Inform the signal operator again when you are clear of the crossing.

Open crossings
271. These have no gates, barriers, attendant or traffic lights but will have a 'Give Way' sign. You should look both ways, listen and make sure there is no train coming before you cross.

Accidents and breakdowns
272. If your vehicle breaks down, or if you have an accident on a crossing you should
- get everyone out of the vehicle and clear of the crossing immediately
- use a railway telephone if available to tell the signal operator. Follow the instructions you are given
- move the vehicle clear of the crossing if there is time before a train arrives. If the alarm sounds, or the amber light comes on, leave the vehicle and get clear of the crossing immediately.

Tramways

273. You **MUST NOT** enter a road, lane or other route reserved for trams. Take extra care where trams run along the road. The width taken up by trams is often shown by tram lanes marked by white lines, yellow dots or by a different type of road surface. Diamond-shaped signs give instructions to tram drivers only.
Law RTRA sects 5 & 8

274. Take extra care where the track crosses from one side of the road to the other and where the road narrows and the tracks come close to the kerb. Tram drivers usually have their own traffic signals and may be permitted to move when you are not. Always give way to trams. Do not try to race or overtake them.

275. You **MUST NOT** park your vehicle where it would get in the way of trams or where it would force other drivers to do so.
Law RTRA sects 5 & 8

276. Tram stops. Where the tram stops at a platform, either in the middle or at the side of the road, you **MUST** follow the route shown by the road signs and markings. At stops without platforms you **MUST NOT** drive between a tram and the left-hand kerb when a tram has stopped to pick up passengers.
Law RTRA sects 5 & 8

277. Look out for pedestrians, especially children, running to catch a tram approaching a stop.

278. Cyclists and motorcyclists should take extra care when riding close to or crossing the tracks, especially if the rails are wet. It is safest to cross the tracks directly at right angles.

Light signals controlling traffic

Traffic Light Signals

| RED means 'Stop'. Wait behind the stop line on the carriageway | RED AND AMBER also means 'Stop'. Do not pass through or start until GREEN shows | GREEN means you may go on if the way is clear. Take special care if you intend to turn left or right and give way to pedestrians who are crossing | AMBER means 'Stop' at the stop line. You may go on only if the AMBER appears after you have crossed the stop line or are so close to it that to pull up might cause an accident | A GREEN ARROW may be provided in addition to the full green signal if movement in a certain direction is allowed before or after the full green phase. If the way is clear you may go but only in the direction shown by the arrow. You may do this whatever other lights may be showing. White light signals may be provided for trams |

Flashing Red Lights

Alternately flashing red lights mean YOU MUST STOP.

At level crossings, lifting bridges, airfields, fire stations, etc

Motorway signals

Do not proceed further in this lane

Change lane

Reduced visibilty ahead

Lane ahead closed

Temporary maximum speed limit and information message

Leave motorway at next exit

Temporary maximum speed limit

End of restriction

Lane control signals

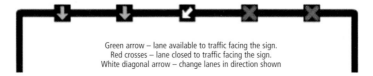

Green arrow – lane available to traffic facing the sign.
Red crosses – lane closed to traffic facing the sign.
White diagonal arrow – change lanes in direction shown

Signals to other road users

Direction indicator signals

I intend to move out to the
right or turn right

I intend to move in to the left or
turn left or stop on the left

Brake light signals

Reversing light signals

I am applying the brakes

I intend to reverse

These signals should not be used except for the purposes described.

Arm signals

For use when direction indicator signals are not used, or when necessary to reinforce direction indicator signals and stop lights. *Also for use by pedal cyclists and those in charge of horses.*

I intend to move in to
the left or turn left

I intend to move out to
the right or turn right

I intend to slow
down or stop

Signals by authorised persons

Stop

Traffic approaching
from the front

Traffic approaching from
both front and behind

Traffic approaching
from behind

To beckon traffic on

From the side

From the front

From behind*

Arm signals to persons controlling traffic

I want to go straight on

I want to turn left;
use either hand

I want to turn right

*In Wales, bilingual signs appear on emergency services vehicles and clothing

Traffic signs

Signs giving orders

Signs with red circles are mostly prohibitive. Plates below signs qualify their message.

Entry to 20 mph zone

End of 20 mph zone

School crossing patrol

Maximum speed limit

National speed limit applies

Stop and give way

Give way to traffic on major road

No vehicles except bicycles being pushed

Give priority to vehicles from opposite direction

No vehicle or combination of vehicles over length shown

No vehicles over height shown

No vehicles over width shown

No goods vehicles over maximum gross weight shown (in tonnes) except for loading and unloading

No overtaking

No motor vehicles

Manually operated temporary STOP and GO signs

No buses (over 8 passenger seats)

No towed caravans

No vehicles carrying explosives

No right turn

No left turn

No U-turns

No cycling

WEAK BRIDGE

No vehicles over maximum gross weight shown (in tonnes)

No entry for vehicular traffic

No waiting

No stopping (Clearway)

URBAN CLEARWAY
Monday to Friday

No stopping during times shown except for as long as necessary to set down or pick up passengers

Parking restricted to permit holders

No stopping during period indicated except for buses

Note: Although *The Highway Code* shows many of the signs commonly in use, a comprehensive explanation of the signing system is given in the booklet *Know Your Traffic Signs*, which is on sale at booksellers. The booklet also illustrates and explains the vast majority of signs the road user is likely to encounter. The signs illustrated in *The Highway Code* are not all drawn to the same scale. In Wales, bilingual versions of some signs are used including Welsh and English versions of place names. Some older designs of signs may still be seen on the roads.

Signs with blue circles but no red border mostly give positive instruction.

One-way traffic (note: compare circular 'Ahead only' sign)

Ahead only

Turn left ahead (right if symbol reversed)

Turn left (right if symbol reversed)

Keep left (right if symbol reversed)

Route to be used by pedal cycles only

Segregated pedal cycle and pedestrian route

Minimum speed

End of minimum speed

Mini-roundabout (roundabout circulation – give way to vehicles from the immediate right)

Vehicles may pass either side to reach same destination

Buses and cycles only

Trams only

Pedestrian crossing point over tramway

With-flow bus and cycle lane

Contra-flow bus lane

With-flow pedal cycle lane

Warning signs Mostly triangular

Distance to 'STOP' line ahead

Crossroads

Junction on bend ahead

T-junction

Staggered junction

Distance to 'Give Way' line ahead

The priority through route is indicated by the broader line.

Sharp deviation of route to left (or right if chevrons reversed)

Double bend first to left (symbol may be reversed)

Bend to right (or left if symbol reversed)

Roundabout

Uneven road

Plate below some signs

Dual carriage-way ends

Road narrows on right (left if symbol reversed)

Road narrows on both sides

Two-way traffic crosses one-way road

Two-way traffic straight ahead

Traffic signals

Traffic signals not in use

Slippery road

Steep hill downwards

Steep hill upwards

Gradients may be shown as a ratio i.e. 20% = 1:5

Warning signs – continued

School crossing patrol ahead (some signs have amber lights which flash when children are crossing)

Frail elderly people (or blind or disabled as shown) crossing road

Pedestrians in road ahead

Pedestrian crossing

Traffic queues likely ahead

Cycle route ahead

Side winds

Hump bridge

Worded warning sign

Risk of ice

Risk of grounding

Light signals ahead at level crossing, airfield or bridge

Level crossing with barrier or gate ahead

Level crossing without barrier or gate ahead

Level crossing without barrier

Trams crossing ahead

Cattle

Wild animals

Wild horses or ponies

Accompanied horses or ponies

Quayside or river bank

Opening or swing bridge ahead

Low-flying aircraft or sudden aircraft noise

Falling or fallen rocks

Available width of headroom indicated

Overhead electric cable; plate indicates maximum height of vehicles which can pass safely

Tunnel ahead

Distance over which road humps extend

Other danger; plate indicates nature of danger

Soft verges

Direction signs Mostly rectangular Signs on motorways – blue backgrounds

At a junction leading directly into a motorway (junction number may be shown on a black background)

On approaches to junctions (junction number on black background)

Route confirmatory sign after junction

Downward pointing arrows mean 'Get in lane'
The left-hand lane leads to a different destination from the other lanes

The panel with the inclined arrow indicates the destinations which can be reached by leaving the motorway at the next junction

Signs on primary routes – green backgrounds

On approaches to junctions

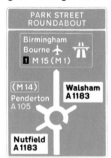

On approaches to junctions

Blue panels indicate that the motorway starts at the junction ahead.
Motorways shown in brackets can also be reached along the route indicated.
White panels indicate local or non–primary routes leading from the junction ahead.
Brown panels show the route to tourist attractions.
The name of the junction may be shown at the top of the sign.
The aircraft symbol indicates the route to an airport.
A symbol may be included to warn of a hazard or restriction along that route.

Route confirmatory sign after junction

At the junction

On approach to a junction in Wales (bilingual)

Signs on non-primary and local routes – black borders

On approaches to junctions

Green panels indicate that the primary route starts at the junction ahead. Route numbers on a blue background show the direction to a motorway. Route numbers on a green background show the direction to a primary route.

At the junction

Direction to toilets with access for the disabled

Other direction signs

Picnic site

Ancient monument in the care of English Heritage

Direction to camping and caravan site

Advisory route for lorries

Tourist attraction

Route for pedal cycles forming part of a network

Route for pedestrians

Diversion route

Recommended route for pedal cycles to place shown

Symbols showing emergency diversion route for motorway and other main road traffic

Holiday route

Direction to a car park

Information signs All rectangular

Start of motorway and point from which motorway regulations apply

Area in which cameras are used to enforce traffic regulations

Traffic has priority over oncoming vehicles

No through road for vehicles

Hospital ahead with Accident and Emergency facilities

Tourist information point

End of motorway

Parking place for solo motorcycles

Advance warning of restriction or prohibition ahead

'Countdown' markers at exit from motorway (each bar represents 100 yards to the exit). Green-backed markers may be used on primary routes and white-backed markers with black bars on other routes. At approaches to concealed level crossings white-backed markers with red bars may be used. Although these will be erected at equal distances the bars do not represent 100 yard intervals.

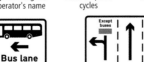
Motorway service area sign showing the operator's name

Recommended route for pedal cycles

With-flow bus lane ahead

Entrance to controlled parking zone

End of controlled parking zone

Bus lane on road at junction ahead

Appropriate traffic lanes at junction ahead

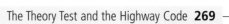

Road works signs

Road works

Loose chippings

Road works 1 mile ahead

End of road works and any temporary restrictions

Temporary hazard at road works

Temporary lane closure (the number and position of arrows and red bars may be varied according to lanes open and closed)

Lane restrictions at road works ahead

One lane crossover at contraflow road works

Signs used on the back of slow-moving or stationary vehicles warning of a lane closed ahead by a works vehicle. There are no cones on the road

Slow moving or stationary works vehicle blocking a traffic lane. Pass in the direction shown by the arrow

Mandatory speed limit ahead

Road markings Across the carriageway

Stop line at signals or police control

Stop line at 'Stop' sign

Stop line for pedestrians at a level crossing

Give way to traffic on major road

Give way to traffic from the right at a roundabout

Give way to traffic from the right at a mini-roundabout

Along the carriageway

| Edge line | Centre line See Rule 106 | Hazard warning line See Rule 106 | Double white lines See rules 107 and 108 | Diagonal hatching See Rule 109 | Lane line See Rule 110 |

Along the edge of the carriageway

Waiting restrictions

Waiting restrictions indicated by yellow lines apply to the carriageway, pavement and verge. You may stop to load and unload or while passengers board or alight unless there are also loading restrictions as described below. The times at which the restrictions apply are shown on nearby plates or on entry signs to controlled parking zones. If no days are shown on the signs, the restrictions are in force every day including Sundays and Bank Holidays. White bay markings and upright signs (see below) indicate where parking is allowed.

Red Route stopping controls

Red lines are used on some roads instead of yellow lines. In London the double and single red lines used on Red Routes indicate that stopping to park, load/unload or to board and alight from a vehicle (except for a licensed taxi or if you hold an Orange Badge) is prohibited. The red lines apply to the carriageway, pavement and verge. The times that the red line restrictions apply are shown on nearby signs, but the double red line ALWAYS means no stopping at any time. On Red Routes you may stop to park, load/unload in specially marked boxes and adjacent signs specify the times and purposes and duration allowed. A box MARKED IN RED indicates that it may only be available for the purpose specified for part of the day (eg between busy peak periods). A box MARKED IN WHITE means that it is available throughout the day.

YELLOW OR RED LINES CAN ONLY GIVE A GUIDE TO THE RESTRICTIONS AND CONTROLS IN FORCE AND SIGNS, NEARBY OR AT A ZONE ENTRY, MUST BE CONSULTED.

No waiting at any time

No waiting during times shown on sign

Waiting is limited to the times and duration shown

No stopping at any time

No stopping during times shown on sign

Parking is limited to the times and duration shown

Only loading may take place at the times shown for up to a maximum duration of 20 minutes

On the kerb or at the edge of the carriageway

Loading restrictions on roads other than Red Routes

Yellow marks on the kerb or at the edge of the carriageway indicate that loading or unloading is prohibited at the times shown on the nearby black and white plates. If no days are indicated on the signs the restrictions are in force every day including Sundays and Bank Holidays.
ALWAYS CHECK THE TIMES SHOWN ON THE PLATES.
Lengths of road reserved for vehicles loading and unloading are indicated by a white 'bay' marking with the words 'Loading Only' and a sign with the white on blue 'trolley' symbol. This sign also shows whether loading and unloading is restricted to goods vehicles and the times at which the bay can be used. If no times or days are shown it may be used at any time. Vehicles may not park here if they are not loading or unloading.

No loading or unloading at
any time

No loading or unloading at
the times shown

Loading bay

Other road markings

Keep entrance clear of stationary vehicles, even if picking up or setting down children

Warning of 'Give Way'
just ahead

Parking space
reserved for vehicles
named

See Rule 217

See rule 120

Box junction See Rule 150

Do not block that part of
the carriageway indicated

Indication of traffic lanes

Vehicle markings

Large goods vehicle rear markings

Motor vehicles over 7500 kilograms maximum gross weight and trailers over 3500 kilograms maximum gross weight

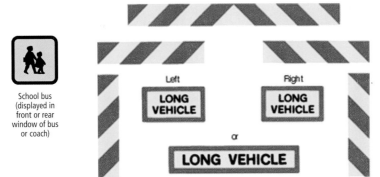

School bus (displayed in front or rear window of bus or coach)

Left

LONG VEHICLE

Right

LONG VEHICLE

or

LONG VEHICLE

The vertical markings are also required to be fitted to builders' skips placed in the road, commercial vehicles or combinations longer than 13 metres (optional on combinations between 11 and 13 metres)

Hazard warning plates

Certain tank vehicles carrying dangerous goods must display hazard information panels

2YE
1089

FLAMMABLE LIQUID
3

Newtown-on-Moors
(0123) 45678

The above panel will be displayed by vehicles carrying certain dangerous goods in packages

The panel illustrated is for flammable liquid. Diamond symbols indicating other risks include:

TOXIC
6

Toxic substance

OXIDIZING AGENT
5.1

Oxidising substance

COMPRESSED GAS
2

Non-flammable compressed gas

RADIOACTIVE
7

Radioactive substance

SPONTANEOUSLY COMBUSTIBLE
4

Spontaneously combustible substance

CORROSIVE
8

Corrosive substance

Projection markers

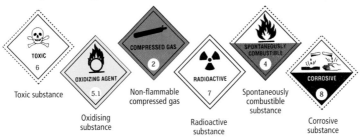

Side marker

End marker

Both required when load or equipment (eg crane jib) overhangs front or rear by more than two metres

Annexes

1. Choosing and maintaining your bicycle

Make sure that

- you choose the right size of cycle for comfort and safety
- lights and reflectors are kept clean and in good working order
- tyres are in good condition and inflated to the pressure shown on the tyre
- gears are working correctly
- the chain is properly adjusted and oiled
- the saddle and handlebars are adjusted to the correct height.

You **MUST**
- ensure your brakes are efficient
- at night, use lit front and rear lights and have an efficient red rear reflector.

PCUR reg 6 & RVLR no 18

2. Motorcycle licence requirements

If you have a provisional motorcycle licence, you **MUST** satisfactorily complete a Compulsory Basic Training (CBT) course. You can then ride on the public road, with L plates (in Wales either D plates, L plates or both can be used), for up to two years. To obtain your full motorcycle licence you **MUST** pass a motorcycle theory test and then a practical test.

Law RTA 1988 sect 97

If you have a full car licence you may ride motorcycles up to 125cc and 11kW power output, with L plates (and/or D plates in Wales), on public roads, but you **MUST** first satisfactorily complete a CBT course if you have not already done so.

If you have a full moped licence and wish to obtain full motorcycle entitlement you will be required to take a motorcycle theory test if you did not take a separate theory test when you obtained your moped licence. You **MUST** then pass a practical motorcycle test.

Note that if CBT was completed for the full moped licence there is no need to repeat it, but if the moped test was taken before

1/12/90 CBT will need to be completed before riding a motorcycle as a learner.
Law MV(DL)R reg 42(1) & 69(1)

Light motorcycle licence (A1): you take a test on a motorcycle of between 75 and 125cc. If you pass you may ride a motorcycle up to 125cc with power output up to 11kW.

Standard motorcycle licence (A): if your test vehicle is between 120 and 125cc and capable of more than 100 kph you will be given a standard (A) licence. You will then be restricted to motorcycles of up to 25 kW for two years. After two years you may ride any size machine.

Direct or Accelerated Access enables riders over the age of 21, or those who reach 21 before their two-year restriction ends, to ride larger motorcycles sooner. To obtain a licence to do so they are required to
- have successfully completed a CBT course
- pass a theory test, if they are required to do so
- pass a practical test on a machine with power output of at least 35kW.

To practise, they can ride larger motorcycles, with L plates (and/or D plates in Wales), on public roads, but only when accompanied by an approved instructor on another motorcycle in radio contact.

You **MUST NOT** carry a pillion passenger or pull a trailer until you have passed your test.
Law MV(DL)R reg 16

Moped Licence Requirements

Mopeds are up to 50cc with a maximum speed of 50 kph.

To ride a moped, learners **MUST**
- be 16 or over
- have a provisional moped licence
- complete CBT training.

You **MUST** first pass the theory test for motorcycles and then the moped practical test to obtain your full moped licence.

If you passed your driving test before 1 February 2001 you are qualified to ride a moped without L plates (and/or D plates in Wales), although it is recommended that you complete CBT before riding on the road. If you passed your driving test after this date you **MUST** complete CBT before riding a moped on the road.
Laws MV(DL)R reg 43

Note. For motorcycle and moped riders wishing to upgrade, the following give exemption from taking the motorcycle theory test
● full A1 motorcycle licence
● full moped licence, if gained after 1/7/96.
Laws MV(DL)R reg 42

3. Motor vehicle documentation and learner driver requirements

Documents

Driving Licence. You **MUST** have a valid signed driving licence for the category of vehicle you are driving. You **MUST** inform the Driver and Vehicle Licencing Agency (DVLA) if you change your name and address.
Law RTA 1988 sect 87

Insurance. You **MUST** have a valid insurance certificate covering you for third party liability. Before driving any vehicle, make sure that it has this cover for your use or that your own insurance gives you adequate cover. You **MUST NOT** drive a vehicle without insurance.
Law RTA 1988 sect 143

MOT. Cars and motorcycles **MUST** normally pass an MOT test three years from the date of the first registration and every year after that. You **MUST NOT** drive a vehicle without an MOT certificate, when it should have one. Driving an unroadworthy vehicle may invalidate your insurance. Exceptionally, you may drive to a pre-arranged test appointment or to a garage for repairs required for the test.
Law RTA 1988 sects 45, 47, 49 & 53

Vehicle Registration Document. Registration documents are issued for all motor vehicles used on the road, describing them (make, model, etc.) and giving details of the registered keeper.

You **MUST** notify the Driver and Vehicle Licensing Agency in Swansea as soon as possible when you buy or sell a vehicle, or if you change your name or address. For registration documents issued after 27 March 1997 the buyer and seller are responsible for completing the registration documents. The seller is responsible for forwarding them to DVLA. The procedures are explained on the back of the registration documents.

Law RV(R&L)R regs 10, 12 & 13

Vehicle Excise Duty. All vehicles used or kept on the roads **MUST** have a valid Vehicle Excise Duty disc (tax disc) displayed at all times. Any vehicle exempt from duty **MUST** display a nil licence.

Law VERA sect 29

Production of documents. You **MUST** be able to produce your driving licence and counterpart, a valid insurance certificate and (if appropriate) a valid MOT certificate, when requested by a police officer. If you cannot do this you may be asked to take them to a police station within seven days.

Law RTA 1988 sects 164 & 165

Learner drivers

Learners driving a car **MUST** hold a valid provisional licence. They **MUST** be supervised by someone at least 21 years old who holds a full EC/EEA licence for that type of car (automatic or manual) and has held one for at least three years.

MV(DL)R reg 16

Vehicles. Any vehicle driven by a learner **MUST** display red L plates. In Wales, either red D plates, red L plates, or both, can be used. Plates **MUST** conform to legal specifications and **MUST** be clearly visible to others from in front of the vehicle and from behind. Plates should be removed or covered when not being driven by a learner (except on driving school vehicles).

Law MV(DL)R reg 16 & sched 4

You **MUST** pass the theory test (if one is required) and then a practical driving test for the category of vehicle you wish to drive before driving unaccompanied.

Law MV(DL)R reg 40

4. The road user and the law
Road traffic law

The following list can be found abbreviated throughout the Code. It is not intended to be a comprehensive guide, but a guide to some of the important points of law. For the precise wording of the law, please refer to the various Acts and Regulations (as amended) indicated in the Code. Abbreviations are listed below.

Most of the provisions apply on all roads throughout Great Britain, although there are some exceptions. The definition of a road in England and Wales is 'any highway and any other road to which the public has access and includes bridges over which a road passes'. In Scotland, there is a similar definition which is extended to include any way over which the public have a right of passage. It is important to note that references to 'road' therefore generally include footpaths, bridle-ways and cycle tracks and many roadways and driveways on private land (including many car parks). In most cases, the law will apply to them and there may be additional rules for particular paths or ways. Some serious driving offences, including drink-driving offences, also apply to all public places, for example public car parks.

Functions of Traffic Wardens Order 1970	FTWO
Highway Act 1835 or 1980 (as indicated)	HA
Horses (Protective Headgear for Young Riders) Regulations 1992	H(PHYR)R
Motor Cycles (Protective Helmets) Regulations 1980	MC(PH)R
Motorways Traffic (England & Wales) Regulations 1982	MT(E&W)R
Motorways Traffic (Scotland) Regulations 1995	MT(S)R
Motor Vehicles (Driving Licences) Regulations 1999	MV(DL)R
Motor Vehicles (Wearing of Seat Belts) Regulations 1993	MV(WSB)R
Motor Vehicles (Wearing of Seat Belts by Children in Front Seats) Regulations 1993	MV(WSBCFS)R
Pedal Cycles (Construction & Use) Regulations 1983	PCUR
Public Passenger Vehicles Act 1981	PPVA
Road Traffic Act 1988 or 1991 (as indicated)	RTA
Road Traffic (New Drivers) Act 1995	RT(ND)A
Road Traffic Regulation Act 1984	RTRA
Road Vehicles (Construction & Use) Regulations 1986	CUR
Road Vehicles Lighting Regulations 1989	RVLR
Road Vehicles (Registration & Licensing) Regulations 1971	RV(R&L)R
Roads (Scotland) Act 1984	R(S)A
Traffic Signs Regulations & General Directions 1994	TSRGD
Vehicle Excise and Registration Act 1994	VERA
Zebra, Pelican and Puffin Pedestrian Crossings Regulations and General Directions 1997	ZPPPCRGD

5. Penalties

Parliament has set the maximum penalties for road traffic offences. The seriousness of the offence is reflected in the maximum penalty. It is for the courts to decide what sentence to impose according to circumstances.

The penalty table, see over, indicates some of the main offences, and the associated penalties. There is a wide range of other more specific offences which, for the sake of simplicity, are not shown here.

The penalty points and disqualification system is described below.

Penalty points and disqualification

The penalty point system is intended to deter drivers from following unsafe driving practices. The court **MUST** order points to be endorsed on the licence according to the fixed number or the range set by Parliament. The accumulation of penalty points acts as a warning to drivers that they risk disqualification if further offences are committed.

A driver who accumulates 12 or more penalty points within a three year period must be disqualified. This will be for a minimum period of six months, or longer if the driver has previously been disqualified.

For every offence which carries penalty points the court has a discretionary power to order the licence holder to be disqualified. This may be for any period the court thinks fit, but will usually be between a week and a few months.

In the case of serious offences, such as dangerous driving and drink-driving, the court **MUST** order disqualification. The minimum period is 12 months, but for repeat offenders or where the alcohol level is high, it may be longer. For example, a second drink-drive offence in the space of 10 years will result in a minimum of three years' disqualification.

Furthermore, in some serious cases, the court **MUST** (in addition to imposing a fixed period of disqualification) order the offender to be disqualified until they pass a driving test. In other cases the court has a discretionary power to order such disqualification. The test may be an ordinary length test or an extended test according to the nature of the offence.

Laws RTRA sects.28,29,34,35 and 36

Penalty table

Offence	Maximum penalties			
	IMPRISONMENT	FINE	DISQUALIFICATION	PENALTY POINTS
*Causing death by dangerous driving	10 years	Unlimited	Obligatory– 2 years minimum	3–11 (if exceptionally not disqualified)
*Dangerous driving	2 years	Unlimited	Obligatory	3–11 (if exceptionally not disqualified)
Causing death by careless driving under the influence of drink or drugs	10 years	Unlimited	Obligatory– 2 years minimum	3–11 (if exceptionally not disqualified)
Careless or inconsiderate driving	-	£2,500	Discretionary	3–9
Driving while unfit through drink or drugs or with excess alcohol; or failing to provide a specimen for analysis	6 months	£5,000	Obligatory	3–11 (if exceptionally not disqualified)
Failing to stop after an accident or failing to report an accident	6 months	£5,000	Discretionary	5–10
Driving when disqualified	6 months (12 months in Scotland)	£5,000	Discretionary	6
Driving after refusal or revocation of licence on medical grounds	6 months	£5,000	Discretionary	3–6
Driving without insurance	-	£5,000	Discretionary	6–8
Driving otherwise than in accordance with a licence	-	£1,000	Discretionary	3–6
Speeding	-	£1,000 (2,500 for motorway offences)	Discretionary	3–6 or 3 (fixed penalty)
Traffic light offences	-	£1,000	Discretionary	3
No MOT certificate	-	£1,000	-	-
Seat belt offences	-	£500	-	-
Dangerous cycling	-	£2,500	-	-
Careless cycling	-	£1,000	-	-
Cycling on pavement	-	£500	-	-
Failing to identify driver of a vehicle	-	£1,000	Discretionary	3

* Where a court disqualifies a person on conviction for one of these offences, it must order an extended retest. The courts also have discretion to order a retest for any other offence which carries penalty points: an extended retest where disqualification is obligatory, and an ordinary test where disqualification is not obligatory.

New drivers. Special rules apply to drivers within two years of the date of passing their driving test if they passed the test after 1 June 1997 and held nothing but a provisional (learner) licence before passing the test. If the number of penalty points on their licence reaches six or more as a result of offences they commit before the two years are over (including any they committed before they passed the test), their licence will be revoked. They must then reapply for a provisional licence and may drive only as learners until they pass a theory and practical driving test.

Law RT(ND)A

Note. This applies even if they pay by fixed penalty. Drivers who already have a full licence for one type of vehicle are not affected by this when they pass a test to drive another type.

Other consequences of offending

Where an offence is punishable by imprisonment then the vehicle used to commit the offence may be confiscated.

In addition to the penalties a court may decide to impose, the cost of insurance is likely to rise considerably following conviction for a serious driving offence. This is because insurance companies consider such drivers are more likely to have an accident.

Drivers disqualified for drinking and driving twice within 10 years, or once if they are over two and a half times the legal limit, or those who refused to give a specimen, also have to satisfy the Driver and Vehicle Licensing Agency's Medical Branch that they do not have an alcohol problem and are otherwise fit to drive before their licence is returned at the end of their period of disqualification. Persistent misuse of drugs or alcohol may lead to the withdrawal of a driving licence.

6. Vehicle maintenance, safety and security

Vehicle maintenance

Take special care that lights, brakes, steering, exhaust system, seat belts, demisters, wipers and washers are all working. Also

- lights, indicators, reflectors, and number plates **MUST** be kept clean and clear
- windscreens and windows **MUST** be kept clean and free from obstructions to vision

- lights **MUST** be properly adjusted to prevent dazzling other road users. Extra attention needs to be paid to this if the vehicle is heavily loaded
- exhaust emissions **MUST NOT** exceed prescribed levels
- ensure your seat, seat belt, head restraint and mirrors are adjusted correctly before you drive
- items of luggage are securely stowed.

Law: many regulations within CUR cover the above equipment and RVLR regs 23 & 27

Warning displays

Make sure that you understand the meaning of all warning displays on the vehicle instrument panel. Do not ignore warning signs, they could indicate a dangerous fault developing.

- When you turn the ignition key, warning lights will be illuminated but will go out when the engine starts (except the handbrake warning light). If they do not, or if they come on whilst you are driving, stop and investigate the problem, as you could have a serious fault.
- If the charge warning light comes on while you are driving, it may mean that the battery isn't charging. This must also be checked as soon as possible to avoid loss of power to lights and other electrical systems.

Tyres

Tyres **MUST** be correctly inflated and be free from certain cuts and other defects.

Cars, light vans and light trailers MUST have a tread depth of at least 1.6mm across the central three-quarters of the breadth of the tread and around the entire circumference.

Motorcycles, large vehicles and passenger carrying vehicles MUST have a tread depth of at least 1mm across three-quarters of the breadth of the tread and in a continuous band around the entire circumference. **Mopeds** should have visible tread.

Laws CUR reg 27

If a tyre bursts while you are driving, try to keep control of your vehicle. Grip the steering wheel firmly and allow the vehicle to roll to a stop at the side of the road.

If you have a flat tyre, stop as soon as it is safe to do so. Only change the tyre if you can do so without putting yourself or others at risk – otherwise call a breakdown service.

Tyre pressures. Check weekly. Do this before your journey, when tyres are cold. Warm or hot tyres may give a misleading reading.

Your brakes and steering will be adversely affected by under-inflated or over-inflated tyres. Excessive or uneven tyre wear may be caused by faults in the braking or suspension systems, or wheels which are out of alignment. Have these faults corrected as soon as possible.

Fluid levels

Check the fluid levels in your vehicle at least weekly. Low brake fluid may result in brake failure and an accident. Make sure you recognise the low fluid warning lights if your vehicle has them fitted.

Before winter

Ensure that the battery is well maintained and that there are appropriate anti-freeze agents in your radiator and windscreen bottle.

Other problems

If your vehicle
- pulls to one side when braking, it is most likely to be a brake fault or incorrectly inflated tyres. Consult a garage or mechanic immediately
- continues to bounce after pushing down on the front or rear, its shock absorbers are worn. Worn shock absorbers can seriously affect the operation of a vehicle and should be replaced
- smells of anything unusual such as burning rubber, petrol or electrical; investigate immediately. Do not risk a fire.

Overheated engines or fire

Most engines are water cooled. If your engine overheats you should wait until it has cooled naturally. Only then remove the coolant filler cap and add water or other coolant.

If your vehicle catches fire, get the occupants out of the vehicle quickly and to a safe place. Do not attempt to extinguish a fire in the engine compartment, as opening the bonnet will make the fire flare. Call the fire brigade.

Petrol stations

Never smoke or use a mobile phone on the forecourt of petrol stations as this is a major fire risk and could cause an explosion.

Vehicle security

When you leave your vehicle you should
- remove the ignition key and engage the steering lock
- lock the car, even if you only leave it for a few minutes
- close the windows completely
- never leave children or pets in an unventilated car
- take all contents with you, or lock them in the boot. Remember, for all a thief knows a carrier bag may contain valuables. Never leave vehicle documents in the car.

For extra security fit an anti-theft device such as an alarm or immobiliser. If you are buying a new car it is a good idea to check the level of built-in security features. Consider having your registration number etched on all your car windows. This is a cheap and effective deterrent to professional thieves.

7. First aid on the road

In the event of an accident, you can do a number of things to help, even if you have had no training

1. Deal with danger

Further collisions and fire are the main dangers following an accident. Approach any vehicle involved with care. Switch off all engines and, if possible, warn other traffic. Stop anyone from smoking.

2. Get help

Try to get the assistance of bystanders. Get someone to call the appropriate emergency services as soon as possible. They will need to know the exact location of the accident and the number of vehicles involved.

3. Help those involved

DO NOT move casualties still in vehicles unless further danger is threatened. **DO NOT** remove a motorcyclist's helmet unless it is essential. **DO NOT** give the casualty anything to eat or drink.

DO try to make them comfortable and prevent them from getting cold, but avoid unnecessary movement. **DO** give reassurance confidently to the casualty. They may be shocked but prompt treatment will minimise this.

4. Provide emergency care
Follow the **ABC of First aid**

A is for **Airway** – check for and relieve any obstruction to breathing. Remove any obvious obstruction in the mouth. Breathing may begin and colour improve.

B is for **Breathing** – if breathing does not begin when the airway has been cleared, lift the chin and tilt the head very gently backwards. Pinch the casualty's nostrils and blow into the mouth until the chest rises; withdraw, then repeat regularly once every four seconds until the casualty can breathe unaided.

C is for **Circulation** – prevent blood loss to maintain circulation. If bleeding is present apply firm hand pressure over the wound, preferably using some clean material, without pressing on any foreign body in the wound. Secure a pad with a bandage or length of cloth. Raise the limb to lessen the bleeding, provided it is not broken.

5. Be prepared
Always carry a first aid kit. You could save a life by learning emergency aid and first aid from a qualified organisation, such as the local ambulance services, the St John Ambulance Association and Brigade, St Andrew's Ambulance Association, the British Red Cross or any suitable qualified body.

This Code between rules 1 and 278, is issued with the Authority of Parliament (laid before both Houses of Parliament June 1998) and appears in the law described as follows:

A failure on the part of a person to observe any provision of **The Highway Code** shall not itself render that person liable to criminal proceedings of any kind, but any such failure may in any proceedings (whether civil or criminal and including proceedings for an offence under the Traffic Acts, the Public Passenger Vehicles Act 1981 or sections 18 to 23 of the Transport Act 1985) be relied upon by any party to the proceedings as tending to establish or negative any liability which is in question in those proceedings.

Road Traffic Act 1988

Index

References are to rule numbers, except those numbers given in *bold italic*, which refer to the annexes

Index

Index

Part 5

Glossary

Accelerate
To make the vehicle move faster by pressing the right-hand pedal.

Advanced stop lines
A marked area on the road at traffic lights, which permits cyclists or buses to wait in front of other traffic.

Adverse weather
Bad weather that makes driving difficult or dangerous.

Alert
Quick to notice possible hazards.

Anticipation
Looking out for hazards and taking action before a problem starts.

Anti-lock brakes
Brakes that stop the wheels locking so that you are less likely to skid on a slippery road.

Aquaplane
To slide out of control on a wet road surface.

Articulated vehicle
A long vehicle that is divided into two or more sections joined by cables.

Attitude
The way you think or feel, which affects the way you drive. Especially, whether you are patient and polite, or impatient and aggressive.

Automatic
A vehicle with gears that change by themselves as you speed up or slow down.

Awareness
Taking notice of the road and traffic conditions around you at all times.

Black ice
An invisible film of ice that forms over the road surface, creating very dangerous driving conditions.

Blind spot
The section of road behind you which you cannot see in your mirrors. You 'cover' your blind spot by looking over your shoulder before moving off or overtaking.

Brake fade
Loss of power to the brakes when you have been using them for a long time without taking your foot off the brake pedal. For example, when driving down a steep hill. The brakes will overheat and not work properly.

Braking distance
The distance you must allow to slow the vehicle in order to come to a stop.

Brow
The highest point of a hill.

Built-up area
A town, or place with lots of buildings.

Carriageway
One side of a road or motorway. A 'dual carriageway' has two lanes on each side of a central reservation.

Catalytic converter
A piece of equipment fitted in the exhaust system that changes harmful gases into less harmful ones.

Chicane
A sharp double bend that has been put into a road to make traffic slow down.

Child restraint
A child seat or special seat belt for children. It keeps them safe and stops them moving around in the car.

Clearway
A road where no stopping is allowed at any time. The sign for a clearway is a red cross in a red circle on a blue background.

Coasting
Driving a vehicle without using any of the gears. That is, with your foot on the clutch pedal and the car in neutral.

Commentary driving
Talking to yourself about what you see on the road ahead and what action you are going to take – an aid to concentration.

Comprehensive insurance
A motor insurance policy that pays for repairs even if you cause an accident.

Concentration

Keeping all your attention on your driving.

Conditions

How good or bad the road surface is, volume of traffic on the road, and what the weather is like.

Congestion

Heavy traffic that makes it difficult to get to where you want to go.

Consideration

Thinking about other road users and not just yourself. For example, letting another driver go first at a junction, or stopping at a zebra crossing to let pedestrians cross over.

Contraflow

When traffic on a motorway follows signs to move to the opposite carriageway for a short distance because of roadworks. (During a contraflow, there is traffic driving in both directions on the same side of the motorway.)

Coolant

Liquid in the radiator that removes heat from the engine.

Defensive driving

Driving safely without taking risks, looking out for hazards and thinking for others.

Disqualified

Stopped from doing something (eg driving) by law, because you have broken the law.

Distraction

Anything that stops you concentrating on your driving, such as chatting to passengers or on your mobile phone.

Document

An official paper or card, eg your driving licence.

Dual carriageway

One side of a road or motorway, with two lanes on each side of a central reservation.

Engine braking – see also gears

Using the low gears to keep your speed down. For example, when you are driving down a steep hill and you want to stop the vehicle running away. Using the gears instead of braking will help to prevent brake fade.

Environment

The world around us and the air we breathe.

Exceed

Go higher than an upper limit.

Exhaust emissions

Gases that come out of the exhaust pipe to form part of the outside air.

Field of vision

How far you can see in front and around you when you are driving.

Filler cap

Provides access to the vehicle's fuel tank, for filling up with petrol or diesel.

Fog lights

Extra bright rear (and sometimes front) lights which may be switched on in conditions of very poor visibility. You must remember to switch them off when visibility improves, as they can dazzle and distract other drivers.

Ford

A place in a stream or river which is shallow enough to drive across with care.

Four-wheel drive (4WD)

On a conventional vehicle, steering and engine speed affect just two 'drive' wheels. On 4WD, they affect all four wheels, ensuring optimum grip on loose ground.

Frustration

Feeling annoyed because you cannot drive as fast as you want to because of other drivers or heavy traffic.

Fuel consumption

The amount of fuel (petrol or diesel) that your vehicle uses. Different vehicles have different rates of consumption. Increased fuel consumption means using more fuel. Decreased fuel consumption means using less fuel.

Fuel gauge

A display or dial on the instrument panel that tells you how much fuel (petrol or diesel) you have left.

Glossary

Gantry

An overhead platform like a high narrow bridge that displays electric signs on a motorway.

Gears

Control the speed of the engine in relation to the vehicle's speed. May be hand operated (manual) or automatically controlled. In a low gear (such as first or second) the engine runs more slowly. In a high gear (such as fourth or fifth), it runs more quickly. Putting the car into a lower gear as you drive can create the effect of engine braking – forcing the engine to run more slowly.

Handling

How well your vehicle moves or responds when you steer or brake.

Harass

To drive in away that makes other road users afraid.

Hard shoulder

The single lane to the left of the inside lane on a motorway, which is for emergency use only. You should not drive on the hard shoulder except in an emergency, or when there are signs telling you to use the hard shoulder because of roadworks.

Harsh braking (or harsh acceleration)

Using the brake or accelerator too hard so as to cause wear on the engine.

Hazard warning lights

Flashing amber lights which you should use only when you have broken down. On a motorway you can use them to warn other drivers behind of a hazard ahead.

High-sided vehicle

A van or truck with tall sides, or a tall trailer such as a caravan or horse-box, that is at risk of being blown off-course in strong winds.

Impatient

Not wanting to wait for pedestrians and other road users.

Inflate

To blow up – to put air in your tyres until they are at the right pressures.

Instrument panel

The car's electrical controls and gauges, set behind the steering wheel. Also called the dashboard.

Intimidate

To make someone feel afraid.

Involved

Being part of something. For example, being one of the drivers in an accident.

Jump leads

A pair of thick electric cables with clips at either end. You use it to charge a flat battery by connecting it to the live battery in another vehicle.

Junction

A place where two or more roads join.

Liability

Being legally responsible.

Manoeuvre

Using the controls to make your car move in a particular direction. For example turning, reversing or parking.

Manual

By hand. In a car that is a 'manual' or has manual gears, you have to change the gears yourself.

Maximum

The largest possible; 'maximum speed' is the highest speed allowed.

Minimum

The smallest possible.

Mirrors

Modern cars have a minimum of three rear view mirrors: one in the centre of the windscreen, and one on each front door. Additional mirrors may be required on longer vehicles, or when towing a high trailer such as a caravan. Some mirrors may be curved (convex or concave) to increase the field of vision. The mirror on the windscreen can be turned to anti-dazzle position, if glare from headlights behind creates a distraction.

Mobility

The ability to move around easily.

Monotonous

Boring. For example, a long stretch of motorway with no variety and nothing interesting to see.

MOT

The test that proves your car is safe to drive. Your MOT certificate is one of the important documents for your vehicle.

Motorway

A fast road that has two or more lanes on each side and a hard shoulder. Drivers must join or leave it on the left, via a motorway junction. Many kinds of slower vehicles – such as bicycles – are not allowed on motorways.

Multiple-choice questions

Questions with several possible answers where you have to try to choose the right one.

Observation

The ability to notice important information, such as hazards developing ahead.

Obstruct

To get in the way of another road user.

Octagonal

Having eight sides.

Oil level

The amount of oil needed for the engine to run effectively. The oil level should be checked as part of your regular maintenance routine, and the oil replaced as necessary.

Pedestrian

A person walking.

Pegasus crossing

An unusual kind of crossing. It has a button high up for horse riders to push (Pegasus was a flying horse in Greek legend).

Pelican crossing

A crossing with traffic lights that pedestrians can use by pushing a button. Cars must give way to pedestrians on the crossing while the amber light is flashing. You must give pedestrians enough time to get to the other side of the road.

Perception

Seeing or noticing (as in Hazard Perception).

Peripheral vision

The area around the edges of your field of vision.

Positive attitude

Being sensible and obeying the law when you drive.

Priority

The vehicle or other road user that is allowed by law to go first is the one that has priority.

Provisional licence

A first driving licence. all learner drivers must get one before they start having lessons.

Puffin crossing

A type of pedestrian crossing that does not have a flashing amber light phase.

Reaction time

The amount of time it takes you to see a hazard and decide what to do about it.

Red route

You see these in London and some other cities. Double red lines at the edge of the road tell you that you must not stop or park there at any time. Single red lines have notices with times when you must not stop or park. Some red routes have marked bays for either parking or loading at certain times.

Red warning triangle

An item of safety equipment to carry in your car in case you break down. You can place the triangle 45m behind your car on the same side of the road. It warns traffic that your vehicle is causing an obstruction. (Do not use these on motorways.)

Residential areas

Areas of housing where people live. The speed limit is 30mph or sometimes 20mph.

Road hump

A low bump built across the road to slow vehicles down. Also called 'sleeping policemen'.

Rumble strips

Raised strips across the road near a roundabout or junction that change the sound the tyres make on the road surface, warning drivers to slow down. They are also used on motorways to separate the main carriageway from the hard shoulder.

Glossary

Safety margin
The amount of space you need to leave between your vehicle and the one in front so that you are not in danger of crashing into it if the driver slows down suddenly or stops. Safety margins have to be longer in wet or icy conditions.

Separation distance
The amount of space you need to leave between your vehicle and the one in front so that you are not in danger of crashing into it if the driver slows down suddenly or stops. The separation distance must be longer in wet or icy conditions.

Security coded radio
To deter thieves, a radio or CD unit which requires a security code (or pin number) to operate it.

Single carriageway
Generally, a road with one lane in each direction.

Skid
When the tyres fail to grip the surface of the road, the subsequent loss of control of the vehicle's movement is called a skid. Usually caused by harsh or fierce braking, steering or acceleration.

Snaking
Moving from side to side. This sometimes happens with caravans or trailers when you drive too fast, or they are not properly loaded.

Staggered junction
Where you drive cross another road. Instead of going straight across, you have to go a bit to the right or left.

Steering
Control of the direction of the vehicle. May be affected by road surface conditions: when the steering wheel turns very easily, steering is 'light', and when you have to pull hard on the wheel it is described as 'heavy'.

Sterile
Clean and free from bacteria.

Stopping distance
The time it takes for you to stop your vehicle – made up of 'thinking distance' and 'braking distance'.

Supervisor
Someone who sits in the passenger seat with a learner driver. They must be over 21 and have held a full driving licence for at least three years.

Tailgating
Driving too closely behind another vehicle – either to harass the driver in front or to help you in thick fog.

Tax disc
The disc you display on your windscreen to show that you have taxed your car (see Vehicle Excise Duty, below).

Thinking distance
The time it takes you to notice something and take the right action. You need to add thinking distance to your braking distance to make up your total stopping distance.

Third party insurance
An insurance policy that insures you against any claim by passengers or other persons for damage or injury to their person or property.

Toucan crossing
A type of pedestrian crossing that does not have a flashing amber light phase, and cyclists are allowed to ride across.

Tow
To pull something behind your vehicle. It could be a caravan or trailer.

Traffic calming measures
Speed humps, chicanes and other devices placed in roads to slow traffic down.

Tram
A public transport vehicle which moves along the streets on fixed rails, usually electrically powered by overhead lines.

Tread depth
The depth of the grooves in a car's tyres that help them grip the road surface. The grooves must all be at least 1.6mm deep.

Turbulence
Strong movement of air. For example, when a large vehicle passes a much smaller one.

Two-second rule

In normal driving, the ideal minimum distance between you and the vehicle in front can be timed using the 'two-second' rule. As the vehicle in front passes a fixed object (such as a signpost), say to yourself 'Only a fool breaks the two second rule'. It takes two seconds to say it. If you have passed the same object before you finish, you are too close – pull back.

Tyre pressures

The amount of air which must be pumped into a tyre in order for it to be correctly blown up.

Vehicle Excise Duty

The tax you pay for your vehicle so that you may drive it on public roads.

Vehicle Registration Document

A record of details about a vehicle and its owner.

Vehicle watch scheme

A system for identifying vehicles that may have been stolen.

Vulnerable

At risk of harm or injury.

Waiting restrictions

Times when you may not park or load your vehicle in a particular area.

Wheel balancing

To ensure smooth rotation at all speeds, wheels need to be 'balanced' correctly. This is a procedure done at a garage or tyre centre, when each wheel is removed for testing. Balancing may involve minor adjustment with the addition of small weights, to avoid wheel wobble.

Wheel spin

When the vehicle's wheels spin round out of control with no grip on the road surface.

Zebra crossing

A pedestrian crossing without traffic lights. It has an orange light, and is marked by black and white stripes on the road. Drivers must stop for pedestrians to cross.

Part 6

Answers to Questions

ALERTNESS – SECTION 1

1 C	2 BDF	3 C	4 D	5 C	6 C	7 C	8 C	9 B
10 D	11 AC	12 ABCD	13 AD	14 AB	15 AB	16 ABCD	17 C	18 B
19 D	20 B	21 C	22 B	23 B	24 ABE	25 C	26 B	27 B
28 D	29 C	30 C	31 C	32 A	33 D	34 D		

ATTITUDE – SECTION 2

35 D	36 A	37 C	38 B	39 C	40 D	41 D	42 B	43 B
44 BCD	45 ABE	46 A	47 D	48 B	49 A	50 A	51 B	52 A
53 A	54 C	55 A	56 B	57 D	58 D	59 D	60 A	61 A
62 B	63 C	64 A	65 C	66 A	67 C	68 B	69 C	70 DE
71 B	72 D	73 B	74 C	75 D	76 B	77 C	78 A	79 A
80 B	81 A							

SAFETY AND YOUR VEHICLE – SECTION 3

82 B	83 AB	84 ABF	85 BEF	86 C	87 ACF	88 C	89 B	90 A
91 D	92 C	93 D	94 D	95 D	96 A	97 AE	98 D	99 B
100 D	101 D	102 A	103 B	104 BCDF	105 D	106 D	107 BC	108 BC
109 A	110 D	111 C	112 A	113 B	114 B	115 D	116 C	117 D
118 D	119 D	120 B	121 B	122 B	123 D	124 AB	125 ABF	126 ABC
127 ABC	128 BDF	129 D	130 ADE	131 BDF	132 D	133 B	134 CDE	135 B
136 B	137 C	138 B	139 DE	140 A	141 C	142 B	143 D	144 D
145 D	146 B	147 C	148 A	149 B	150 D	151 A	152 C	153 A
154 B	155 AB	156 A	157 D	158 B	159 BCD	160 C	161 CD	162 A
163 A	164 D	165 C	166 B	167 B	168 B	169 D	170 ABE	171 ADE
172 D								

SAFETY MARGINS – SECTION 4

173 D	174 D	175 BC	176 B	177 D	178 D	179 C	180 B	181 BC
182 A	183 ACE	184 B	185 A	186 B	187 A	188 B	189 AE	190 C
191 B	192 C	193 BDEF	194 B	195 D	196 A	197 C	198 A	199 AD
200 C	201 B	202 B	203 B	204 C	205 C	206 B	207 B	208 BC
209 C	210 C	211 B	212 C	213 D	214 BC	215 B	216 ACE	217 D
218 D	219 D	220 A	221 D	222 BD	223 D	224 B	225 A	226 D
227 A	228 B							

HAZARD AWARENESS – SECTION 5

229 D	230 CD	231 B	232 C	233 A	234 D	235 ACE	236 D	237 C
238 A	239 C	240 C	241 D	242 B	243 B	244 A	245 A	246 A
247 C	248 C	249 CD	250 A	251 B	252 A	253 C	254 BF	255 B
256 AE	257 A	258 D	259 D	260 C	261 B	262 B	263 C	264 A
265 B	266 B	267 CD	268 B	269 D	270 B	271 A	272 A	273 D
274 A	275 B	276 AE	277 C	278 B	279 BC	280 D	281 B	282 B
283 C	284 D	285 C	286 CD	287 AC	288 AB	289 A	290 A	291 B
292 A	293 ABC	294 C	295 C	296 C	297 ABE	298 C	299 D	300 D
301 C	302 C	303 D	304 ABD	305 ABC	306 D	307 C	308 AB	309 B
310 B	311 CD	312 D	313 ACE	314 ABE	315 A	316 A	317 D	318 D
319 A	320 D	321 A	322 B					

VULNERABLE ROAD USERS – SECTION 6

323 D	324 D	325 C	326 C	327 B	328 D	329 D	330 AD	331 B
332 C	333 D	334 A	335 D	336 D	337 B	338 D	339 B	340 D
341 D	342 C	343 AC	344 C	345 C	346 A	347 D	348 C	349 D
350 ABC	351 C	352 B	353 B	354 AC	355 ABD	356 B	357 D	358 A
359 D	360 A	361 D	362 D	363 A	364 A	365 C	366 C	367 C
368 D	369 ACE	370 D	371 B	372 A	373 C	374 D	375 C	376 C
377 A	378 D	379 D	380 A	381 A	382 B	383 B	384 D	385 C
386 C	387 B	388 C	389 AE	390 D	391 C	392 C	393 B	394 B
395 D	396 D	397 A	398 C	399 C	400 D	401 D	402 B	403 D
404 D	405 B	406 B	407 C					

OTHER TYPES OF VEHICLE – SECTION 7

408 B	409 A	410 A	411 B	412 B	413 D	414 B	415 A	416 BC
417 B	418 D	419 A	420 A	421 A	422 C	423 B	424 B	425 D
426 D	427 D	428 B	429 B	430 B	431 B	432 AC	433 BD	434 B
435 B	436 D							

VEHICLE HANDLING – SECTION 8

437 C	438 ACE	439 A	440 CD	441 D	442 A	443 BDF	444 C	445 D
446 C	447 DE	448 D	449 B	450 C	451 D	452 C	453 D	454 D
455 C	456 C	457 BD	458 BD	459 D	460 B	461 C	462 CE	463 C
464 D	465 A	466 A	467 C	468 B	469 ABDF	470 A	471 D	472 B
473 B	474 AB	475 BD	476 A	477 ACD	478 B	479 A	480 C	481 B
482 A	483 A	484 C	485 C	486 A	487 B	488 C	489 D	490 B
491 D	492 ABD	493 D	494 C	495 C	496 C	497 D	498 D	499 A

MOTORWAY RULES – SECTION 9

500 ADEF	501 ADEF	502 D	503 D	504 D	505 D	506 A	507 B	508 C
509 BE	510 C	511 A	512 C	513 A	514 D	515 A	516 C	517 C
518 C	519 C	520 C	521 C	522 B	523 C	524 B	525 B	526 A
527 B	528 B	529 D	530 CDF	531 C	532 D	533 C	534 D	535 A
536 B	537 B	538 D	539 C	540 A	541 B	542 D	543 A	544 D
545 D	546 A	547 C	548 B	549 B	550 C			

RULES OF THE ROAD – SECTION 10

551 C	552 B	553 D	554 B	555 A	556 C	557 D	558 ADF	559 BDEF
560 AD	561 A	562 B	563 A	564 B	565 A	566 D	567 A	568 D
569 D	570 C	571 A	572 ACE	573 B	574 C	575 D	576 BD	577 B
578 A	579 D	580 C	581 A	582 B	583 CDE	584 B	585 AE	586 B
587 A	588 ABD	589 A	590 B	591 B	592 A	593 D	594 A	595 D
596 C	597 D	598 D	599 BEF	600 D	601 D	602 D	603 C	604 C
605 D	606 A	607 A	608 A	609 C	610 B	611 A	612 D	613 AB
614 A	615 D	616 D	617 A	618 D	619 B	620 ABC	621 D	622 A
623 D	624 A	625 A						

ROAD AND TRAFFIC SIGNS – SECTION 11

626 D	627 D	628 A	629 A	630 B	631 A	632 D	633 B	634 D
635 D	636 D	637 A	638 C	639 B	640 D	641 C	642 B	643 A
644 B	645 B	646 C	647 C	648 A	649 C	650 B	651 C	652 B
653 D	654 D	655 C	656 D	657 C	658 B	659 C	660 D	661 A
662 D	663 B	664 D	665 B	666 A	667 A	668 A	669 A	670 B
671 B	672 A	673 D	674 ACEF	675 C	676 A	677 A	678 C	679 D
680 B	681 C	682 B	683 B	684 B	685 B	686 D	687 A	688 C
689 A	690 C	691 D	692 A	693 C	694 B	695 D	696 A	697 B
698 B	699 C	700 C	701 A	702 A	703 C	704 B	705 C	706 D
707 C	708 ACD	709 B	710 A	711 C	712 D	713 C	714 B	715 A
716 A	717 C	718 BDF	719 A	720 C	721 C	722 B	723 B	724 A
725 C	726 A	727 B	728 A	729 B	730 D	731 D	732 B	733 A
734 A	735 D	736 C	737 D	738 C	739 B	740 C	741 C	742 A
743 B	744 D	745 B	746 B	747 A	748 D	749 A	750 B	751 B
752 D	753 C	754 B	755 A	756 B	757 A	758 C	759 A	760 B
761 A	762 A	763 C	764 C	765 A	766 B	767 C	768 B	769 A
770 C	771 ACE	772 A	773 A	774 C	775 C	776 B	777 B	778 B
779 B	780 B	781 A						

DOCUMENTS – SECTION 12

782 C	783 B	784 B	785 BE	786 C	787 C	788 B	789 D	790 AB
791 D	792 D	793 D	794 C	795 CDE	796 CD	797 B	798 B	799 C
800 ABF	801 BCE	802 ABE	803 BD	804 D	805 A	806 C	807 ABD	808 D
809 B	810 C							

ACCIDENTS – SECTION 13

811 A	812 BCDE	813 B	814 ABE	815 A	816 ACF	817 A	818 ABD	819 ACE
820 DEF	821 ABE	822 ACF	823 AE	824 ACDE	825 C	826 BC	827 CDE	828 A
829 B	830 B	831 BDE	832 B	833 C	834 D	835 CD	836 D	837 C
838 C	839 B	840 D	841 B	842 BDE	843 C	844 A	845 B	846 AB
847 A	848 A	849 B	850 B	851 D	852 C	853 C	854 B	855 D
856 C	857 ABD	858 A	859 CD	860 CE	861 C	862 DEF	863 B	864 C
865 A	866 A	867 BE	868 ABCE	869 ADE	870 A	871 D	872 B	873 C
874 D	875 A	876 D	877 B	878 A	879 BE			

VEHICLE LOADING – SECTION 14

880 AD	881 A	882 D	883 A	884 D	885 BD	886 D	887 B	888 A
889 D	890 BC	891 A	892 A	893 C				

Useful Contacts

AA Driving School
0800 60 70 80
www.theAA.com

Driving Standards Agency (DSA)
You can book your Theory or Practical Test

Online: www.dsa.gov.uk

By phone: 0870 010 1372

By fax: 0870 010 2372

Welsh speakers: 0870 010 0372

Minicom: 0870 010 7372

To book your Theory Test you will need:

- The driver number on your licence
- Your debit/credit card details

To book your Practical Test you will need:

- The driver number on your licence
- Theory Test pass date and certificate number
- Driving school code (if known)
- Your preferred date
- Unacceptable days or periods
- If you can accept a test at short notice
- Disability or any special circumstances
- Your credit/debit card details

Saturday and weekday evening tests are available at some driving test centres. The fee is higher than for a driving test during normal working hours on weekdays. Evening tests are available during the summer months only.

Pass Plus scheme
For information on the Pass Plus scheme ask your Advanced Driving Instructor

Online: www.passplus.org.uk

Phone the DSA: 0115 901 2633

Driver and Vehicle Licensing Agency (DVLA)
www.dvla.gov.uk

For enquiries about your driving licence
Phone: 0870 240 0009

Or write to:
Customer Enquiries (Drivers) Unit
DVLC
Swansea
SA6 7JL

For queries about vehicle registration and licensing
Phone: 0870 240 0010

Or write to:
Customer Enquiries (Vehicles) Unit
DVLC
Swansea
SA99 1BL

The Highway Code
www.thehighwaycode.gov.uk

St John Ambulance
www.sja.org.uk
08700 10 49 50

St Andrew's Ambulance Association
www.firstaid.org.uk

Personal Information

My driver number

Driving instructor's name and
phone number

Driving instructor's number

Theory Test date and time

Theory Test pass date

Theory Test certificate number

Driving school code

Practical Test date and time

Acknowledgements

Illustrations: Chris Orr & Associates
Editor: Pam Stagg